Revealed

Using Remote Personality Profiling to Influence, Negotiate and Motivate

Revealed

John Taylor
Consultant, UK

Adrian Furnham
Professor of Psychology, University College London, UK

and

Janet Breeze
Consultant, Oman

palgrave
macmillan

First published 2014 by
PALGRAVE MACMILLAN

Palgrave Macmillan in the UK is an imprint of Macmillan Publishers Limited, registered in England, company number 785998, of Houndmills, Basingstoke, Hampshire RG21 6XS.

Palgrave Macmillan in the US is a division of St Martin's Press LLC, 175 Fifth Avenue, New York, NY 10010.

Palgrave Macmillan is the global academic imprint of the above companies and has companies and representatives throughout the world.

Palgrave® and Macmillan® are registered trademarks in the United States, the United Kingdom, Europe and other countries.

ISBN 978–1–137–29198–1

This book is printed on paper suitable for recycling and made from fully managed and sustained forest sources. Logging, pulping and manufacturing processes are expected to conform to the environmental regulations of the country of origin.

A catalogue record for this book is available from the British Library.

A catalog record for this book is available from the Library of Congress.

Typeset by MPS Limited, Chennai, India.

For Hedge and my special girls (JB)

Ronnie, Isabella, Jack, and Bobby (JT)

For Alison and Benedict: revealing why I spend so long in the office (AF)

Contents

List of Figures and Tables

Figures

Tables

Preface

Revealed is a natural extension to *Bad Apples* (Furnham and Taylor, 2011). It builds on the themes of *Bad Apples: Identify, Preventing, and Manage Negative Behaviour at Work*. But having established that there are things we can do to reduce the risks, colleagues and clients wanted more. They could see the dangers and they had their 'Due Diligence' reports on people, but these related to what the individual had done in the past and their current financial, personal, and employment status. In general these reports did not analyze behavioral patterns that could predict their future actions, their real preferences nor their *Dark Side*.

We were challenged by some clients to do go further and, perhaps reflecting our own *Dark Side*, we accepted the challenge. On a couple of tasks we could not meet or interact with the subject or any of his close associates. The challenge then was to produce a report on the basis of open source material and interviews with people who knew the subjects as work colleagues. It took time because we were creating a new process and our evidence had to be strong and verifiable. A frequent problem was that there was too much open source material and narcissists in particular like to put stuff on their Facebook or Linked-in pages – not much of it reliable for our analytical purposes.

But we persevered and the reports were well received and proved accurate and useful to the client.

As the process developed, we identified six facets of an individual that we believe are important in identifying the influences on their behaviors: cultural origins, biographical background, intelligence, personality, Dark Side traits, and their deep-seated motivations. Many clients are only interested in the last two, but we need to analyze all six aspects in order to have confidence in our judgments of the *Dark Side* and motivations.

Revealed provides the background to our methodology and details of the scientific and research data we use.

One of our dilemmas was which case studies to choose for inclusion in the book. We have many examples, some of which of course are confidential to the client. We have described well-known figures, others less known and occasionally we have disguised the subject. We hope that together these demonstrate not only the rich insights the process can provide but also how it is feasible to gather the information on which to make judgments remotely.

Our aim has always been to provide the understanding and tools to help people make better predictions of what others are likely to do in the future. In this process, wise readers will also become better informed about the influences on their own behaviors and therefore how best to manage them in order to be effective in business or when dealing with others with whom they wish to manage their relationship more skillfully. We also hope it will be of broader interest to biographers and all those intrigued by human behavior.

Acknowledgments

The book would be much weaker without the help, contribution, and chiding of others. Geert Hofstede, Robert Cialdini, and Robert Hogan have provided much of the academic backbone for the book. They have their credits in the text and bibliography, but they provide much more than just the citations we provide. Melvyn Payne is always there to help us interpret apparently contradictory behaviors; David Charters embarrasses us by telling the world of our powers (but cleverly appealing to our narcissistic and histrionic tendencies); Barry Roche, generous and kind, while never letting an opportunity to tease or stimulate go by; Anthony Banks, Philippa Charlton, Peter Wilson, and Jane Attwood for their commercial insights and encouragement; Dave Watson and Laura Day for their insights and encouragement.

Sarika Breeze, Aimee Hutchinson, and Luke Treglown contributed enormously with their research and practical help with case studies. Jane Ness as always ensured as best she could that JT's disorganized traits were manageable. Her support and assistance make her very special.

Acknowledgments quite properly make references to the often unseen contributions of family. They have to tolerate distance and absentmindedness in the belief that there is some great thinking process happening. Their faith is essential to our well-being: This was for Christopher a first experience and who, despite being under enormous pressure himself, is forever there, a wise voice of counsel and source of loving and unstinting support. Alison and Aly have been here before; your support, tolerance, and love are not taken for granted – thank you.

chapter 1

Introduction

A significant number of studies done over 40 years suggest that there is a one in two chance that executives will fail in some significant way. According to Michael Watkins, author of *First 90 Days*, 64 per cent of new executives hired from outside will not succeed in their new jobs. Similarly the Corporate Leadership Council data suggest that 40 per cent of newly appointed executives will derail within the first 18 months. The demands on business leaders and senior managers have never been greater, nor have the costs of poor selection.

64 per cent of new executives hired from outside will not succeed in their new jobs

We value executives with strong powers of persuasion, an ability to secure the best deal, to build networks and work alongside people of different cultures. Success in negotiation, entering a new country or gaining market intelligence usually comes down to building relationships of trust, liking and agreement with key individuals and decision-makers, both within and outside our organizations. Particularly in a competitive international context, this requires heightened understanding of whom we are dealing with and how their perceptions and approach might differ from our own.

> *When dealing with people, remember we are not dealing with creatures of logic; we are dealing with creatures of emotion, creatures bristling with prejudices and motivated by pride and vanity.* (Carnegie, 1936)

Revealed addresses the urgent business challenge of understanding better the people on whom we depend for success. The methodology it presents – *Remote Personality Profiling (RPP)* – helps identify and manage the risks that a senior business leader will under-perform, particularly when under pressure. It also helps us identify and manage differences between our approach and that of others we might want to influence, negotiate with or motivate. The aim is to really 'get under the skin' of an individual: to get a 'full picture' of that person and to understand 'what makes them tick'.

So, how do we ensure that we recruit the right person to the job? How can we use knowledge of an individual to influence, negotiate, motivate and manage them more effectively? These are perhaps the principal uses of RPP, but it has many other applications. Through RPP we can paint a picture of an individual who interests or matters to us, for whatever reason. A political leader, past or present, an artist or scientist. Someone whose achievements or actions set them apart from the rest. The criminal, spy or tyrant whose deeds remain unexplained. Someone whom perhaps we research in order to draw wider lessons regarding why individuals behave the way they do. Though it borrows ideas from both, RPP is more than psychobiography or personal profiling.

Revealed is a valuable aid to negotiators in business and public life, to headhunters and recruiters, heads of security looking for the insider threat, fiction writers and biographers. It would also be useful for intelligence officers looking for potential human sources.

The six elements of RPP

Based on extensive and rigorous academic research and their combined inter-national expertise in the fields of psychology and business, the authors believe that there are six main elements affecting an individual's attitudes, character-istic behaviors and motivation (see Figure 1.1). These are outlined below and explained in detail in Chapters 2–7.

Chapter 2: Culture and clan

The culture and society into which a person is born and in which they are raised has a profound impact on how they view the world, relate to others and tend to behave in everyday situations. Lack of familiarity with the manifestations of another's cultural background, both superficial – body language, rituals and

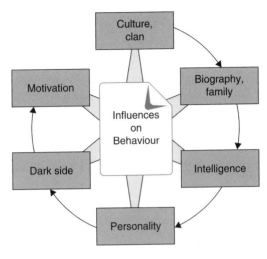

FIG 1.1 / **The six dimensions**

other practices – and underlying – values and beliefs – is perhaps the single greatest cause of failed international business dealings. We identify reliable sources of information regarding cultural differences at both levels.

Chapter 3: Biography and family

Against the context of culture and clan, this chapter examines those experiences unique to an individual that are likely to have the greatest impact. Socioeconomic background, family and key relationships and misfortunes, especially in early life, are hugely influential in shaping or dictating life choices and attitudes. We also look at how physical appearance, gender and sex differences, sexuality, age, class, illness, travel and work experiences affect how we behave and are perceived.

Baroness Thatcher's early years – living above the family grocery store, regular attendance to the local Methodist church, wartime experiences and exposure to politics, particularly through her father who served as alderman and mayor of Grantham – are widely considered to have shaped her attitudes towards individual responsibility, entrepreneurship, economic policy and patriotism, as well as her decision to enter politics.

Chapter 4: Intelligence

Often overlooked or downplayed by assessors, particularly in selection for senior posts, many experts identify intellect as the most reliable overall predictor of an individual's performance in a job. If broken down and analysed in relation to specific requirements or learning environments it can maximize individual contributions and development potential. In this chapter we define and look at how general, multiple and executive intelligence, learning quotient and thinking styles affect performance and behaviors. We also look at gifts or strengths identified by Positive psychologists as contributing to overall performance.

Chapter 5: Personality

While some people can adapt, personality traits are fairly fixed from our late teens. A comprehensive trait assessment is a powerful tool in understanding under what conditions an individual will be at ease and operate most effectively. There is a broad international agreement on different personality traits (the preferences of each individual), and they lend themselves to remote assessment, obviating the need for standard personality tests. In this chapter we describe the Big Five basic personality traits and highlight the significance of the related concepts of 'multiple intelligences', trust and integrity. We also examine 'personality misfits' and those aspects of personality that are broadly considered most desirable in an employee.

Chapter 6: The dark side

Particularly at senior levels, hitherto masked 'dark side' traits, sometimes called personality disorders and mental health issues, can surface with devastating impact. In this chapter we look at DSM-IV personality disorders in the context of Hogan and Hogan's work, identifying 12, remarkably common, dark side traits. We supplement this with recommendations regarding how to weed out potential 'derailers' and manage associated problems.

Chapter 7: Motivation

The sum of the previous elements, motivation is ultimately what leads individuals to behave in a particular way. Motivation is more prone to change than other elements and is often hard to fathom. As outlined in the chapter, consciously and sub-consciously we adopt defence mechanisms to explain motivations that are deep-seated and sometimes unpalatable, both to us and to others. But, perhaps more than any of the other elements, identification of consistent/constant underlying motivations gives vital clues as to how best to approach and manage others. In this chapter, in addition to clarifying some key concepts and popular motivation theories, we describe nine motivations that we believe encapsulate thinking on the topic and provide a useful framework for assessment.

The general format for each of the above chapters is:

- Clear definition of the element and exploration of why it is important by highlighting associated risks
- A simplified overview of dominant theories regarding its impact on behavior
- Highlighting of those aspects which the authors identify as most useful in the context of RPP
- General conclusions and a short recommended reading list (supplemented by a classic alphabetical bibliography at the end of the book).

Chapter 8: Remote personality profiling

This chapter provides step-by-step guidance to collecting the evidence and building a subject's profile using the RPP Research Questionnaire. The methodology is simple and requires no specialized background in personality assessment. Taken together with the information provided in the preceding chapters, it can be analysed to reveal any risks or sensitivities of which the assessor should be aware in their dealings with the subject. To illustrate our approach we present the case study of Alphafox who has had a successful international business career, but whose remote personality profile would indicate some cause for concern. The RPP Questionnaire is presented in full in Annex I.

Chapter 9: Managing extremes

There are many possible approaches to managing and influencing people. In this chapter, as well as highlighting some important general considerations, we introduce our RPP Framework (Annex 2) as a means to ensure that these as well as RPP research findings are taken fully into account. We provide a wealth of tips in relation to the six elements and, where meaningful, also direct the reader towards appropriate heuristic tools. Primary amongst these are Cialdini's 'weapons of influence', supplemented by the influence of logic which we have introduced. All of these are described later in this Introduction. Once again, we illustrate our approach using the case study of Alphafox, recommending how to make an initial pitch for his cooperation and also manage him on a long-term basis.

Chapter 10: Case studies

This chapter comprises eight case studies. Six of these are well-known figures: Stephen Hawking, John Lennon, Margaret Thatcher, Mohamed Al-Fayed, Angela Merkel, Steve Jobs and Edward Snowden. The other two are profiles of individuals whose identities have been disguised – Indigo, an Iranian official, and Silverod, a Saudi businessman. As with Wolfman, an Indian national (this chapter), and Alphafox (Chapter 8), a Spanish entrepreneur, these profiles conclude with headline recommendations for managing or otherwise influencing the subject. All four were commissioned from the authors and their colleagues @RemoteProfiler.com. For further information and assistance please contact **info@remoteprofiler.com**.

Why remote personality profiling?

There are a number of techniques and approaches to understanding people better: what they are really like, what motivates them, what they will do in the future. One of the best known is *Offender or Criminal Profiling*. This can take many forms (a clinical, geographic, typological approach), but the primary aim in most cases is to identify (and then detain) a criminal or criminal gangs. There is also *Psychobiography*, more than biography in that it attempts to use psychological theories to interpret, explain, as well as describe, a person's (living or dead) behavior. It tends to focus on motives and on how particular events shaped people.

People profiling involves collecting a great deal of information, verifying this and putting it together in some meaningful way. There are essentially three ways of doing this:

1. The Typological approach
   This usually involves having a set of pre-existing types or categories and trying to see which one the subject best fits. It is attractively simple but tends to overlook significant data and to simplify rather than clarify. People are too easily 'fitted' into pre-ordained boxes that may not capture sufficiently the important complexities and inconsistencies of human behavior.
2. The Algorithmic approach
   This method is derived from multivariate statisticians who collect specific data that they 'feed' into a mathematical model which weights, processes and combines the data in a particular way. There is a pre-ordained formula: the sort of thing that actuaries use when making their calculations. It

appears to be very scientific but can be misleading given the nature of what is 'fed in' and the evidence for the particular algorithm. The formula may not easily be able to cope with the sort of data we have, for example, concerning a person's motivation.

3. The Thematic approach

   This involves making a semi-clinical and experiential judgment based on a weighting of factors. It differs from the algorithmic approach in that the gestalt judgement has to be based on clinical judgement. Inevitably this requires considerable training in the field to ensure conclusions are both reliable and insightful.

Biographers, criminologists and historians use these methods extensively. They are called into question for a variety of reasons: the tendency to attribute too little force to the situation the target person finds themselves in, rather than their individual personality and motivation (called actor–observer bias). Next, the tendency to seek for, and give unwarranted emphasis to, information that fits one's theory about the target person (confirmation bias). There are also difficulties in relation to understanding how people of different culture and gender view the world. Some tend to over-emphasize the power of certain very specific (often early life) events and become 'pathologizing psychoanalysts'.

For us there are three aspects to RPP that make it uniquely insightful, reliable and accurate.

Remote

This essentially means trying to understand an individual without being able to interview or test them face-to-face. It can be remote in the sense of distance both in space and in time. There are many reasons why it may not be possible to interview a person that one is attempting to profile. They may be the subject of a posthumous biography or someone who, for a variety of reasons, may not wish to be researched or who requires sensitive handling.

The advent of the World Wide Web in particular has meant that there is a massive amount of information available about individuals that they cannot easily control or hide. Not all of it, of course, is accurate. It can include or be supplemented by audio recordings or video footage of the subject, copies of their speeches or writing, as well as published and unpublished accounts of them. RPP relies on tapping into this information. By providing lists of questions in relation to all areas of assessment – identifying what to look for – and guidance regarding what the data collected means, *Revealed* determines what is most pertinent and can reliably be used to come to sound and verifiable conclusions.

An additional method of collecting information remotely is to interview those who knew or know the subject well. They may be friends, family members, fellow school and university students, workplace colleagues or contacts and others who know them through perhaps religious or leisure activities. What they know and what they are prepared to say is of essence. People know very different things about people as a function of the length and type of relationship that they have had with them. Their observations may be very astute or rather superficial. Clearly, the more people who really know the target person and are willing to disclose their observations the better. Again, *Revealed* directs the researcher towards asking the right questions and allowing for personal bias.

Personality

This is shorthand, and possibly a misnomer, as can be seen from the RPP model we advocate a far wider approach than standard personality assessment.

We try to understand how the person sees the world: how their life journey has shaped them and the impact of many factors on their development. By presenting some of the most rigorously tested and academically accepted psychological theories and models, *Revealed* guides the researcher towards collecting and integrating into assessment the information that is most meaningful in determining how people feel, think and act.

Profiling

For us, a profile is a rich and dynamic description of an individual, on which an understanding of them can be built and their habitual or likely behaviors identified. RPP attempts to *fully* understand (describe and explain) an individual as well as how, when and what might change in their lives. *Revealed* presents clearly and concisely the elements that come together to make them who they are, presenting established and validated theories and taxonomies to give a structure to the information-gathering process.

How relevant is RPP to today's business world?

Today we know more about the psychology of human behavior than ever before, and yet in business we rarely apply this knowledge consistently, holistically and to greatest effect. People most often want to form a favourable impression and, especially in business, there is no lack of experts offering advice or training on how to present ourselves in the best possible light, on how to dissimulate, hiding less favourable aspects of our character and abilities. In the international context the scope for misinterpretation and misunderstanding is yet greater. All too often we allow ourselves to be taken in.

There are over 10,000 psychometric and intelligence tests available to help us get below the surface of a subject. However, particularly at senior levels, they are rarely administered. Overviews of earlier career experience, which typically focus on the positives, are limited in their scope and usefulness for assessing competence and predicting performance in different, and often more challenging, roles. In contrast, RPP helps identify influences and patterns of behaviors that in the past may have been tolerated or overlooked, but which may escalate under increased pressure. They may call into question a candidate's suitability or suggest ways in which they can be better managed in future.

Externally, formal assessment is unlikely to be an option, and background research, if conducted at all, tends to focus on biographical data rather than personality, intellect and motives, though clearly these would provide additional valuable personal insights. In both spheres, we are often blinded by status and qualifications and rely too much on instinct and first impressions, even across cultural divides, despite the obvious and proven risks. The 'science' is essentially missing.

We might assume that human assessment is too complex; that the information on which we can make a valid assessment is simply too diverse and inaccessible; that there are simply too many variables to take into account when seeking to predict and influence behaviors. In this context, no wonder we rely on gut feelings and tried and tested strategies. *Revealed* dispels the myth that the science of understanding people better is for the experts alone. That it is only available in the context of existing standard assessment procedures, with the subject's cooperation and access to extensive time and resources. It also debunks the idea, particularly prevalent in the West, that individuals are inscrutable and have a high degree of control over their behaviors and how we interpret them.

Revealed explains how to build a profile of an individual – their mind-set, behavior and motivation. It presents a simple, comprehensive methodology – RPP – that builds on recent advances in human assessment, particularly in the fields of work psychology and personality disorders, and enables even the non-expert to peel back the layers, revealing the person within.

Through RPP we can build a profile that gives vital insights into an individual's background, intellect, values, behavioral preferences and motivations. Such a profile can have a decisive impact on, for example, our pitch for new business or philanthropic funding, or a manager's ability to perform effectively at a high level. It shows that, for example, without 'grilling' a potential donor or senior manager or asking them to submit to tests, we can assess how they are likely to react to a proposal. It can highlight the risk that a technically brilliant manager is being promoted beyond their level of comfort or competence. In sum, it is a methodology that provides the means of seeing someone with fully open and fresh eyes. Armed with these human insights, and taking other external factors into account, we can make more informed decisions and devise more effective influencing, negotiating, motivation and management strategies.

In essence *Revealed* attempts to answer three questions:

- Why does a subject feel, think and behave the way they do? It identifies key elements influencing them and the likely consequences of them taking on certain roles or behaving in specific situations.
- What evidence do we need to look for to assess their 'fit' in a role or organization and when do we need to handle the subject with particular care and sensitivity? It enables us to assess their needs and expectations and map them against reliable RPP research findings
- How can we more effectively identify and manage differences between their drives, preferences and approach and our own? It outlines general principles and illustrates how tried and tested influencing strategies can be adapted in the light of RPP research findings.

Revealed moves from theory to practice with emphasis on the practical. It sets out clearly what to look out for and links behavioral and other indicators to sound conclusions. Guidance on collecting and interpreting data is brief. Questions are clear and, even if our research cannot answer all of them immediately, they serve to highlight areas of interest or concern in our future dealings. It presents detailed case studies to illustrate how we can assess suitability or 'fit' for a particular role, and suggests strategies to influence and motivate in a manner that takes full account of a subject's background, personality and abilities and our own personal preferences or conditioning.

The assessor is then only left to factor in the context: the opportunities or constraints which a specific role or situation may bring. Can, for example, a senior appointee be encouraged to manage his behaviors through friendly awareness-raising or training? Can weaknesses or strengths be managed through team-working or a fresh allocation of responsibilities? In a negotiation or pitch for funding, given time or financial limitations, which would be the most effective tactics to build trust, put them at their ease, highlight common ground or elicit valuable information?

RPP is a fresh approach made possible by increasing access to World Wide Web materials. Assessments are comprehensive – not just focused on some aspects of character and behavior – and can be made from afar. It uses open sources of information, without the individual's cooperation, specialist expertise or significant resources. While designed primarily to help organizations appoint the right people, particularly leaders and senior executives, and to gain commercial advantage in external business dealings, RPP has many more applications.

Examples of how RPP might be used

Matching internal and external candidates to sensitive or critical roles: Are they truly suitable?

Human resource professionals, executive boards and stakeholder managers, all have to decide on the level of competency, trust and commitment to an organization's goals, often without recourse to standard assessment procedures.

Before negotiations began the Chairman and Board of Omega approached us for a profile of Alphafox (identity disguised), a well-known Spanish entrepreneur and prospective investor in the company and as such a potential board member. Having deployed RPP we concluded that Alphafox could be an asset, in that he is bright enough for the position and is sociable when in public. He is highly driven, will win new business and drive a good bargain.

However, our research also raised concerns. He demonstrates a degree of volatility and scepticism. This might make him a difficult partner and team member. If he perceives he has been wronged he is likely to turn against the company and will be quick to litigate.

For full case study, see Chapters 8 and 9

Are there indicators that the favoured internal executive responds poorly to stress? What situations might make them derail? Are they being promoted beyond their level of competence intellectually, and is their thinking style conducive to a leadership role? Will a board member be discreet and prove committed to and effective in lobbying on the company's behalf? Is an NGO representative being considered by a company for an advisory role likely to be genuinely interested in finding new forms of collaboration with the private sector? Might they become a whistle-blower?

Negotiating, sometimes across cultural divides: what are their personal preferences and natural behaviors?

Businessmen, diplomats and politicians all have to negotiate – it is a significant part of most people's work life. Knowing more about the person on the other side of the table has to be a real advantage. What will an Argentine expect in terms of deference? What motivates a venture capitalist? How can we best present a proposal, given a potential funder's intellect and thinking style? Where will an informant feel most at ease? How can we strike up rapport with a valuable contact? Taken all together, what is our best approach?

Robert, a British businessman, sits down opposite his counterpart for the first discussions about what could turn out to be the biggest contract his company has ever won. How does he maximize his chance of success? Clearly much depends on his interlocutor. His approach with Frank, a sharp-witted but somewhat introverted American engineer and senior procurement manager, could be to fly in and present data-rich documentation and introduce specialists able to answer technical questions, followed up by an invitation for a beer in a quiet hotel bar to discuss further points of interest before heading for the airport.

But with Ahmed, a Saudi sheikh, second son in the family-owned business, the approach Robert takes is different. He has familiarized himself with cultural mores, knows the sheikh has no formal qualifications in his field and has some indications of the sheikh's arrogant and self-confident character. His approach, over the course of several invitations and meetings, will involve respect and flattery through acknowledgement of his family's status and relations to the king, of his personal achievements and primary interest – horse racing – and the subtle presentation of evidence suggesting Robert's networks and credentials as the most senior regional representative of a successful MNC. Robert's assumption is that the contract's financial and technical details will be passed down to others and then formally and publicly approved by the sheikh at a later stage.

Building an individual's profile: what are all the elements that come together to make someone who they are?

This application is the one most akin to criminal profiling. Biographers, investigators, the intelligence services, legal and financial institutions, biographers, journalists, even just a curious bystander, may want or benefit from having a more complete understanding of why an individual behaves in the way they do. What factors contributed to a politician's drive or commitment to a particular cause? Can we conclude that this whistle-blower is likely to be reliable? What personal factors will constrain a foreign contact from responding positively to a request for privileged information? To what degree can we

Walter Isaacson (2011) in his biography of Steve Jobs writes *'He was not a model boss or human being, tidily packaged for emulation. Driven by demons, he could drive those around him to fury and despair. But his personality and passions and products were all interrelated, just as Apple's hardware and software tended to be, as if part of an integrated system.'*

He was a character whose unconventional appearance and manner would hardly have singled him out in 1977, aged 22, as one of the world's most successful future entrepreneurs. What led him to become so is the subject of endless speculation in the same way as figures such as Hitler, Marilyn Monroe, Nelson Mandela and Baroness Thatcher continue to enthral.

conclude that a trader was 'rogue' rather than the institution being at fault? The assessor of course can also benefit by heightening their awareness of their own 'programming' that may lead to poor decisions or judgments of character.

Influence and persuasion

Inherent in RPP assessment is the question of how to persuade others and whether we can use the same tactics whatever their personality or motivation. Many of us search for ways to influence and persuade others in order to reap the most benefit from these individuals. Recent research suggests that a simple way of persuading others is through taking advantage of their 'reptilian brain'. Certain brain areas respond quickly and automatically to stimuli in order to guide our behavior. Many decisions are made unconsciously and instinctively without us being aware of the lack of rational thought behind our actions.

Those wishing to influence others' behavior can take advantage of *heuristics*, experience-based, intuitive problem-solving strategies that individuals commonly use in order to speed up decision-making processes. Kahneman and Frederick (2002) suggest that cognitive heuristics work through a process of attribute substitution. According to their theory, when a complex judgment of a target attribute is made, this is substituted with a heuristic attribute that is simpler to calculate. So, without conscious awareness, a simpler question is answered than the originally cognitively straining issue.

Heuristics are generally advantageous to decision-making, as they require minimal cognitive effort. However, in certain situations they can lead to cognitive biases. There is also potential for others to take advantage of them. Cialdini (2001) proposes six key principles of persuasion, rooted in heuristics, which can be employed to influence others.

As highlighted above, influence of this kind derives from our reliance on emotional rather than rational appeal. The strength of those emotions varies amongst individuals, and strategies must take this into account. A really tough person is not likely to be greatly influenced by an approach from an individual who tries to use charm or social proof; someone motivated by security and caution is not going to be very impressed by something which is untried and scarce.

We believe that people are also influenced by a seventh principle of persuasion, *logic*. This principle is also subject to emotion. More often than not people like to believe that the decision they take is based on evidence and sound reasoning and can be persuaded that it is by another's carefully reasoned presentation of argument or fact.

Reciprocity	When we are given something by another person, or treated well, we feel obliged to reciprocate in kind. Cialdini suggests that all human societies subscribe to this rule. As humans we do not feel happy being indebted to someone and so offer something in return for what they have provided or done. Extensive experimental research confirms the existence of such a social norm, wherein a favour received is returned.
Commitment and consistency	We have a drive to be consistent. When we make a commitment to do something, we experience personal and interpersonal pressure to behave as we have in the past or have suggested that we will. Inconsistency is frowned upon and considered to be an undesirable personality trait by society, and so is avoided. Making even a small commitment can result in significant behavioral changes over a longer period. As an example, individuals have been found to be increasingly willing to purchase a product related to a cause to which they have previously committed (e.g. buying a washing powder brand which makes a donation to a rainforest protection charity).
Social proof	We use others' behavior to determine what is correct and accepted. Cialdini quotes sales expert Cavett Robert, suggesting that 'since 95 per cent of the people are imitators and only 5 per cent initiators, people are persuaded more by the actions of others than by any proof we can offer.' This effect has found to be so strong as to persuade people against their own instincts. In Asch's (1951) famous experiments, 75 per cent of participants agreed with confederates who presented the same incorrect answer regarding the similarity in length of three lines.
Authority	We are trained from birth to trust and abide by instructions given by figures of authority. We automatically trust them and rely on their authority to shortcut decision-making. Once an individual in a position of authority has given an order, we tend to stop thinking about the situation and to respond as suggested without much further thought.
Scarcity	Products will be more popular when they are available for 'a limited time only', or when they are in short supply and likely to sell out – 'only 10 iPhones left in store'. Furthermore, if you have information that few other people possess, it becomes more precious and can command a higher price.
Liking	People tend to be persuaded easily by those whom they like. Physical attractiveness plays a role, with research showing that we believe good-looking individuals have more desirable traits such as kindness and intelligence. We like those who resemble us, this seeming to be the case whether we are alike in terms of opinions, personality or lifestyle. Cooperating and having to work together to achieve mutual goals also results in liking. We develop liking for those who compliment us, believing and accepting these compliments, as well as developing positive feelings towards those who have praised us.

Chapter 9 – Managing Extremes – offers suggestions as to which of the above might prove most effective in relation to different subject profiles. These incorporate and supplement the tips given throughout the book.

How to use this book

Behavioral extremes, areas of difference and hidden, surprising or unexplained aspects of a subject can be risks, both in the short and longer term. Above all our aim in writing this book has been to provide practical guidance and tools to help identify and manage such risks in relation to the subject selected for assessment.

Descriptions of the six elements and guidance to direct the reader towards drawing up an accurate profile of their subject (and indeed themselves) are provided throughout the book. There are also two tools – the RPP Research Questionnaire, introduced in Chapter 8 – Remote Personality Profiling, produced in summary in Annex 1 and the RPP Framework introduced in Chapter 9 – Managing Extremes and reproduced in Annex 2.

The RPP Research Questionnaire is designed specifically for use by a basic researcher. Completed (or even part completed) it can provide a solid basis for identifying risk areas in relation to a subject. If the researcher reads the material contained in Chapters 2–7, it will clearly provide valuable additional background information, but familiarity with the material is not a must.

The RPP Framework is essentially a planning tool whose purpose is to ensure that all relevant research is taken into account and allied to appropriate 'tips and tools of influence'. It can be used by an individual or as the basis for team discussion.

We recommend that, as they go through the book, readers use the RPP Framework in Annex 2, applying the knowledge acquired from the book to a specific subject, 'influencer' and scenario. To conduct a fuller analysis of an individual, using more specialist techniques, we suggest you contact us at info@remoteprofiler.com.

Conclusion

In *Revealed* each of the elements we analyse has been the focus of numerous academic studies and exhaustively examined by business and management gurus. What we have done is to bring the wealth of their research and knowledge together and present it in a simplified form. Thus, as illustrated by the summarized version of a Remote Profiler report below, extensive expertise can be readily applied to a subject of interest, even by the non-expert.

Case study: Wolfman

This remote personality profile is based on a real subject, but client and subject identities have been disguised. All of the terms we use will be fully explained in the course of *Revealed*.

The brief

Aardvik, a Norwegian oil company, identified an Indian national, Wolfman, as a useful person to appoint as a non-executive board member, specifically to assist them develop their oil and gas exploration work in South Asia. Aardvik do not yet have a permanent base in South Asia but have been awarded a concession and the prospects look good. Before approaching Wolfman they have asked for a remote personality profile to help them make the approach and to formulate their offer.

Cultural Background – Implications of being Indian

In Indian society management tends to be decisive and aggressive. Norwegians rather tend towards intuition and consensus, preferring to resolve conflict through compromise and resolution. In India careers are compulsory for men but optional for women; indeed, in India there is a much lower share of working women in professional jobs. In India money is generally prioritized over more leisure time. The reverse is true in Norway.

In more individualist societies, such as Norway, hiring and promotion decisions are supposed to be based on skills and rules only, whereas in more collectivist societies, such as in India, decisions take into account the employees 'in group' – in general relationships are more important than the task.

India generally is a larger 'power distance' society than Norway. This means that the ideal boss is a benevolent autocrat, or 'God father'. Privileges and status symbols are the norm in India but frowned upon in small power distance countries such as Norway.

The differences between Indian and Norwegian cultures are quite profound. The question is how much does Wolfman reflect his society's values and practices? He is intelligent and well travelled; he will therefore be well aware that societies differ and he appears tolerant of these differences. Nonetheless, in dealing with him it would be wise to allow for his cultural background.

A further factor to take into account is his wife's origins. She comes from Kerala, a south-western state where women play a much more significant role in the family – some even describe the state as matriarchal. This is often mentioned by Wolfman. He will have a much more tolerant attitude to 'gender equality' than many of his compatriots.

Culturally, there are two dimensions where Norway and India differ significantly. Norway has a low score for power distance. This means that Norwegians tend to be independent; hierarchy is for convenience only. Power is decentralized and managers count on the experience and knowledge of their team members. Employees expect to be consulted. People from India on the other hand accept un-equal rights and paternalistic leadership; the attitude to managers is formal; communication is top down; and negative feedback is never offered to more senior people.

The second difference is in the scale of masculinity. Norway scores second lowest which means they value consensus and sympathy for the underdog; incentives such as free time and flexibility are favoured, an effective manager is a supportive one and decision-making is achieved through involvement. Indians like to show off their success and power, and work is often the centre of one's life and visible symbols of success in the work place are important. However, India is also a very spiritual society where humility and abstinence is

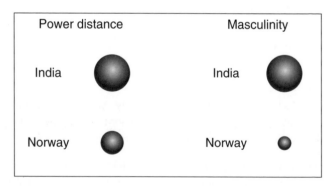

FIG 1.2 Cultural differences: Norway/India

Source: Based on data from www.geert-hofstede.com.

also valued. It is also worth noting that Wolfman's wife comes from Kerala, a state known for its matriarchal approach to life. Wolfman has always worked long hours and given total support to his political masters. But he is not ostentatious and often defers to his wife (see Figure 1.2).

Biographical information – Privileged and loving

Wolfman was born in Tamil Nadu in 1942 and married Samu from Kerala in 1961. He had one younger brother who died in his teens. Wolfman was deeply upset by his brother's death but was greatly comforted by the extended family support. They have no children and have a stable loving relationship. Wolfman comes from a wealthy family and he enjoyed a privileged upbringing. He attended university in New Delhi and achieved excellent results. He went on to Oxford where he received a DPhil in Mathematics.

In 1965 he joined the Indian Foreign Service and became ambassador to a major European country. He became special advisor to the Indian Prime Minister in 1997 and has remained loyal to the Indian Congress party since. He was appointed a special economic advisor to the former Prime Minister Manmohan Singh and has just retired from that post.

He and his wife are in good health and have homes in Delhi (a small flat but in a wealthy area) and Tamil Nadu. They enjoy reading and walking. Occasionally they go overseas but usually this has been when Wolfman travels for business. He has recently taken up a part-time professorial post at Bangalore University.

Intellect – Clever

Wolfman has a superior intellect and remains inquisitive and open to new ideas. He is an acknowledged expert in early Hindu scientific achievements. His knowledge of European Renaissance art is also impressive.

Personality – Introvert and well adjusted

Wolfman is relatively introvert but has no problem being in large crowds. His wife is much more extravert and Wolfman often leaves his wife to make the running in social situations. Wolfman then quietly joins the group and goes on to impress. They are a good team.

TABLE 1.1   Wolfman's five-factor personality profile

Introvert	↔	Extravert
Stable	↔	Neurotic
Open	↔	Closed
Agreeable	↔	Tough
Conscientious	↔	Disorganized

He responds well to stress and we judge him to be quite tough despite his genial manner. He appears well organized, but this could be because he can employ staff to take on his administration (see Table 1.1).

The Dark Side – Reserved and dutiful

Wolfman has no obvious high-risk habits or behaviors. There is evidence to suggest that he can be reserved and independent. He stands up to criticism, can misread social cues and unintentionally bruise others. He is very dutiful – unassuming, mannerly. He rarely challenges policy decisions and consults regularly (see Table 1.2).

TABLE 1.2   Wolfman's Dark Side risks

	Some risk	High risk
Reserved	◆	
Dutiful		◆

Motivations and values – Traditional, humble and hard working

Throughout his career Wolfman has set achievement as his prime motivator. He has held senior positions in government and clearly enjoys the power and influence this gives him. He is religious and regularly visits his local Hindu temple. He is also patriotic. There is a mischievous side to Wolfman, and he is willing to take risks though, as he has become older, he is probably more measured in his personal risk-taking.

It is also worth noting what he is not: he is not hungry for recognition of his work or achievements, except perhaps from his immediate superior. However, he does respond positively to well-placed compliments. He is not commercial, which in India is extraordinary. There has never been any suggestion that he is corrupt or accepted any bribe.

He leads and enjoys a pretty simple life: he does not drink alcohol, unless it is thought socially necessary, eats lightly and simply, and does not court big society events.

General assessment

Wolfman would be an asset to any company working in India. He clearly has high-level contacts and is a hard worker. He is clever and well adjusted, showing no real personality extremes. He will be modest – to the point of questioning whether he really can offer anything of value to this unknown world (to him) of commercial activity.

He will argue his case but in the end will accept the decision of his superior – if he respects them. As he has become older he will have learnt how to question and while dutiful we judge he is not blind in his obedience.

The biggest issue for a Norwegian company employing Wolfman is the cultural differences. Wolfman is a deeply patriotic person – worldly but Indian.

Recommendations

We recommend:

- Wolfman will only work for a company if he believes that it is for the good of India. He will be loyal to his employers, but if there is conflict between them and India, he will always opt for the latter.
- While not a vain man he will respond to compliments on his vast experience and intellect.
- Help him understand the ways of Norway and Norwegian culture; he will understand the differences intellectually, but find it hard to absorb the differences. Show interest in and respect for his culture.
- Involve his wife wherever possible – she is close to him and a strong influence. She is also a charming dinner companion and is more assertive than most Indian women, though not relative to those who come from Kerala.

Recommended reading

Carnegie, D. (1936) *How to Win Friends and Influence People*. New York: Pocket Books.
Cialdini, R (2001) *Influence: The Psychology of Persuasion*. New York: Quill.

chapter **Culture**

In 'Outliers' (2008) Malcolm Gladwell provides a life and death example of why culture matters and is the starting point for understanding people. Faced with problems as they came into land, an analysis of flight recordings concludes that the Korean Air first captain acted wholly consistently with his societal norms. He evidently had concerns but did not raise them with the senior pilot using direct language. He adhered to strict hierarchy rules and sought to maintain surface harmony, avoiding possible offence by suggesting his superior was failing to react appropriately. The pilot, who had earlier complained of tiredness, simply did not register the seriousness of the first officer's concerns. Even in the face of imminent disaster, the first pilot's default behaviors were so deeply ingrained, and his assumption that the pilot would understand so strong, that he failed to step in with catastrophic consequences.

The importance of culture in shaping our attitudes and behavior is reflected in the fact that it is the first element we address in RPP (see Figure 2.1). The above example illustrates the degree to which our cultural background is an inescapable and hugely influential factor in shaping our attitudes and behavior. International air safety measures have now been introduced which factor in the need for explicit, internationally neutral communication in the cockpit and with air traffic control.

Equally in business, acknowledging cultural incompatibilities or differences and taking appropriate action to manage or mitigate them is essential, both in specific situations and in longer-term relationship-building. In negotiation

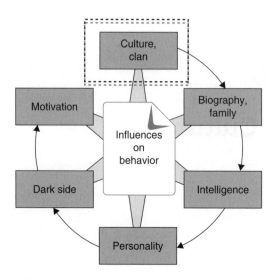

FIG 2.1 / **The six dimensions: culture**

with foreign counterparts, understanding that 'no' might mean 'yes but I don't want to openly disagree' can save much frustration and misdirected energy.

In this era of globalizing business, many of us are used to dealing with people of different cultural backgrounds. We generally do so with good intent and can access extensive sources of guidance on intercultural management and negotiation. And yet, often we are caught out by cultural differences surfacing and getting in the way. The 2012 EIU report – Competing across borders – cites 51 per cent and 49 per cent of research respondents, respectively, as stating that 'differences in cultural traditions' and 'different workplace norms' are the greatest threats to the smooth functioning of cross-border relationships. Bribery and corruption is an example of potential culture clash. 'Wasta' (a concept originating in the Arab tribal system suggesting the use of personal influence in decision-making, amounting to nepotism in many Western eyes) is just part of the way things operate in many parts of the Middle East and North Africa. In the same way that in India or Nigeria a bribe or 'dash' is a widely accepted manner of boosting the salary of an under-paid government official but is punishable by law in a US or British businessman's home country. Getting the right results is open to varying methods and interpretations, and a failure or inability to apply local rules can be a real stumbling block. Many business contacts in the region will be aware of the sensitivities but may have to grapple with the expectations of family, friends and others.

It is in situations where we need to deal outside our own culture(s), such as when we travel abroad, that we become most acutely aware of not only the practical but also the usually unexpressed, emotional value they have for us. We have to learn new rules and should, although usually don't, hesitate before attributing meaning and significance to what we see and hear. Without investment in understanding the cultural context and how the people who matter to us are influenced by it, and by their broader cultural background, we are thrown off balance and sometimes at considerable disadvantage.

The term 'culture' is used in relation to various groupings – national, religious, ethnic, gender, age and organizational being just some. The relevance of some of these to the remote personality profiler is discussed in Chapter 3 – Biographical Information. This chapter explores in greater depth the impact of national culture. Recently the field has attracted many business researchers and it illustrates well the wide scope and multiple layers of cultural impact. Here, as throughout *Revealed*, we seek to highlight in particular those frequently overlooked and underestimated risks that arise from hidden and hard-to-quantify differences which, if we fail to manage, can result in lost advantage and, on occasions, real damage to relationships that matter.

Those national cultures, which we experience in early life, tend to be those with which we have greatest affiliation and comfort and to which we default, particularly under pressure. Understanding a person's cultural background, and the degree to which it influences them, therefore, becomes hugely important. Without this knowledge, we may wrongly assume what they value, misinterpret their words and actions or handle them inappropriately. We would tend to see them primarily through our own cultural lens, frequently underestimating hidden differences in outlook and motivation. Being a member of minority or ethnic group, being of a certain age or nationality may be of no significance, but then again it might be. We need to find out, by understanding the individual, context and requirements of the situation or role.

Culture is an ill-defined concept. In this chapter we first try to bring clarity to the term and explain why culture(s) are important to us, illustrating ways and means by which 'group norms' are embedded in us during childhood and later life. We then examine a variety of approaches to identifying and measuring differences between national cultures and

Culture is an ill-defined concept.

how they can be applied to common work situations. Finally, we provide a framework to facilitate assessment of when – both in relation to a specific subject and situation – those differences are likely to surface and require us to adapt our own default culturally shaped approach. Thus, we demist the lens through which the remote personality profiler is likely to see the subject and explore a range of options for handling them.

Situational management by stealth:

When we sent delegations to Greece, we always insisted that meetings took place in non-smoking venues. That way we could always be sure that one of our counterparts would be out of the room at any given point. Highest per capita consumption of cigarettes in the world!

Source: Former British diplomat.

What is culture?

Ask someone to define culture, let alone the one under which they operate, and it will usually draw slightly blank stares. They may be more forthcoming when describing their *organizational* culture, described forcefully in staff handbooks and PR materials though, as we all know, these often reflect management aspirations rather than reality (think UK banking sector).

But when it comes to national culture they will often resort to far vaguer notions such as 'democratic', 'Islamic' or, in the case of UK, 'pluralistic' or even the get-out of 'multi-cultural'.

In *Culture and Anarchy*, published in the late 1860s, Matthew Arnold gave an early definition of culture as 'the best which has been thought and said'. Nowadays it has wider and often more negative connotations (again the banks come to mind), and we would be harangued if we were to suggest that one national culture is intrinsically better than another. So a more useful definition, certainly in terms of national culture as discussed in detail in this chapter, might be that put forward by Triandis who says *'Culture is to society what memory is to individuals. In other words, culture includes traditions that tell 'what has worked' in the past. It also encompasses the way people have learned to look at their environment and themselves, and their unstated assumptions about the way the world is and the way people should act.'* But an agreed definition will be forever elusive!

Cultures are learnt and it takes years for most foreigners to pick up practices, let alone understand the subtle meanings behind them. In Kate Fox's amusing and insightful book *Watching the English* she lists eight, at first sight rather nebulous, English rules just for queuing in a pub (and imagine the confusion when the English don't for once form an orderly queue). We don't explain them here in full – it takes the author several pages to do so – but even their titles give us an idea of the challenge of getting to grips with culture:

• Sociability rule
• Invisible-queue rule
• Pantomime rule
• The rules of Ps and Qs
• The rules of regular speak
• The rules of coded Pub-talk
• The rules of pub argument
• The free association rule
  Fox (2004)

Cultures are pervasive, which can be explained by the fundamental human desires and needs they address, providing their members with:

• tried and tested solutions, obviating the need to reinvent the wheel and draw conclusions based on limited knowledge;
• a sense of security, well-being and control over the environment;
• a framework through which to interpret and make sense of the world;
• patterns of behavior which enable them to live together harmoniously and productively.

Cultures evolve wherever there are groups whose members find benefit or need to work or co-exist and are used to distinguish one group from another. Ethnic cultures sometimes assert themselves to overcome oppression, professional cultures to promote common standards, and company cultures ultimately in order to protect and promote their shareholder value proposition. When we use terms such as 'working class' in reference to an individual, it's shorthand for a whole gamut of assumptions regarding how they think and behave. They may subsequently be proven inaccurate, but it's a starting point at least.

A whole mix of factors come together to form a national culture or identity. We tend to associate more laid-back attitudes with warmer climates, for example. Religious movements, historical and political events, improvement in economic conditions and exposure to other ways of life can all change the systems or rules – written and unwritten – under which we operate. Superficially the change can seem rapid and quite significant, but research indicates that at national level cultures are quite constant. Even radical developments, such as we have seen recently in the Middle East and North Africa, mask a much slower pace and shallower depth of change in traditional values and practices.

Cultures are embedded in us from birth and serve us well. They enable us to live in groups and problem-solve. They have far more influence over us than the Western world, in particular, tends to assume. Knowing about the environment in which an individual is raised – their early experiences with authority, whether brought up a Christian or Muslim, the institutions they attend – is always a useful backdrop to engaging substantively with them. But what can we learn about their country of origin and the national cultures that have influenced them to help us build relationships and get things done? What are the observable and, crucially, less obvious aspects of culture that confound the business traveler? Can they be managed effectively and, if so, how? We need to look at how and which cultures are embedded in us to find out.

How is culture embedded in us?

Kluckhohn (1954) talks about explicit and implicit culture, the former being what people talk about and can specify more readily (written procedures, artifacts, role models and rituals), and the latter more related to feelings, what is taken for granted and what exists on the fringes of awareness.

By way of example, consider a meeting at an international oil company. Before it starts you get a health and safety briefing and have observed coming in numerous signs alerting you to potential hazards. When you chat at length with an employee, you realize that health and safety are organizational priorities. Encouraging staff to intervene on safety issues, even when it is just a senior manager not holding the handrail in head office, may seem excessive until you realize the purpose behind it. On an oilrig it is imperative, and avoiding death is of critical importance to the company. Signaling high-level commitment makes H&S part of the DNA of the company, not just a practical response to a real and specified danger.

All of us are subject to cultural influences, made up of a complex combination of 'systems' from birth. They teach individuals what matters, what works and what is expected of them in order to continue to live in the group. What this oil company has realized is that it is often the less visible aspects that have greatest impact and that they carry over into many different spheres of life, eventually forming our default behaviors and attitudes. Theirs is a version of the methods deployed by a mother, or others close to you as a child, and society at a later stage.

Organizational cultures can have profound impacts on individuals but early and persistent exposure to explicit and implicit 'cultural primes' over the course of a lifetime has a far deeper impact on us. This is achieved through two mutually reinforcing processes.

Enculturation

Kottak (2011) says enculturation *'teaches an individual the accepted norms and values of the culture or society where the individual lives'*. He who says that culture is *'one of the foundations and boundary conditions upon and within which the individual and his potentialities develop'* (Goodman, 1967), puts forward the notion of boundaries that grant acceptance to members, as well as control and protect. As such, little wonder that enculturation takes place early on in an individual's life in the proximal environment, usually through parents, family members and significant others, primarily during childhood. In seeking to care and protect us, and equip us with the tools we need to survive and thrive in life, those around us pass on, largely subconsciously, the combined wisdom of the group.

These are the influences to which individuals are most persistently exposed. As such they are also the influences of which they are least consciously aware, which they find the most difficult to control and to which they have the greatest emotional attachment. Here we choose to define them in terms of national culture, but in Chapter 3 we discuss at length individual differences in the way a child is brought up, perhaps, for example, in a poor single-parent family, and how that might affect a child and later adult.

Different cultures bring children up very differently. The practice of the mother and new-born staying at home or with close family members for a period of 40 days is still common in Japan, India, Turkey and Greece, despite the exigencies of modern life. Contrast that with other cultures that encourage early stimulation and loud, proud and varied interaction both within and outside the home. Some cultures, often those less economically developed, put greater emphasis on family ties, loyalty and respect for authority. This differing attitude toward dependence is likely to have long-term effects and distinguish the members of one culture from another. Other largely subconscious efforts have been shown to impact the development of social rather than analytical intelligence, although both can be developed in later life.

Conroy, Hess, Azuma and Kashiwagi (1980) highlight how the language that mothers chose when chastising children would tend to reinforce wider held beliefs regarding the importance of the individual relative to the group. In collectivist Japan, where group interests tend to be promoted over individual, Japanese mothers were shown to be prone to stress the feelings of others through expressions such as 'It will be annoying to them if you misbehave', whereas mothers from individualistic United States were more likely to emphasize rules and authority structures that the child is supposed to have internalized through expressions such as 'You know better than that.'

Hsu (1953) also comments on cultural differences in child-rearing practices between the Chinese and Americans. American families attribute greater importance to the growing child than to those bringing them up. In such a context, he points out that given the environment is sensitive to *the child*, they are less likely to develop *social sensitivity*. A Chinese upbringing would tend to reduce a child's sense of self-importance and oblige them to be sensitive to others and their *environment*. Goodman (1967) agrees, suggesting that self-importance as a child results in adults being more assertive, attention-demanding and undervaluing the importance of others. It may also make them feel relatively indifferent toward rules and authority but, on a more positive note, be conducive to boldness, assurance and a sense of autonomy.

Socialization

Socialization takes place in the wider, distal environment, generally through more deliberate, targeted interventions by schools and other institutions. The underlying values tend to be consistent with those promoted in the proximal environment. Both emerge from a country or community's unique experience of ecological factors, history, language, wars and religions and are sustained through the efforts of its group members. For example, a strong concern for keeping order and respecting authority will be reflected in schools, usually the first environment outside the family to which a child is exposed on a consistent basis. In general, a preference for non-participative teaching methods will reinforce the idea of traditional wisdom and respect for an authority figure. The habit engendered amongst pupils of not speaking up and challenging the teacher may translate into more submissive behaviors as adults and at work.

Brody (1992) reviews studies on ethnic differences in intelligence amongst African Americans. He found that mothers are more important than fathers in intellectual socialization and that, in black-white unions where the mother is white, the child scored on average nine points higher in IQ tests than in those unions where the mother was black. He concludes that differing socialization practices are largely accountable.

How can we get a handle on culture?

Galtung (1981) is one of a number of authors and researchers to have observed differences between Oriental and Occidental intellectual styles. The former he sees as characterized by a more holistic approach to reality and more dialectic approach to understanding it as a totality with built-in contradictions evolving over time. The Occidental style is characterized by an atomistic conception of reality, combined with deductive approach to understanding – dividing reality into a number of small parts, linking them together to form highly impressive deductive pyramids.

Hall (1976) distinguishes between high and low context cultures to explain differences in communication styles. In a high context culture, such as China and many other Asian countries, most information is found in the physical context or internalized in the person, while very little is in the explicit, transmitted part of the message. In relatively low-context cultures, such as the United States, Scandinavia and Germany this is less the case. This could go some way toward explaining, for example, why punchy Powerpoint presentations are more popular in less field-dependent countries in terms of getting messages across than in many parts of Asia.

Such studies provide fascinating insights into the enormous scope and depth of culture's impacts. Reaching consensus on the extent and form of impact, however, is hampered by a number of factors. Some approach culture from a universalist perspective – looking for differences in basic psychological functions and processes; and others from a relativist – looking for evidence of similarities. Some study it as external to the individual, others as internal. In terms of country-comparative studies, some are considered to have used an excessively Western-biased emic approach and to have incorporated too few countries to draw valid conclusions. Even if nationally comparable data fields are agreed, some ask whether the data generated can be meaningfully and reliably applied to the assessment of individuals, given the difficulties of isolating one influence (say innate intelligence) from another (say a truly inspirational teacher).

There is broad agreement, however, that there is considerable divergence between different nationalities in terms of how, largely subconsciously, we:

- select and process information;
- give meaning to what we see and hear;
- behave in routine or ritualized situations;
- judge to what extent those around us share our view about what matters.

Entering another country or dealing with someone with a different cultural background leads us automatically to make distinctions, at least in terms of explicit culture and practices, and manage them to a degree. Acknowledging them is likely to enable us to be better prepared, both emotionally and pragmatically on subsequent visits.

In effect, we see everything through a cultural lens. This means, for example, that:

- We tend to attribute similar meanings to body language and other para-lingual communication. Often this is misleading. Staring someone straight in the eye in India is disrespectful whereas to avoid doing so suggests evasiveness in other countries. An American might interpret falling silent in a meeting as acquiescence or shyness whereas in fact his Chinese counterpart just doesn't want to openly disagree. Even the extent to which we focus on the content of speech rather than body language and other contextual factors has been shown to differ.
- We deploy behaviors that are inappropriate or misunderstood in another cultural context. A Russian may raise his voice and an American bang his fist while this would be completely unacceptable to a Singaporean or Japanese in most situations. All humans have been shown to experience similar emotions but the intensity of feeling in relation to certain situations and the manner in which those emotions are expressed vary. So Ekman and Friesen (1975) talk of 'display rules' masking emotions.
- We develop ethnocentric views and stereotypes, subconsciously seeking out evidence to support our assumptions and prompting us to make simplified assumptions about what matters to others and how they will act. The Swiss will always be slaves to time, the Germans to rules, the English are perfidious, the Spanish put things off until mañana and the Dutch are unbearably direct. Some of these may have validity but are just aspects of national identity which our subject may not possess.

National personality profiles

As stated above, one of the ways in which we define cultures is by associating particular characteristics with members of a group or nationality – we stereotype. There is, naturally enough, more divergence between citizens of a country than between national profiles. But research does indicate that there is some truth to the notion that citizens of a country share personality traits or at least that culture exercises significant impact on the relative weight or desirability associated with given personality traits and their related social behaviors.

The Revised NEO Personality Inventory (NEO PI-R), developed by Costa and McCrae and introduced in Chapter 5 – Personality, measures individuals on a scale of Extraversion, Agreeableness, Conscientiousness, Neuroticism and Openness to experience. Cheung et al. argue that a sixth dimension, related to Interpersonal Relatedness, is necessary to highlight the value attached to this quality in China and other collectivist countries. However, Costa and McCrae's model is generally considered reliable when used worldwide to define personality.

Based on the NEO PI-R, McCrae and Terracciano have drawn up over 50 country personality profiles that show that certain personality types are more prevalent in some countries than others. Thus, we can say that on average Italians are more extravert than Filipinos, and the Japanese more neurotic than the Swedes. Hofstede's four main value dimensions discussed below are strongly associated with each of the personality traits. They are, for example, negatively correlated with an acceptance of unequal power distribution and positively with individualism. Geographically proximate cultures often have similar profiles, and there is a clear contrast between European, US, Asian and African cultures.

Others have found also evidence of national-level characteristics. Heine (2005) concludes that the Japanese and others from more interdependent/collectivist countries tend to self-enhance less than others who perceive themselves more independent. Church and Katigbak (1992) found that American students placed greater stress on good grades and personal achievement than Filipinos who stress preparation for getting a good job and receiving approval from others. Readily accessible country-comparative data on these and many other work-related issues however is lacking.

Zhang, Kohnstamm, Slotboom, Elphick and Cheung (2002) compared free descriptions of children by parents and found Chinese parents of school-age children generated many more descriptors, mostly critical, in the domain of conscientiousness. They suggest that these findings reflect the Chinese high achievement orientation and show that classification (for trait descriptions) is sensitive to cultural differences. Academic achievement by children is often more crucial to a family at that point than other life concerns. This might imply a preoccupation with self-discipline and maintaining social order through the rest of life.

Sagan (1977) states that *'While our behavior is still significantly controlled by our genetic inheritance, we have, through our brains, a much richer opportunity to blaze new behavioral and cultural pathways on short timescales.'* Hofstede and McCrae disagree on the relative importance of genetic versus cultural factors, but both would agree that it is a very broad-brush approach to cultural assessment.

So how else can we conceptualize national culture in a way that helps us understand some of the less obvious ways in which the members of one national group differ from another?

Value dimensions

Geert Hofstede is a Dutch professor in Organizational Anthropology and International Management, and is the most eminent and cited researcher in the field of intercultural management. He defines culture as *'The collective programming of the mind that distinguishes the members of one group or category of people from others' mental programming.'* Hofstede's value dimensions have framed substantial pieces of subsequent cultural research and guidance. Originally based on research at IBM in the 1970s, this has been updated and his value dimensions expanded to six as follows:

- *Power distance* – the extent to which the less powerful members of institutions and organizations within a country accept that power is distributed unequally.
- *Individualism* – the degree of interdependence a society maintains among its members.
- *Masculinity/femininity* – fundamentally describes what motivates people, wanting to be the best (masculine) or liking what you do (feminine).
- *Uncertainty avoidance* – the extent to which the members of a culture feel threatened by ambiguous or unknown situations and have created beliefs and institutions that try to avoid these.

- *Pragmatism*[1] – the degree to which people relate to the past when dealing with the present and future and accept that much that happens around us cannot be explained.
- *Indulgence* – the extent to which people try to control their desires and impulses.

Seventy-five plus countries have been measured on the basis of these dimensions. Not surprisingly perhaps, the United States emerges as the most individualistic nation, whereas central and Latin American countries are at the bottom with Pakistan and Indonesia not far behind.

Hofstede has provided useful tools on his website. Free of charge is the country comparison tool, which, as the name suggests, enables us to compare different cultures. www.geert-hofstede.com/countries.html.

Using this tool to compare, for example, the United States and Japan, the charts reveal that there are significant differences in the Individualism, Masculinity, Uncertainty Avoidance and Pragmatism dimensions.

The accompanying descriptions describe how the United States is more individualistic, less masculine (assertive), more comfortable with uncertainty and much less pragmatic – for the Japanese the challenge is not to know the truth but to live a virtuous life.

Hofstede's publications analyze several societal and organizational-level behaviors on the basis of these dimensions. Dimensions can be combined to show, for example, that in low power distance and low masculinity countries, such as Sweden and Denmark, attitudes toward leaders tend to be that status counts for little, there is sympathy for the underdog and consultation is preferred over decisiveness.

Of Hofstede's six dimensions those of most relevance to RPP are, we believe, the first four. Below we highlight some of the main characteristics associated with each (see Table 2.1).

Triandis provides a useful breakdown of the attributes associated with people from individualist and collectivist countries, but also warns that many countries contain elements of each, and individuals cannot reliably be categorized as one or the other just because of where they were raised.

Hofstede is opposed to using nation-level data to assess individuals, and clearly there are dangers and limitations. Personalities, motivations and beliefs vary more within than between nations. But the nation-level data, and observations regarding how they play out at a societal or organizational level,

TABLE 2.1 A description of the six fundamental dimensions of culture

Low Power Distance High	
Independent	Dependent
Convenient hierarchy	Hierarchy essential
Equal rights/power	Privileges
Superiors accessible	Superiors inaccessible

Individualism	Collectivism
Self – I	The group – we
Loosely-knit social framework	Group opinion
Individual opinions	Implicit communication
Explicit communications	Face/shame
Loss of self-respect/guilt	

Masculine	Feminine
Clear objectives & targets	Changeable objectives & targets
Achiever admired	Sympathy for the underdog
Assertive/confrontational	Consensus
Competition, even amongst colleagues	'Independent' cooperation
Seeks material rewards	Values quality of life
	Modest

Low Uncertainty Avoidance High	
Low need for structure & rules	Need for structure & rules
Risk-taking	Security
Emotions concealed	Emotions revealed
Relaxed	Strong beliefs and intolerance of unorthodoxy
Practice more than principles	

Pragmatic	Normative
Don't expect to be able to explain everything	Like to explain everything
Focus on virtue rather than absolute truth	Truth-seekers
Adaptable to new circumstances	Respect traditions
Careful with money	Tend not to save for the future
Persevere in seeking results	Quick results

Indulgence	Restraint
Unfettered enjoyment of life	Suppress gratification of needs
Fun-seekers	Strict social norms

Source: Based on data at www.geert-hofstede.com (May 2014).

do provide a good starting point for assessment. It would be true to say that, *on average*, someone from an individualist, low uncertainty avoidance country would develop more diverse in-groups to meet their needs rather than rely on family or traditional in-groups. They would also *on average* seek greater self-reliance, expect greater freedom of choice and feel more comfort with untried and untested methods and innovation than someone from a more traditional, collectivist, uncertainty-avoiding society.

Cultural differences

Fons Trompenaars is a business writer and management consultant who has compiled a database based on questionnaires completed by over 30,000 participants since 1987. He defines culture as *'the way in which a group of people solves problems and reconciles dilemmas'* and identifies seven dimensions on which national cultures vary.

- *Universalism versus particularism* – how clearly and consistently rules are set out and applied.
- *Individualism versus communitarianism* – how strongly people identify with the group and its interests versus their own.
- *Neutral versus emotional* – the extent of suppression of emotion and emotional expression.
- *Specific versus diffuse* – whether you prioritize the relationship or the task.
- *Achievement versus ascription* – whether you are judged primarily on personal efforts and their results or on the status you have in terms of family, education, age, etc.
- *Time* – the relative importance of past, present and future and whether you see time as sequential or cyclical.
- *Attitudes to the environment* – is it something we control or are we controlled by it?

Cross-cultural psychologists rarely mention Trompenaars, partly perhaps because he does not publish country scores but also due to questions over methodology. As with Hofstede, however, he does provide numerous useful examples of how differences play out at the organizational and individual levels. His dimensions are, however, complementary to Hofstede's dimensions, in that they develop similar themes and draw attention to different aspects of behavior.

An awareness of a nation-level tendency to control the visible and audible signs of anger and other emotions is of significance. By knowing, for example, that harmony within the group is important (as in more collectivist countries such as Japan) and that there is a tendency to mask emotions, we can allow for that and seek to identify what 'display rules', to use Ekman and Friesen's term, are in force in that particular environment. This combination of knowing what provokes an emotional response in one society – what they value or hold up as important – and how that emotion is likely to be expressed gives us greater insight into their mind-set and motivation.

The World Values Survey is a useful source of information regarding 'systems' or sub-cultures in operation in different societies and the predominant views that they engender. Started in 1981 the latest of six waves was in 2014. It maps values associated with religious, political, economic and social life and publishes freely available data online (www.worldvaluessurvey.org). It shows that there are two major dimensions on which cultures vary – traditional versus secular-rational values and survival versus self-expression values. Traditional societies emphasize the importance of religion, parent–child ties, deference to authority and traditional family values. They tend to have high levels of national pride and nationalistic outlook. Secular-rational are broadly the opposite. Survival values focus on economic and physical security, are relatively ethnocentric in their outlook and have low levels of trust and tolerance. Self-expression values are more tolerant of difference and demand greater involvement in economic and political life.

Also relevant in this context are what Triandis terms 'cultural syndromes' according to which countries can be classified:

- *Complexity* – the level of citizens' access to information and divergent groups.
- *Tightness and looseness* – concepts developed further by Gelfand, to describe the degree of 'felt accountability' and pressure to conform to societal norms.
- *Individualist/collectivist* – as outlined by Hofstede. Individualist countries socialize people to look after themselves and their immediate family only – and collectivist to be relatively dependent on, and loyal to, in-groups.

Where countries and their 'systems' are on a scale of exposure to and tolerance of different opinions, behaviors and beliefs and those systems' centrality to society's functioning provide the boundary conditions for interaction, certainly amongst its members but also for those doing business there. Often, taking time to consider the country from which someone comes is fundamentally important to business dealings and in explaining different mind-sets and motivations. If, for example, seeking to influence the manager of a family-owned company who was born and brought up in Saudi Arabia, important considerations would be that you are dealing with someone who will likely feel a strong sense of loyalty to certain in-groups (in particular his clan), and more widely the royal family. He will have had relatively limited exposure to new ideas and other points of view through the media and educational institutions (both of which are tightly controlled) and who will, in their own country, be expected at all times to adhere to Sharia law and key tenets of Islam (prioritizing philanthropy toward a local community, for example, over 'win-win' business).

Other sources of guidance

The search for meaningful categories by which to compare countries continues. Some are promising. Bond and Leung's social axiom project, for example, has found significant differences between countries based on two dimensions – social cynicism (a negative view of human nature, which correlates with Hofstede's collectivism dimension) and dynamic externality (the degree to which beliefs are focused on religiosity and a belief that effort will ultimately lead to justice). House et al. (2004) looked at leadership styles considered the most effective in different countries. However, at the current time we believe the comparative frameworks outlined in the previous section represent the 'best available'.

Certainly, they are those most frequently applied by business writers who are also the source of a range of useful insights and guidance in intercultural management and cross-cultural encounters. Nancy Adler, for example, looks at motivation, leadership and decision-making. Others combine aspects of the research with more personal observational data. Books listed at the end of this chapter illustrate and explain further country-specific greetings and rituals and underlying values such as 'haji' (shame) in Japan or 'face-saving' in Arab countries. When preparing for meetings with foreign counterparts this, and guidance such as that outlined below, is often indispensable in helping to avoid faux pas and misunderstandings.

Negotiation styles

In his book *Cross-Cultural Business Behaviour*, Richard Gesteland (2012) categorizes nationalities in relation to their negotiation-style. The main distinctions he makes are:

- Deal-focus v Relationship-focus.
- Informal (Egalitarian) v Formal (Hierarchical).
- Rigid-Time (monochromic) v Fluid-Time (polychromic).
- Emotionally Expressive v Emotionally Reserved Cultures.

Of these, Gesteland indicates the most significant is the difference between deal and relationship-focused cultures. He points out how this impacts communications styles, with deal-focused cultures being more direct, preferring clarity, whereas relationship-focused want to preserve above all harmony, meaning they are uncomfortable with and avoid when possible giving criticism or bad news. This may lead to frustration and misunderstanding.

He illustrates some wider implications, such as whether someone is judged as being sincere or corrupt. Sincerity in relationship-focused cultures is associated with someone who always helps, whereas in deal-focused with someone who is honest and frank. Ways and means of getting things done evolve in response. Gesteland states there are correlations between high levels of corruption and relationship-focused, strongly hierarchical and polychronic societies. They also tend to be poorer and more bureaucratic. In such societies it is more readily accepted to use contacts or pay off lowly civil servants to get to decision-makers to speed things up.

Time

Trompenaars and Hofstede discuss ways in which cultures shape the way people think and talk about time. Some but not all differences in attitudes toward time cause very evident problems.

Collett (1994) develops further the time theme, making useful distinctions and exploring some of the practical implications arising from them, for example, as regards punctuality. He categorizes some countries as *time-bound* (Germany, Britain, Switzerland and Scandinavia) and others as *time-blind* (Spain, Portugal and Greece). Time-bound emphasize schedules, deadlines, time wasting, time-keeping and a fast pace of life. Time-blind societies are more relaxed and casual about time. Hence what is late in one society is not necessarily so in the other. As societies become more time-bound they have a more competitive attitude to time, and so 'fast' is better. Hence fast-living, fast-eating, fast-tempo manic-type work behavior emphasizing 'catching up' and not being 'left-behind'. Time-bound societies see time as linear, time-blind as cyclical. Time-bound societies centre work around clocks, schedules, delivery dates, agendas and deadlines. This can make for serious misunderstandings.

Collett also points out various other time-related distinctions that relate specifically to the world of work. The first is the time-blind culture's inability to distinguish between sacred and profane time. The former is for eating, family and sleeping. Profane time is used for everything else. Hence, in Spain meetings can easily be interrupted: time is not dedicated solely to the meeting. There is also the distinction between *mono-* and *poly*-chronic time.

Time-bound societies are *monochronic* – they do one thing at a time. Time-blind are *polychronic* happily ignoring appointments, schedules, deadlines and tolerating interruption. Third there is the issue of *time-orientation*: past, present and future. Thus, the British are thought to be interested more in the distant and recent past and, therefore, do not invest so much in the future, while the Germans have a longer view of the future investing in basic research, education and training.

Attitudes to time are also influenced by personality, meaning some important distinctions can be made at an individual level. One such distinction is between *the time estimator* and *the time contractor*. To the former 'I shall see you at 6.30' means any time around 6.30 (i.e. 6.05, 6.45), while to the latter that is a promise or a contract. If a time estimator is married to or works with a time contractor all hell is frequently cut loose as their expectations and misunderstandings are challenged!

Equally there are those fixated in the past, those obsessed only with the present, and those looking only to the future. Remembering past experiences and lessons is valuable. Concentrating on the 'now' is important. Thinking about and planning for the future is good. But to be always backward looking means you miss current opportunities, and to be overly future oriented ignores current problems which impact on how you get to the future.

Recently Zimbardo in America identified five key individual approaches to the time perspective.

• The *'past-negative' type*: focuses on negative personal experiences that still have the power to upset and cause feelings of bitterness and regret.
• The *'past-positive' type:* takes a nostalgic view of the past, with a 'better safe than sorry' approach that may hold them back.
• The *'present-hedonistic' type*: is dominated by pleasure-seeking impulses, and reluctant to postpone feeling good for later gain.
• The *'present-fatalistic' type*: doesn't enjoy the present but feels trapped in it, unable to change the future, feels powerless.
• The *'future-focused' type*: is ambitious, focused on goals, and has a sense of urgency.

Similar differences can be observed in organizations. Some do time-urgency seriously. Time is a measurable variable. Others seem much more relaxed. Some are amnesic about the past, believing it pointless to look back. Others are obsessed with the future paying top dollar for strategy consultants to predict and possibly control the future.

Moving from the general to the specific

In this chapter we have described and provided references to sources that describe those values and practices that might be considered broadly characteristic of individuals sharing a national culture. In Chapter 3 – Biographical Information, we adopt a similar approach when considering other 'group' influences such as class, age and gender. This is the general starting point for RPP in relation to all elements explored in *Revealed*. We describe what is typical of a particular 'type' and then assess the extent to which our subject appears to 'fit the mould' based on what we know about them. The scope of observational and other data available to us in making these assessments is presented throughout Chapters 2–7, and detailed guidance on data collection is given in Chapter 8. It is this research that enables us to move from general analysis of cultural influences to analysis of our specific subject.

We know early influences in particular have a profound effect on all of us through the processes of enculturation and socialization. It is also clear that some national cultures exert greater or less influence, conformity, loyalty and dependency on their citizens than others and that the systems that make up a culture may be more or less pertinent to the situation at hand.

Individuals do not absorb all aspects of a particular culture in equal measure and can develop knowledge and sensitivity to other cultures over the course of their lifetime. If we learn our Saudi subject has enjoyed travelling extensively, worked harmoniously in a multinational company with foreign colleagues, has attended one of the most prestigious universities and, when he travels abroad, is not adverse to the odd glass of Scotch, it tells us something about the extent to which he fundamentally identifies with his culture of birth and gives an indication of how autonomous he is likely to feel, both in terms of mind-set and motivation. Such knowledge will be particularly relevant when meeting outside his home country as he will be less constrained by psychological and other restrictions.

So what specific factors might mean that the cultures to which our subject has been exposed exert greater or lesser influence over how they think and behave?

Nobody behaves entirely consistently over time or when faced with similar challenges or dilemmas. The situation will always be a major determinant of attitudes and behavior, and so whatever we know about an individual and his cultural background has to be analyzed in the context of a specific role or situation.

Neyer and Harzing (2008) use the concept of 'strong' and 'weak' situations to help explain the degree of impact of national culture on behaviors. 'Strong' situations are those where the likelihood of national differences asserting themselves above other factors is reduced, 'weak', exacerbated. A strong situation might be one where, for example, organizational procedures are clearly set out, where there is mutual interest in achieving rapid resolution of a problem, or where the negotiator is well versed in local practices or has built a relationship of trust. Weak might be when the chief negotiator is stressed, and as a result fails to manage culturally inappropriate behavior or make concessions to get the job done. This suggests that the 'strength' of a situation in cultural terms can be managed, given awareness of some of the less or more helpful potential contributory factors.

Karau and Williams (1993) found that in the United States individuals put less effort into a task when working with others than when working alone and that there was a similar degree of 'social loafing' in Asian Pacific countries. However, when asked to complete more complex tasks Asian Pacific groups worked harder in groups than when alone. Similar studies were conducted by Earley (1993) in the United States, Israel and China and demonstrated that, except for amongst Americans, there were similar effects when group members were known to each other and believed they were working for the good of the group. In the United States they worked harder when they believed to be working alone

Of the three 'syndromes' identified by Triandis, the individualism-collectivism dimension popularized by Hofstede has been the focus of most attention and has produced a rich research in the field of social psychology across cultures. This is because it addresses issues relating to self-construal – how related someone feels to particular group(s) within a society.

Markus and Kitayama (1991) have looked at how independent self-construal (often associated with the United States) and interdependent self-construal (often associated with Asian countries) impact cognition, motivation and emotion-associated behaviors. Kağıtçıbaşı (2005) has also studied how interdependent, independent (the latter characteristic of more socially and economically developed countries) and autonomous-relational family models (combining elements of both) affect individuals. Such studies have application at national not individual level where personality and life experiences have far greater relevance but also provide interesting insights into typical behaviors, for example, of how individuals are likely to react to failure in the broader national context.

Ward, Bochner and Furnham (2001) looks at social identity and intergroup relations in the context of an individual's acculturation. He suggests that an individual's experience will be affected by:

• individual characteristics;
• the permanence of, and motivation for, cross-cultural relocation;
• the broader social context, in particular cultural pluralism and the extent of apparent prejudice and discrimination and how they affect self-esteem, psychological well-being and social skills acquisition.

Essentially in RPP we need to take similar considerations into account. Questions are:

• In a given situation, what cultures matter to our subject, that is, what is their predominant social/cultural identity?
• Do they have the right personality and background to be able to adapt to other cultures?
• Do they perceive the need to do so – that is, are they motivated to accommodate or bridge differences with another culture(s)?
• What factors in the broader environment will support or undermine the process of 'bridge-building' or 'fit' and can they be managed effectively?

Gibson, Maznevski and Kirkman (2009) suggest aspects of personality and personal history that are key in affecting the extent of impact of national culture on an individual's perception, values, beliefs and behaviors (see Table 2.2).

Neyer and Harzing's study of cross-cultural behavior at the European Commission found that experience of other cultures and of working in a foreign language tended to facilitate or foster 'norms' to reduce conflict. But it also found that under time pressure to complete tasks this was not the case, increasing culturally determined behaviors in terms both of styles of criticizing and of task versus relationship orientation.

Certainly, with greater exposure a subject is likely to take less for granted and show greater flexibility in dealing cross-culturally, but other aspects of personality and motivation will also come into play. Does the subject perceive the need to invest in learning different cultural norms or to adapt his approach to negotiations or tasks? Some of these considerations are captured by the concept of 'cultural intelligence' that has become popular in recent years and is discussed further in Chapter 3 –Biographical Information. It emphasizes the importance of being adaptable, willing to make concerted efforts to identify and understand differences and drawing up strategies and acting while taking them fully into account. In a sense this addresses the issues of motivation and

TABLE 2.2   How culture impacts on perceptions and culture

Areas of cultural impact	Personality	Other
Perception – do you see what I see? 'The process by which individuals select, organise and evaluate stimuli from the external environment.' (Singer 1976)	Openness – inquiring intellect and independence of thinking results in individuals being more open to ways of perceiving others than those typical of their nature culture – more independent	Familiarity with other cultures
Values – what is important? 'Values are: 1. Concepts or beliefs 2. That pertain to desirable end states or behaviors 3. That transcend specific situations 4. That guide selection or evaluation or behavior and events and 5. Ordered by relative importance.' Schwartz	Social adaptability/ extraversion and interpersonal involvement result in individuals being more likely to change their values to fit the social setting	Extent of identification with a particular culture
Beliefs – what is related to what?	Conformity – tendency to match oneself to others and follow social norms, demonstrating friendly compliance	Strongest when native to a particular culture rather than acculturated
Behavior – what will I do? System of expectancies – what kinds of behavior the individual anticipates being rewarded or punished for	Conscientiousness/ constraint implying a degree of caution in behavior	Self-efficacy – judgment of capability to accomplish a certain level of performance meaning more willing to step outside culturally prescribed behaviors

analysis of the possible obstacles to successful cross-cultural dealings. We, and ideally our subject, have to be motivated to overcome obstacles and assess the best strategies to do so.

In Chapter 8 – Remote Personality Profiling, we present the case study of Alphafox, a potential board member to a British company. In terms of personality, he is assessed as having relatively high scores on extraversion and inquisitiveness but would tend to be disorganized rather than conscientious, neurotic and low on agreeability. In business dealings and over his lifetime he has had a lot of exposure to different cultures, but primarily two. His parents are Spanish and he was brought up and educated in the UK. Both countries might be assessed high in terms of complexity, and looseness, but Spain is more collectivist than the UK and he maintains strong family links. On this basis, in terms of life experiences we can conclude that he is likely to be fairly aware of and skilled in adapting to the British culture and that, from a national cultural perspective at least, there is little danger of misunderstanding or antipathy. He may still be loyal to particular in-groups, rather than forming new alliances readily, but this is not considered a primary influence on his motivation, which is assessed to be personal vanity, need for power, fun and materialism which are more related to personality than culture.

Influencing different personality types

In the introduction we gave an overview of Cialdini's six strategies of influence (p XX) to which we added our own – logic or reason. These are discussed in greater detail in Chapter 9 – Managing Extremes. All of these influencers have been shown to have universal application. In other words, each can be deployed effectively with subjects from different cultural backgrounds although their effectiveness will vary. Below we consider how.

While there are many different ways of measuring culture, we link our seven influencers to Hofstede's six cultural dimensions outlined earlier in this chapter, indicating which are likely to make the greatest contribution to achieving successful outcomes.

Power distance

Those from cultures where authority is conferred unquestioningly and age revered will tend to be the most influenced by someone who is senior or older. At the other end of the scale, where authority can be questioned, people are more likely to respond to logic, reason and scarce expertise.

Individualism

Those from collectivist societies will tend to respond well to social proof, particularly if rooted in their own society, and to commitment and consistency. Individualistic societies may respond well to scarcity and logic.

Masculinity

Those from countries high on this score will tend to be motivated by achievement and competition; they will see the advantage of reciprocation and scarcity will be attractive. Those who value caring and quality of life will respond to liking and social proof.

Uncertainty avoidance

Those who are comfortable with uncertainty will probably not be too influenced by any one factor, though if they like the influencer it will have some impact. Those who want more certainty in their life will value commitment, consistency and authority. They also tend to appreciate logical approaches in problem-solving.

Pragmatism

Those low on pragmatism need to have the truth and will respond well to logic, authority and commitment. At the other end of the scale, those comfortable with there not being an explanation for everything in life will be influenced by liking and reciprocity.

Indulgent

Indulgent societies will be influenced by liking, reciprocity and scarcity. More restrained societies by commitment and consistency, social proof and authority.

Culture as risk

What then are the risks for the negotiator, the recruiter or the team builder of ignoring or having insufficient insights into the dimensions identified above? We identify three primary risks:

- Stereotyping: while, as demonstrated in this chapter, members of a culture would tend to have a lot in common and abide by the same 'rules', individuals are always just that, individual.
- Only acknowledging differences in overt cultural practices, such as the etiquette of greetings, while underestimating the more important, but less obvious, value differences. These shape perceptions, problem-solving and provide a sense of security and well-being.
- Attributing the wrong meaning to actions and behaviors due to our own cultural lens. Body language varies, motivation varies, the strength of feeling varies, the degree of conformity expected varies. We need to take this into account in interpreting and reacting to our subject's behaviors.

Conclusion

Our cultural background has a profound impact on how we think, feel and behave. In this chapter we discuss the impact of national culture most extensively. But the processes described in this chapter by which culture is embedded in us can equally be applied to such influences as social class, religion and the generation into which we were born, discussed in Chapter 3 – Biographical Information. Having established generalizations regarding what it means to belong to one or other culture, the remote personality profiler should then look for evidence of the extent to which the subject can be considered typical or rather deviates from the norm.

When we move outside our culture(s) of birth, we invariably need to adapt to, or at least allow for, differences in practices and outlooks of which we ourselves are usually only vaguely aware. Hofstede's value dimensions provide the most useful country-comparative data currently available to help us anticipate problems that may arise when dealing cross-culturally and to cater for them. Taken with more detailed guidance regarding practices, they enable us to anticipate and manage those differences more effectively.

The following framework provides a summary of the key considerations pertaining to whether, in the context of profiling, a situation is likely to be 'strong' or weak' and suggests some questions which help clarify other contributory factors.

A FRAMEWORK FOR CULTURAL ASSESSMENT

Enculturation – What do we know about the cultural identity of their parents and other influential figures? Where did they spend their childhood? Who do they choose to socialise with? Are they bilingual?

Socialization – Do we know where they were educated and have worked? Were particular 'national systems', political, religious or other, particularly constraining or influential?

Life experiences – Have they travelled extensively or been exposed to other cultures through work or study, family relations or interest? Are there any indicators that they have rejected their culture of birth or the society in which they are operating/have been acculturated?

Cultural context – Will the setting and members of the group accentuate adherence to particular cultural norms? Is it an environment with which they are familiar or where they are likely to feel at ease?

Other factors/individual measures – What else do we know about the subject e.g. their personality traits, intelligence and character and how these are likely to affect their level of adherence to cultural norms in this situation?

Recommended reading

Hofstede G. (2010) *Cultures and Organisations: Software of the Mind*. McGraw-Hill USA.
Trompenaars F. and Hampden-Turner C. (1997) *Riding the Waves of Culture*. Nicholas Brealey Publishing.
Nydell M.K. (2012) *Understanding Arabs: A Contemporary Guide to Arab Society,* Nicholas Brealey Publishing.
Gesteland R. R. (2005) *Cross-Cultural Business Behaviour* (4th edition).

Biographical Information

Being told someone 'was born with a silver spoon in his mouth' or is of the Hindu caste Shudra, with the function of serving others, prompts people to make assumptions. This may relate to the ease (or difficulty) with which they have reached their position in life or the strength of their aspirations and even abilities. If the reality does not conform to expectations, it sparks interest in their past and what it is about them or what's happened to them that might explain why. The privileged son has founded his own company with no financial backing from his family; the lower caste Indian has risen to the position of manager. How come? What prompted or enabled them to follow these paths?

As Chapter 2 – Culture suggests, when we look into someone's background, and especially their family and early background, we can and do find answers. Nowadays as part of selection procedures business routinely collects a whole range of bio-data, which Lautenschlager and Shaffer (1987) refer to as 'factual kinds of questions about life and work experiences, as well as to items involving opinions, values, beliefs and attitudes that reflect a historical perspective'. Careful examination of this data can provide useful insights into an individual's suitability for a job, their personality and motivation.

There are obvious risks in judging an individual and how they are likely to perform in a job based on CVs, application forms and interviews alone. They will want to present themselves in the best possible light. Often those involved in the assessment process do not allow for their own prejudices or have limited knowledge of, for example, the reputation of foreign educational institutions where someone has studied. They perhaps don't take into account contextual

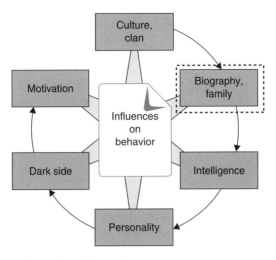

FIG 3.1 The six dimensions: biography

factors such as the organizational culture of a previous employer that allowed a candidate to perform particularly well. Appearance and coaching in how to perform well in interview can also mislead us toward forming a more favorable impression than perhaps is warranted.

These dangers are heightened when we collect and attempt to interpret supplementary biographical material about an individual's early childhood and adolescence – about their family life, relationships and experiences. While understood to be the most formative years, research, and at times intense debate, continues in psychology, psychiatry and psychoanalysis regarding the strength and impact of early influences and events. It is also often difficult to verify facts. Even if true, an assessor might accord them disproportionate significance (unusual and therefore interesting), have unconscious bias or be unaware of any number of other, mitigating or exacerbating factors. Trying to attribute fundamental outlooks and behavior to particular biographical/historical causes is always going to be difficult. If hours spent in a counselor's chair do not always uncover the past, let alone explain the present and predict the future, we must proceed with both realism and caution.

In this chapter, however, we identify elements in a person's past that are generally accepted as having a significant influence on behavior, and particularly those elements that are useful in explaining and anticipating more extreme and potentially disruptive behavioral tendencies. (See Figure 3.1) This will be of interest in personnel selection, but also to the biographer and when dealing with outside contacts. We look at what reliable research tells us about the impact of biographical factors, such as age, sex, physical appearance, class and work experiences, debunking some myths along the way. We also consider the scope and usefulness of information collected by business. We conclude by highlighting the often unanalyzed and non-job-related information that can be our greatest asset when deciding how to manage and otherwise influence business colleagues and others.

So what biographical information gives us clues?

Chapter 2 – Culture focused very much on enculturation and socialization, the two main processes by which individuals adopt the values, beliefs and behaviors espoused by those close to them and present in the wider society in which they live. Biographical research enables us to fill in the details. So while, for example, Alphafox (described in Chapter 8) is Spanish, he was brought up in the UK, meaning that his native culture has not been as significant an influence as it might have been had he moved to the UK later in life. In the same way, although poorer families tend to be less educated and more religious, such general assumptions may not apply to our subject. If we can find out about a subject's relationships, both within and outside the family, life experiences such as historical or political events, their religious practices and their family's economic circumstances, it helps us put the flesh on the bones of our subject, to find out what made the wealthy son and lower-caste Hindu different.

The conditions in which someone is brought up are important to establish. Growing up in rural poverty is different from growing up in a wealthy suburban area and these differences are usually reflected in adult behaviors. Research amongst adults by Inglehart (1997) has shown that socio-economic conditions in childhood are a better predictor of values in adulthood than their current economic situation. Longitudinal studies have also shown it affects cognitive test scores, socio-emotional well-being, physical and mental health, behavioral problems, educational outcomes and future economic status. Brooks-Gunn and Duncan (1997) identify five broad mechanisms by which a child's development is impacted: health and nutrition, the home environment, parental interaction with the child, the parents' mental health and neighborhood conditions.

Growing up in rural poverty is different from growing up in a wealthy suburban area.

Indications that our subject had a poor diet, limited access to educational and other resources, cramped living conditions in high crime areas and stressed parents who worked long hours can help paint a picture. In the same way knowing they lived a life of utter privilege but with an authoritarian and at times cruel parent can help us understand them better.

We cannot hope to unearth extensive details of a subject's background, let alone reliably attribute cause and effect to them. However, below we outline those biographical elements that in recent years have aroused the most interest and/or emerge as having the broadest potential to affect personality and related behaviors. They are likely to be amongst the most significant, and yet their significance is often overlooked or else exaggerated and misinterpreted. We try and put the record straight, outlining useful academic findings along the way.

Parental influence

Abraham Maslow (the much quoted American psychologist) describes his childhood years as dark and unhappy: 'I find it difficult to remember happy experiences. My father loved women, whiskey, and arguing. He did not understand me and viewed me as an idiot. I hated my mother. She could not love anyone. She blackmailed me, believed in the supernatural and was ugly, stingy, ignorant, dirty, cruel, and selfish' Hoffman (1989).

Saudino (2005), a genetic behavioralist, states that most in her field attribute between 20 to 60 per cent of a child's temperament to DNA or genes and the rest to environmental factors. Given how integral most parents are to the environment in which their offspring grow up – in terms of the home they establish, their reactions to poverty or other conditions around them, how they relate to the child and see their future – their influence is clearly worth examining. Some researchers have talked in terms of parental endowments and investments. Endowments are not only genetic predispositions but also values and preferences that parents distil in their children. So, for example, they may place importance on learning and orientation toward the future. If this is the case, although perhaps in short supply, they are likely to choose to invest time and money in their children's education. Parental attitudes toward learning are discussed in Chapter 4 – Intelligence

Parents influence their children's behavior in at least three important ways

and are in turn influenced by a range of factors, such as, for example, the mother's level of education and social class.

According to Gunter and Furnham (2001), parents influence their children's behavior in at least three important ways:

• Through their own behavior they present situations that elicit certain behavior in children, for example, frustration leads to aggression;
• They serve as role models for identification;
• They selectively reward behaviors.

Personality can also be affected by parents; Smernou and Lautenschlagger (1991) found links between biographical data and the personality traits of extraversion and neuroticism. Parental pressure to succeed and the style of parental discipline (authoritarian in particular) were seen to nurture neuroticism. Extraversion was associated with memories of a warm, supportive family background in which parents encouraged their children to engage in various activities and paid them plenty of attention. Satisfying relationships with parents and other family members were important to extraverts.

The psychotherapist, Lowen (1984) states, 'All my narcissistic patients have had the experience of being deeply humiliated in childhood by parents who used power as a means of control. In many cases, the power is physical force. ... Spankings are a common form of such physical abuse.' Physical punishment is not the only way to humiliate a child; criticism that makes the child feel worthless, inadequate or stupid can have just as damaging an effect.

Absence of parent figure and other misfortunes

The interest of the psychiatrist and psychoanalyst is of course excited when attachment is threatened or broken, hence the study of 'separation anxiety'. Threats of abandonment create intense anxiety but, according to Bowlby, they can also arouse anger, sometimes to an intense degree, especially in adolescents. The anger can easily become counter-productive and dysfunctional as the child uses any method to attempt to persuade the parent not to carry out the threat. As with behaviors caused by stress or anxiety at home, these can set up patterns of difficult behavior and concepts of self-worth which last into adulthood.

John Bowlby's Attachment Theory grew out of a pamphlet published immediately after World War II. Commissioned by the United Nations, it recorded the difficulties presented by homeless and orphaned children who usually had direct experience of such separation.

> *All men's misfortunes spring from their hatred of being alone.*
> Jean De La Bruyere (1645–1696)

Parental death is the most studied of the misfortunes, but of course misfortune can come in many forms: absence, physical infirmity, deprivations and the horrors of war or a terrorist act, lack of parental love, divorce, sickness, alcoholism or drug addiction. Support and assistance to mitigate its effects can come from a variety of sources: friendly help from other relatives, school teachers, peers, neighbors, but also from a relatively high cultural-socio-economic status, good medical care and even, as William Therivel (2001) points out, having free time to pursue pleasurable personal interests.

Therivel also recognized the impact of such misfortunes on adult behavior. He considered the combined impact of misfortunes, the level of support available to the child at the time with the intellectual and genetic endowment of the child. His GAM (*Genetic, Assistances and Misfortune*) theory provides a fascinating study of a number of individuals blessed with great skills or qualities. He provides convincing theories to explain why Mozart was a better composer than Salieri, despite their very similar historical, social and intellectual backgrounds. His case studies include Dostoyevsky, Balzac, Goethe, Tolstoy and others.

In Therivel's descriptions those who do not suffer misfortunes are conventional types; this is where most people sit. He is, however, interested in those who do suffer misfortunes and who have a good genetic endowment. They fall into one of two categories, those who have little or no support or assistance and those who do receive support. According to him, this is where talent and serious creativity can be found.

An example of those who endure significant misfortunes but have little support – the 'Crushed' in Therivel's taxonomy – is described in Elsa Ferri's book *Growing Up in a One-Parent Family: A Long-Term Study of Child Development* (1976):

She says, 'the results of the analyses carried out showed that, overall, children in one-parent families had a lower level of attainment in school and were less well-adjusted than their peers from unbroken homes.' She echoes earlier comments suggesting it is not just material help that is needed but also guidance, reassurance and moral support. If it isn't present, then the pressures on a lone parent may become intolerable, with potentially disastrous results for all concerned.

Lowen was conscious of this in his study of narcissists as described above. Therivel also recognizes the dangers. In his chart he places the personality type 'pathological' at the top of his chart – those who have extreme misfortunes and no support.

Birth order

People often attribute certain behaviors and relationships to where someone comes in the family – first, second or perhaps last born. For the remote personality profiler, an obvious attraction of attributing to birth order certain impacts on the subsequent development of an individual might lie in the near certainty of the facts. When you were born and whether you had older and younger siblings are easy to verify.

This area of research has been dominated by Frank Sullaway who, in his book *Born to Rebel* (1996), presented 26 years of statistical evidence to demonstrate how firstborn children behave differently from their younger siblings. His thesis is that children compete for parental attention by creating distinctive niches. Firstborn children tend to be responsible, competitive and conventional. Children born later are more playful, cooperative and rebellious.

Sulloway borrows heavily from Charles Darwin's theories of evolution and his picture, and one of his quotes, adorns the first pages of his book. He provides thousands of birth-order examples, historic and contemporary, to prove his point. His research and arguments are impressive.

It is not surprising therefore to find many followers of his theory. Amongst them Leman (1998) states that the first male, or those born more than five years after their older sibling, have an excellent chance of developing firstborn traits or being 'functional firstborns'. He invites clients to do a quiz to identify which personality traits fit them best:

A. Perfectionist, reliable, conscientious, list maker, well organized, hard driving, natural leader, critical, serious, scholarly, logical, doesn't like surprises, loves computers.
B. Mediator, compromising, diplomat, avoids conflict, independent, loyal to peers, many friends, a maverick, secretive, unspoiled.
C. Manipulative, charming, blames others, seeks attention, tenacious, people person, natural salesperson, precocious, enraging, affectionate, loves surprises.

Sulloway and Leman provide an extensive list of famous people who fit into the categories they identify. Leman found a strong correlation with Sulloway's prediction that firstborn/functional firstborns will choose list A, second born list B and third or lastborn list C.

FIT FOR PURPOSE?

Of 41 US Presidents, Leman found that 23 were first born, a significant proportion, especially given larger family size in the 19th and early 20th centuries.

In Britain, of the first 17, six Prime Ministers and of the 13 since WWII only two (Churchill and Hume) were first born.

It could be argued that the US political system requires someone who has the leadership qualities present in an eldest son: hard driving and natural leaders. In the UK Prime Ministers, except in times of crisis (such as during Churchill's wartime tenure), rise to the top through compromise and diplomacy, developing close political friends and being a mediator; the qualities identified above by Leman as those of the middle child (primus inter pares).

Intriguing and fascinating as these studies are, subsequent analyses challenge Sulloway's main theories. Jefferson, Herbst and McCrae (1998) reported studies that found no significant correlations between personality and birth order. Self-reports using the NEO-PI-R (see Chapter 5 – Personality for a full description of personality measurement) showed little or no association with birth order either, despite very large samples and statistical controls. Peer ratings suggested partial support for Sulloway's hypotheses. According to Jefferson et al. (1998) later-borns are perceived by 'their friends and neighbors as being more sociable, innovative and trusting than firstborns'. Interestingly, the spouses of the individuals concerned did not replicate these peer-rated results.

The debate continues. There are some tempting conclusions to be drawn from the analysis of the impact of birth order on personality and behavior, but the precise impact is not yet sufficiently defined.

Class

All cultures make distinctions based on class and caste that are linked to historical and religious developments. Membership of any one can, much as knowing that one is of a particular nationality, allow us to make certain broad assumptions regarding the influences to which a subject has been exposed and the behaviors and attitudes that would tend to predominate amongst individuals of that group. Belonging to a particular class or caste would tend to mean that you marry or socialize within the same group, have compatible political views and aesthetic preferences and take up similar status occupations. In religions such as Hinduism and Islam, distinctions are often fairly apparent and constant, whereas class membership can be much more difficult to determine and more subject to change.

The results of the Great British Class Survey published in April 2013 indicate a muddying of the waters in terms of class. It makes seven class distinctions: elite, established middle class, technical middle class, new affluent workers, traditional working class, emergent service sector and precariat. The survey was based on Bourdieu's theory (1984) and took into account cultural and social life as well as economic standing. Bourdieu argued that cultural capital (which would incorporate knowledge, skills, education and advantages through which status is obtained or maintained) is the most important. So while the traditional and subtle ways in which class distinctions have been made in the UK and elsewhere – clothing, home furnishings, cooking, entertainment and cultural activities – are still valid, conclusions we can draw are less clear-cut than in the past. From the remote personality profiler's perspective the most interesting subjects are those who have risen well beyond the class into which they were born, usually through education. In most cases this leads to insecurity and a strong desire to be accepted.

Work experiences

What work factors influence people?

- *Early work experience:* For some it is the unadulterated tedium or monotony that powerfully motivates them to avoid similar jobs in the future. For others it is a particular work style or process that they then retain all their lives. This is something that can be identified and selected for.
- *The experience of other people*: It is nearly always an immediate boss, but can be a colleague or peer. They are almost always remembered as either *very bad or very good*: both teach lessons. From a development perspective, it highlights the value of excellent role models or mentor type bosses for the talent group.
- *Short-term assignments*: Project work, standing in for another or interim management. This takes people out of their comfort zone and exposes

them to issues and problems they may never have confronted before so they learn quickly.

- *First major line assignment*: This is often the first promotion, foreign posting or departmental move to a higher position. There are more pressures and accountabilities. Suddenly the difficulties of management become real. Appropriate 'stretch assignments' for talented people as soon as they arrive can have a similar impact.
- *Hardships of various kinds:* Hardship teaches the real value of things: technology, loyal staff, supportive head offices; how resourceful and robust some people can be and how others panic and cave in. It teaches about stress management and the virtues of stoicism, hardiness and a tough mental attitude.
- *Management development*. Some remember and quote their MBA experience, far fewer some specific (albeit expensive) course. One or two quote the experience of receiving 360 degree feedback. More recall a specific coach, because they were either so good or so awful.

Illness

At some stage of their lives most people experience physical illness. There are many stories of how sickly children use their experience to learn some skills. Similarly near death experiences, the loss of a limb or other body part, or an illness that leaves internal scars can profoundly influence people. Lord Owen's *In Sickness and in Power* (2009) documents a number of famous politicians and the illnesses they have had (see Table 3.1 below). His thesis is that their illnesses, both physical and mental, had a direct influence on their behavior, which in turn influenced the way in which they governed.

Age and generations at work

When the decline begins is open to debate, but there is no denying that, as people get older, they experience various symptoms of ageing, both physical and mental. The latter include loss of long-term and working memory, attention and speed of information processing. These can be mitigated by leading healthy, active and cognitively challenging lives and, as at any age, accelerated by fatigue, stress, illness and some forms of medication.

There is evidence that work performance falls with age in jobs that make heavy demands on sensory perceptions, selective attention, working memory

TABLE 3.1 World leaders and their illnesses

Leader name	Title (years)	Related illnesses to hubris
George W. Bush	President of the U.S.A. (2001–2009)	History of alcohol-related problems Over-active Thyroid gland
Jacques Chirac	President of France (1995–2007)	Stroke
Tony Blair	British Prime Minister (1997–2007)	None
Ariel Sharon	President of Israel (2001–2006)	Stoke Cerebral vascular incident (?) Small hole in heart that led to complications Bleeding into the brain – led to medically induced coma
Saddam Hussein	President of Iraq (1979–2003)	Bipolar disorder
Boris Yeltsin	President of Russia (1991–1999)	Lower back pain Cardiac ischemia Reliance on painkillers and alcohol Heart attacks Sleep apnoea Hypothyroidism
George H. W. Bush (Sr).	President of the U.S.A. (1989–1993)	Atrial fibrillation (diagnosed after difficulties when jogging) Thyrotoxicosis
Margaret Thatcher	British Prime Minister (1979–1990)	None
Ronald Reagan	President of the U.S.A. (1981–1989)	One of two politicians diagnosed with Alzheimer's after leaving office Limited attention span
Leonid Brezhnev	General Secretary of the Central Committee of the Communist Party (1964–1982)	High blood pressure Heart attacks Arteriosclerosis of the brain from Alvarez disease Only able to concentrate for around 3 hours a day
Jimmy Carter	President of the U.S.A. (1977–1981)	Haemorrhoids
Josip Broz Tito	President of Yugoslavia (1953–1980)	High blood pressure Heart attacks Cardiomobile – meant he only had 1 or 2 hours of concentration a day
Harold Wilson	British Prime Minister (1974–1976)	One of two politicians diagnosed with Alzheimer's after leaving office

Edward Heath	British Prime Minister (1970–1974)	Hypothyroidism (sometimes referred to as myxoedema Atrial fibrillation of the heart ('rip-roaring heart failure')
Richard Nixon	President of the U.S.A. (1969–1974)	Alcoholic abuse Paranoia
Georges Pompidou	President of France & Co-Prince of Andorra (1969–1974)	Waldenström syndrome Influenza Haemorrhoids
Willy Brandt	Chancellor of the Federal Republic of Germany (1969–1974)	Depressive symptoms that interfered with politics
Lyndon Johnson	President of the U.S.A. (1963–1969)	Heart attacks Depression Acute cholecystitis (caused post-operation depression) Hypersexuality Bipolar - 1
Charles de Gaulle	President of the French Republic (1959–1969)	Depression Malignant Malaria Prostatic adenoma
Lyndon B. Johnson	President of the U.S.A. (1963–1969)	Bipolar 1 disorder
John F. Kennedy	President of the U.S.A. (1961–1963)	Addison's disease Amphetamine abuse
Harold MacMillan	British Prime Minister (1957–1963)	Urinary retention Prostate cancer Hypochondria
Dwight Eisenhower	President of the U.S.A. (1953–1961)	Type 'A' personality Hypertension Crohn's Disease
Anthony Eden	British Prime Minister (1955–1957)	Amphetamine abuse
Winston Churchill	British Prime Minister (1940–1945; 1951–1955)	Major Depressive Disorder: cyclothymic features Alcohol and drug abuse Brain apoplexy
Joseph Stalin	General Secretary of the Central Committee of the Communist Party (1922–1952)	High blood pressure Brain haemorrhaging Paranoia
Franklin D. Roosevelt	President of the U.S.A. (1933–1945)	Minor haemorrhages

(continued)

TABLE 3.1 Continued

Adolf Hitler	Führer of Germany (1934–1945)	Parkinson's disease Hepatitis Heart attacks Neurotic Psychopath – bordering schizophrenia Drug abuse (cocaine; bull testosterone, but not as a replacement of his monorchism) Paranoia
Benito Mussolini	Head of the Italian Government and Duce of Facism (1925–1945)	Bipolar Disorder
Neville Chamberlain	British Prime Minister (1937–1940)	None
Stanley Baldwin	British Prime Minister (1935–1937)	Deafness (thought to be cause of resignation)
James Ramsey MacDonald	British Prime Minister (1929–1935)	Glaucoma Mild dementia
Calvin Coolidge	President of the U.S.A. (1923–1929)	Major Depressive Disorder
Bonar Law	British Prime Minister (1922–1923)	Laryngeal cancer
Warren Harding	President of the U.S.A. (1921–1923)	Heart trouble Depression
David Lloyd George	British Prime Minister (1916–1922)	None
Woodrow Wilson	President of the U.S.A. (1913–1921)	Anxiety Disorder Major Depressive Disorder Personality change due to stroke
Paul Deschanel	President of France (1920)	Elpenor's Syndrome Drug abuse Frontotemporal Dementia
Herbert Asquith	British Prime Minister (1908–1916)	Alcohol abuse Hypertension
Henry Campbell-Bannerman	British Prime Minister (1905–1908)	Heart attacks
Theodore Roosevelt	President of the U.S.A. (1901–1909)	Bipolar disorder

Source: Data taken from various sources including David Owen (2011)

and processing new information. Also in jobs requiring rapid reaction time and physical strength. But overall there is no evidence that productivity falls amongst older workers. Experience can compensate for other shortfalls, for example, enhancing prioritization skills, planning, trouble-shooting abilities and motivation. So, for example, older managers, academics and the like who are required to use their knowledge and judgment without time pressure are likely to perform better than their younger counterparts.

Generations are distinguishable most by their attitudes and values, shaped by their personal experiences. Growing up at a particular time and place often leaves a very strong mark on individuals. After all, societies try to socialize people into a set of beliefs and values about what is right/wrong; good/bad; just/unjust; fair/unfair.

It is not unusual to categorize people of different ages and view them as significantly different, often in a negative light. In the UK the following 'generations' or 'cohorts', amongst others, are identified.

Traditionalists ('Old Fogey's') are, it is said, products of the safe and secure fifties. They were and are cautious, conformist and conservative. They prefer structure and security. They understand loyalty and the concept of a career. They weren't and aren't very mobile and therefore have little experience of any type of diversity. They knew and accepted class divisions inside and outside work and experienced relatively little technological change. Most are now quietly retired doing the garden and falling off the perch at a significant rate.

The Baby Boomers ('The Spoilt Sixties Generation') were indeed shaped by the turbulent 60s, a time when people challenged assumptions and what they saw to be the complacency of their elders. This was the generation of civil rights, Woodstock, moon-landings, sit-ins, hijackings and nuclear power. Think Hippies and Flower-power, but also Vietnam and race riots. The Baby Boomers were anti-conformist and anti-hierarchical. They did not like uniforms or uniformity. They were happy to experiment. After all, sexual intercourse began in 1963. And many enjoyed shocking others. They were rebels with a cause, often disruptive at work. They distrusted authority and like change for change's sake. Some have refused to age gracefully and enjoy shocking their children with their outrageous behavior. The 'alternative' family in the various *Fockers* films nicely sums up the type.

There are plenty of popular books on 'the generations' and they make amusing reading. But they represent just another fad that will soon disappear as will the books to Oxfam bookshops. There is more to understanding employees' attitudes at work than the date they were born.

The impact of travel abroad

Along with other life experiences, permanent moves or shorter periods spent abroad, perhaps as a student or expatriate worker, can have significant impact on how someone thinks, feels and behaves. People who have moved their home to different countries usually have a quite different perspective from those who stayed put.

Oberg (1960) was one of the first to use the term 'culture shock' to describe the possible consequences of such moves and identified six aspects of it.

- Strain because of the effort required to make necessary psychological adaptations;
- A sense of loss and feelings of deprivation about friends, status, profession and possessions;
- Being rejected by and/or rejecting members of the new culture;
- Confusion in role, role expectations, values, feelings and self-identity;
- Surprise, anxiety, event disgust and indignation after becoming aware of cultural differences;
- Feelings of impotence because of not being able to cope with the new environment.

Furnham and Bochner (1986) identify three theoretical approaches to culture shock that help to explain why some people cope with it better than others.

- *Culture learning perspective:* The degree to which an individual acquires culturally relevant social knowledge to cope with and thrive in any new society. This might include knowledge of social etiquette, conflict resolution, non-verbal communication, rules and conventions, forms of polite address, etc. This relates to aspects covered in Chapter 2 – Culture.
- *Stress, coping and adjustment process*: The coping styles of individuals as they attempt to adjust to a new culture. Thus, their personality, social support network, knowledge and skills, and personal demography (age, sex) will, in part, determine how quickly and thoroughly they adapt.
- *Social identity and inter-group relations:* How people see themselves and their group affects how they deal with those from a different group. Stereotyped attributions for the cause of behavior and discrimination against out-groups, but in favor of in-groups, are seen to be a function

of a person's self-identity. Various individual and social forces influence a person's sense of themselves and that, in turn, influences their adaptation to, and acculturation in, the new society.

So, for example, a subject who has a parent from the new country and/or family already resident there is likely to adjust better as they will already be familiar with aspects of the new culture. If, using personality trait dimensions discussed in Chapter 5 – Personality, they are extravert and stable, they are likely to adjust better and if they were 'pulled' to the new country, perhaps by a work opportunity or the appeal of aspects of the life there, rather than being reluctant to leave their own land and then feeling or being made to feel like an outsider on arrival.

Those with greater general confidence levels, often men and older individuals, and who have had greater experience and exposure to other cultures, cope better with such transitions. They may be more suited to expatriate assignments or be more flexible and aware of culture in business dealings.

Livermore (2010) and others suggest that cultural competence or 'cultural intelligence' can be broken down and to some extent taught. Livermore identifies four components of 'CQ':

1. CQ Drive: Showing interest, confidence and drive to adapt cross-culturally – having intrinsic motivation (enjoyment) and extrinsic (tangible benefits) and self-efficacy (confidence)
2. CQ Knowledge: Understanding cross-cultural issues and differences – cultural systems and cultural norms and values
3. CQ Strategy: Strategizing and making sense of culturally diverse experiences – being aware, planning and checking
4. CQ Action: Changing verbal and non-verbal actions appropriately when interacting cross-culturally – focusing on verbal actions, non-verbal actions and speech acts

Physical appearance

How physically attractive you are affects your life, particularly if you are at one extreme or other of physical attractiveness. A highly attractive man or woman is treated by others differently from their peers of average attractiveness. The same is true for those thought unattractive. The issue is made more dramatic by change: the accident that leads to disfigurement, the ageing effect. The dramatic increase in cosmetic surgery is testimony to the importance of physical attractiveness in everyday life.

It is not difficult to describe physical attractiveness in either sex. This is done in terms of height and weight, signs of youth and fitness, body symmetry and movement. Moreover, this is pretty consistent across cultures and time. Like everything else, some people are very attractive and some very unattractive, and most in between. The question is what is the effect on the individual of being at an extreme? It is possible that the highly attractive become narcissistic and the very unattractive very eager to be accepted by others. The latter may shun the limelight and have low self-esteem. The 'small man' or 'Napoleonic complex' is well known: the idea that short men become particularly pugnacious and aggressive to make up for their stature. Equally, beautiful models are often thought of as self-obsessed, demanding and childish. Overweight people are seen as disagreeable, emotionally unstable, incompetent, sloppy, lazy and lacking in conscientiousness. These stereotypes have a large impact on selection, promotion and remuneration. Short people are patronized and thought of as somehow 'unfinished'.

Being noticeably different can have a profound effect on people from an early age. There have been many observations regarding which physical characteristics influence behavior. They seem most significant when unusual or extreme, for example, excessive height or shortness. Researchers have also tried to find a mechanism to explain the degree to which a particular physical characteristic affects people. Thus, some short people are insignificantly influenced by their smallness, while others seem to expend a great deal of energy trying to 'make up for' or compensate for the fact they may be seen in the eyes of others to be weak, childlike and lacking in power.

But is there evidence that physically attractive people are advantaged at work? In a recent and imaginative study on the effect of physical height on workplace success and income, Judge and Cable (2004) set out to test a model that linked height to career success. They suggested various processes that occur in relation to height.

- It predicts *social* esteem or the perceived stature or ascribed status of people.
- It also predicts *self-esteem* (the way we regard ourselves) and that impacts on adjustment. Further social and self-esteem are linked because if tall people are consistently viewed and treated with respect by others their self-worth or self-confidence increases in a self-fulfilling way.
- It is reasonable to assume that social esteem predicts both objective and subjective work performance. The reason for both subjective and objective performance is, they posit, due to possible self-fulfilling processes. People

are more likely to help taller people, boosting the manager's confidence in their performance and so leading them to actually do better.

In three studies their findings were that height was significantly related to career success for both men and women. Moreover height was positively related to income even after controlling for age, sex and weight.

There is plenty of evidence that physical attractiveness has manifold benefits in everyday life also. In 11 meta-analyses Langlois et al. (2000) were able to demonstrate four clear facts. *First*, there is cross-cultural reliability and agreement about attractiveness. *Second*, that both attractive children and adults are judged more positively compared to less attractive control groups, even by people who know them. *Third*, attractive people are treated more positively, and *fourth* exhibit more positive behaviors. There are direct effects, though sometimes moderated by gender, age and familiarity.

In sum, it is likely that a subject's physical appearance, and particularly if it is out of the ordinary in some way, will affect how they are perceived and how they perform. As such it is relevant to the remote personality profiler.

Gender and sex differences

Are males and females psychologically different in terms of ability, personality, motives and so on? Are men more intelligent and women more emotional than men? This area is now so controversial that few wander into it with simple, naïve questions hoping to have them answered. Sex differences have been politicized and arguments, as well as data, are given an ideological, rather than empirical, screening.

Those who believe that *biology is destiny* are quite unsurprised by the sex differences they and others report. The biological determinist view is that *culture and society amplify nature*, which has ensured, through a natural division of labor, that males develop skills for hunting and protection, inclining them to be better at spatial location, stronger and more aggressive than women.

Diametrically opposed is the group that refuses to acknowledge any evidence of sex differences, attributing certain minor variations they might find to *upbringing*. They suggest that it is predominantly *cultural factors that shape sex differences*. In traditional patriarchal societies, from a very early age, young male babies are taught certain attitudes and behaviors quite different from those taught to girls. Some psychologists argue that it is crucially important that we conduct disinterested, impartial, empirical research into the question, whereas others are only happy to report results if they demonstrate no differences.

There are many popular beliefs about the psychological characteristics of the two sexes that have proved to have little or no basis in fact. But there are established differences.

The non-verbal behaviors of women and men differ in a number of interesting ways. Women on average are superior to men in decoding non-verbal cues, particularly facial expressions. Women smile more and engage in more eye contact during social interactions than men do. Men maintain greater personal space and are more expansive in their body movements and postures. Men make more errors in speech than women do and use more 'filled pauses' ('ahs' and 'ums') when they talk.

Men and women, on average, display a number of differences in cognitive or mental abilities. For example, men tend to perform better than women on tests of mathematical and visual-spatial ability, but there is overall female superiority in verbal ability. However, the most recent evidence suggests that this difference in general verbal ability no longer exists but that there may be sex differences favoring women in certain specific verbal skills such as fluency. Some scientists have argued that spatial tasks require bigger brains, which explains the reliable finding that men have bigger brains than women.

Women and men of course display a number of consistent physical differences. Men are stronger than women, particularly at tasks requiring upper body strength. Men show higher levels of general motor activity than women, and women generally have more flexible joints than men.

The realm of affective or emotional functioning has been particularly difficult to study. Boys seem more active and more variable in temperament than girls. Many research studies show greater fear and timidity in girls, but these results tend to be more associated with studies using ratings and self-reports than with those using observational data. After the age of 18 months boys also tend to show greater outbursts of negative emotion in response to frustration than do girls. Boys quite simply are (and remain) more aggressive than girls. Differences in affective functioning are equivocal, but enough studies have reported differences in activity level, fearfulness and emotional responses to frustration to suggest that basic differences in affective functioning may exist. Such differences would not be surprising in the light of hormonal differences between the sexes and the association between temperament and hormone functioning.

In overt behavioral functioning, the evidence suggests that men are higher in aggression and dominance, whereas women are higher in dependence and nurturance-type behavior. The evidence concerning some of these differences is not conclusive but is most reliable for differences in aggression as it comes from a variety of sources: evolutionary, cross-cultural, developmental and biological-hormonal. However, the levels and forms of aggression expressed are highly susceptible to sex-role influences.

Sexuality

It is important to make some distinctions. First there is *sexual identity:* meaning to what extent you feel yourself to be a man or a woman. Second there is *sexual orientation:* which concerns whether you love or are attracted to men or women (or both equally); in short, are you homo, hetero or bi-sexual? Next, there is *sexual preference*. This concerns the things and events that cause a person to become sexually stimulated and excited. Fourthly and lastly, there is *sex role*. This refers to societal expectations for the different sexes.

This is an area of considerable debate, moral outrage and taboo. It is therefore extremely important in the development of any individual, particularly if they are in a minority group, being homo- or bi-sexual. Some suggest that around 10 per cent of the population are (exclusively) homosexual in their orientation and a similar number bi-sexual.

To understand an individual means understanding all aspects of their sexuality. People differ in their sex-drive or libido. They grow up in a society that has many implicit and explicit rules about what is expected and acceptable for males and females of different ages. Sexuality is an area for many of considerable anxiety because they feel abnormal, strange, 'dirty' or perverted. Part of the problem is that people are not always aware of what is 'normal' or acceptable to others in the society. As a consequence much is hidden.

It is not difficult to imagine the effect on an individual of having to hide, disguise or dissimulate such a central part of their life. Thus, some avoid relationships, though an important part of their mental health, while others develop an elaborate cover. If one feels the need from an early age to live a lie it is not surprising that this skill proves very useful in certain aspects of life.

Certainly knowing a person's sexual orientation, preference, history and libido is of keen interest to the profiler. It can be a central feature in their life dictating everything from their job history to their social support network.

How does business assess biographical data?

The first recorded use of biographical data to assess individuals was in 1894 when managers of the Washington Life Insurance Company of Atlanta Georgia were required to answer a list of standardized questions. Some years later Goldsmith (1922) investigated the usefulness of bio-data in selecting people to join the company. He analyzed data concerning 150 salesmen of varying abilities and on the basis of weighted scores and an overall pass mark accepted or rejected them for employment in the life assurance field. By doing this Goldsmith turned the conventional application form into what was called the 'weighted application blank' (WAB) (see Table 3.2).

Thus, a 35-year-old married man (and they were all men!) who had worked in full-time social employment, including some in the insurance industry, had

TABLE 3.2 Example of an early weighted application form

Age		Marital status		Service	
18–20	2				
21–22	1	Married	+1	Full time	+2
23–24	0	Single	1	Part time	2
25–27	+1				
28–29	+2	**Occupation**		Insurance	
30–40	+3				
41–50	+1	Social	+1	Carried	+1
51–60	0	Unsocial	1	Not carried	1
Over 60	1				
Education		**Experience**			+1
		Previous life insurance experience			
8 years	+1	**Confidence**			
10 years	+2	Replies to question: 'what amount of			+1
12 years	+3	insurance are you confident of placing			
		each month?'			
16 years	+2	Does not reply			1

Source: Adapted from Gunter and Furnham (2001).

had 12 years of education, and who was sufficiently confident to say how much insurance business he would generate would score 13 and was a dead cert. A 19-year-old single person with only eight years' education, who had worked in part-time unsocial work with no experience in the life assurance industry and could not answer the confidence question would score 7 and not be offered a job.

It is rare these days to find application forms of this nature, but it is common when applying for jobs, university places or when going through a vetting process to complete application forms which seek a variety of personal details. Their length varies considerably, but at the very least questions are likely to include place of birth and current address, marital status, membership of clubs and organizations, other outside interests, educational and career background, and availability and content of references. Most people completing the forms assume it is primarily for the record – to establish who the person is and to highlight possible problem areas. A married man may well have dependents or limitations on his mobility due to his wife's career; someone who has changed jobs frequently may have issues at work or be easily bored; if they have no outside interests, they are unlikely to be particularly outgoing.

Gunter and Furnham (2001) state that 'the use of biographical details in employment, organization and management research was frowned upon in psychology' (p 31). Experts worried that bio-data instruments lacked objectivity, reliability and validity. However, while the results are not always replicated, some studies suggest that they are useful and that predictive value can be found in the responses to seemingly basic questions. For example, 'does not want a relative contacted in case of emergency' has, in some studies, been shown to be an indicator of employee theft as is, bizarrely, the omission of the middle initial when candidates write their names. Other, seemingly fairly innocent questions might be:

- How often does the subject tell jokes?
- How do they regard their neighbors?
- About how many new friends have they made in the past year?
- Before they were 18 how many times did their family move from one house to another?
- And as an adult from one city, town or country to another?
- While in school, how often did their father, mother or guardian seem to take an interest in how they were doing in class?
- While in high school how many times a week did they go out?

There is no definitive list of biographical items that tend to reveal issues or personality traits likely to be of concern to a broad range of employers. If there were, it might lose its value or at least prompt individuals to be less honest than they already are about their background. The fact that such details can be significant, however, indicates the validity and potential of RPP. Chapter 8 – Remote Personality Profiling lists questions that can be used to get a fuller picture of an individual. When interpreted using information from preceding chapters, weighted and applied to a particular assessment brief, potential risks and all-important considerations come to the fore.

Key risks

What are the key risks inherent in ignoring or having insufficient insights into someone's biographical background? We suggest the following:

- Having done the research on someone's background, favoring them because they are 'similar' to you: we instinctively like people who come from the same village, school or university – this is not scientific and should be avoided.
- Stereotyping people: someone who comes from a different social background or speaks with a strong regional accent should not be judged on that alone; their qualities and skills will be different from the popular view.
- Ignorance or misinterpretation of a traumatic event during their childhood: often this can have a positive effect on a person's personality and motivation, but equally the impact might be negative. Look for the circumstances around the trauma and gain the whole picture.

Conclusion

As highlighted in the previous chapter, familiarizing ourselves with the culture(s) and broader environment in which an individual is raised gives us vital clues as to who they are. In this chapter we present potentially useful biographical data to help us to put flesh on the bones of the subject. The potential range is large, but we should always be aware of information gaps that may put a different slant on our findings and wary of attributing too much importance to any one individual aspect of a subject or their past. As with broad categorizations and stereotypes they may be unreliable or misleading. The myriad relationships, events and experiences which shape us are as complex as we are ourselves, and as difficult to fathom. Some facts, like birth order, have a popular appeal and some tempting inferences, but correlations with any significant behavior are weak. Misfortunes, parental qualities and support elements have a much greater and more generalizable impact, particularly when it comes to identifying the potential causes of negative and disruptive behaviors.

Business has gone some way toward mining straightforward bio-data requests for evidence of strengths, weaknesses and character flaws. It also makes efforts, at least in selection, not to categorize or stereotype individuals according to, for example, gender, age or physical appearance. Some initial assumptions are useful and often verifiable in a subject. But they can also obscure more interesting aspects of a subject's character. It is when we move from the general to the specific that the remote profiler's interest is aroused. If a candidate spent a year in Bangkok as a teenager, it may be noteworthy, but knowing that this was a forced and unhappy move is likely to be more so. How much more does knowing that a candidate came from a single-parent family and worked through school to pay for higher education say about their attitudes and achievements than the academic results?

Even fairly insignificant details unearthed through biographical research can be useful in managing or influencing a subject. Learning that someone places a high premium on thorough preparation, smart dress or punctuality – a legacy from their punctilious mother – can help us present our case better and avoid faux pas. That the subject attended our or a colleague's school or university can help identify common ground or interest and tailor an approach. This in turn helps us build understanding and rapport.

Recommended reading

Gunter, B. and Furnham, A. (2001) *Assessing Potential*. London: Whurr.
Sullaway, F. (1996) *Born to Rebel*. New York: Pantheon.
Therivel, W. (2001) *The GAM/DP Theory of Personality and Creativity*. New York: Kirk House.

Intelligence

How often have you attributed someone's inability to complete satisfactorily a task or undertake a role to a lack of intelligence? 'He's a sausage short of a fry up'. 'The lights are on but nobody's there'. We could probably all list disparaging expressions that hint that someone might not have the cognitive ability to function well at a particular level.

Like so many of the issues we cover in *Revealed*, it is those individuals who are at the extremes that are of most interest: the very bright or surprisingly dim (see Figure 4.1). What effect might it have on someone who as a student was continually and effortlessly top-of-the-class? Equally, how does the person whose family have very high expectations of their academic success cope when they are unable, even with considerable effort, to get the desired results? What exactly does intelligence mean in everyday life and to what extent does it really matter?

We all sense that it does matter in life, that's why we so often pass judgment on whether someone is 'bright' or 'bright enough' and try to create an impression of intelligence. We know that brighter people tend to have educational qualifications and get better jobs in terms of pay. We know also that they tend to be healthier and to live longer. They usually, but not always, make better decisions. They learn faster and, quite rightly, tend to be more self-confident.

What exactly does intelligence mean in everyday life and to what extent does it really matter?

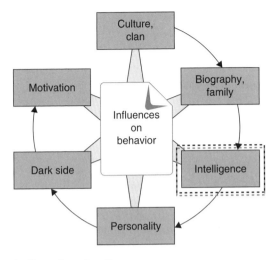

FIG 4.1 / **The six dimensions: intelligence**

But while intelligence is something that we frequently comment on and try to detect in others, in reality in formal assessment we rarely understand it or accord it the importance it deserves. There are not only different levels of intelligence but also different types. We tend to overlook this and read too much into educational qualifications, status and success. A good university degree and other recognized qualifications are certainly useful, but also no prerequisite or guarantee of good performance. Status may have been conferred through family – a son stepping into his father's company shoes – or to a clan member in anticipation of favors returned. A privileged background may give an unwarranted degree and impression of intellectual self-assurance. Personality – being conscientious, extravert and stable – can also lead us to conclude that someone has what it takes intellectually. Even luck might have played a role – simply having come to a manager's attention in a particular job or situation.

These all risk deflecting us from really understanding how intelligent, in terms of both form and level, a candidate, colleague, boss or business contact is and whether they have what it takes to do the job well.

In recent years there has been a move toward examining intelligence in far more depth. Concepts such as 'multiple intelligences' are now part of the management lexicon, and related assessments favored over more traditional Intelligence Quotient (IQ) testing. But how effective and comprehensive are they? We look at some popular approaches to intelligence and 'executive intelligence' assessment, which can be useful and practical supplements to assessing general IQ. Related to these, we also look at the positive psychologists' concept of strengths. These are related in that they provide another approach to assessment and matching individual qualities to needs.

Two other areas are covered in this chapter: differences in thinking or cognitive styles, and learning potential or quotient (LQ). Different roles require different ways of processing information and at times being intellectually curious matters. We suggest factors that identify someone as a convergent versus divergent thinker and a Systematic or Empathizing Type thinker. We also explore those factors that predispose individuals toward acquiring new information and skills.

In our view, together these provide the best overall indicator of how an individual will perform in more senior management posts and will be of interest to anybody keen to delve below surface impressions, into just how able, intellectually, a subject is.

Intelligence as a predictor of success

The definition in the box was coined by 50 intelligence experts in reaction to the controversial book '*The Bell Curve, Intelligence and Class Structure in American Life*' researched and written by Herrnstein and Murray (1994). The Bell curve showed the normal IQ distribution curve, where 68 per cent of the population comes within one standard deviation of the mean, and 95 per cent within two standard deviations (see Figure 4.2).

The controversy around the book arose primarily over the

> '*Intelligence is a very general mental capability that, among other things, involves the ability to reason, plan, solve problems, think abstractly, comprehend complex ideas, learn quickly and learn from experience. It is not merely book learning, a narrow academic skill, or descriptive of test-taking smarts. Rather, it reflects a broader and deeper capability for comprehending our surroundings – "catching on", "making sense" of things, or "figuring out" what to do.*'

reasons for the deviations. In a long article published in *The Wall Street Journal*

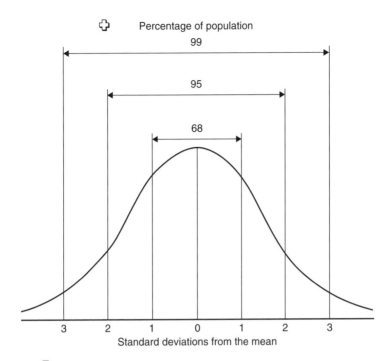

FIG 4.2 / **Bell curve**

the experts refuted some of the conclusions and brought greater clarity to the concept of intelligence and its value. In their view:

- IQ is strongly related (probably more so than any other single measurable human trait) to many important educational, occupational, economic and social outcomes. Its relation to the welfare and performance of individuals is very strong in some arenas of life (education, military training), moderate but robust in others (social competence), and modest but consistent in others (law-abidingness). Whatever IQ tests measure, it is of great practical and social importance.
- A high IQ is an advantage in life because virtually all activities require reasoning and decision-making. Conversely, a low IQ is often a disadvantage, especially in disorganized environments. Of course, a high IQ no more guarantees success in life than a low IQ guarantees failure. There are many exceptions, but the odds for success in our society greatly favor individuals with higher IQs.
- The practical advantages of having a higher IQ increase as life settings become more complex (novel, ambiguous, changing, unpredictable or

multifaceted). For example, a high IQ is generally necessary to perform well in highly detailed, varied or fluid jobs (the professions, management); it is a considerable advantage in moderately complex jobs (crafts, clerical and police work); but it provides less advantage in settings that require only routine decision-making or simple problem solving (unskilled work).

- Differences in intelligence certainly are not the only factor affecting performance in education, training and highly complex jobs (no one claims they are), but how well you think (speed and accuracy of processing), which many call intelligence, and the style in which you think are often the most important factors.

> Members of the same family tend to differ substantially in intelligence (by an average of about 12 IQ points) for both genetic and environmental reasons. They differ genetically because biological brothers and sisters share exactly half their genes with each parent and, on average, only half with each other. They also differ in IQ because they experience different environments within the same family.

- Amongst a selective group, as for example those at graduate school or in special education, other influences on performance comparatively loom larger.

The experts argued that intelligence could be broken down into two useful elements. These correlate to what Cattell (1987) termed '*fluid intelligence*' and '*crystallized intelligence*'. The analogy is to water – fluid water can take any shape, whereas ice crystals are rigid.

Fluid intelligence is effectively the power of reasoning and processing information. It includes the ability to perceive relationships, deal with unfamiliar problems and gain new types of knowledge. Those with higher levels of fluid intelligence would tend to enjoy Sudoku puzzles (which require arithmetic agility and logic to find the right combination of the nine integer numbers for each line and sub box to avoid repetition).

Crystallized intelligence consists of skills and knowledge gained through learning and experience, such as the skills of an accountant, lawyer, mechanic and salesperson. Those with higher crystallized intelligence

> Individuals differ in intelligence due to differences in both their environments and genetic heritage. Heritability estimates range from 0.4 to 0.8 (on a scale from 0–1), most thereby indicating that genetics play a bigger role than does environment in creating IQ differences among individuals.

would tend to enjoy standard crosswords that rely on having acquired a broad vocabulary.

As might be expected, while fluid intelligence peaks before 20 and remains constant with some decline in later years, crystallized intelligence continues to increase as long as the person remains active. Thus, a schoolchild is quicker than a retired citizen at solving a problem that is unfamiliar to both of them, but even the most average older person will perform better when solving problems in their previous area of occupational specialization – using their accumulated knowledge or wisdom.

Standard IQ testing is not common in adults, but cast your mind back to school days, at least in UK, and you will probably remember being assessed to see whether you could hack it at an academically demanding secondary school or would be better pursuing a less demanding or vocational route. Standard IQ tests assess both crystallized and fluid intelligence through a series of questions such as:

- Circle the odd one out in the following number sequence:
  625 361 256 197 144[1]
- Of the following cities, which is the odd one out:
  Oslo London New York Cairo Mumbai Caracas Madrid[2]

Generally we find that scores relating to crystallized and fluid intelligence in (good) IQ tests correlate positively and significantly with one another and that therefore measurement of general intelligence is a good indicator of performance in all areas. In other words people perform at a broadly similar level across all tasks (vocabulary, maths, etc.). As previously stated, such tests have been proven to be highly reliable in predicting future success.

Other intelligence models

Multiple intelligences

Gardner's concept of 'multiple intelligences', made popular by his book of that name first published in 1983, broadens the definition put forward by the experts in *The Wall Street Journal*. It also incorporates elements considered elsewhere in this book, most notably in Chapter 5 – Personality.

'Intelligence, so defined, can be measured, and intelligence tests measure it well. They are among the most accurate (in technical terms, reliable and valid) of all psychological tests and assessments. They do not measure creativity, character, personality or other important differences among individuals, nor are they intended to.'

Gardner defined intelligence as 'the ability to solve problems or to create products that are valued within one or more cultural settings' and went on to specify seven intelligences. He argued that *linguistic/verbal* and *logical/mathematical* are those typically valued in educational settings. *Linguistic* intelligence involves sensitivity to the spoken and written language and the ability to learn languages. *Logical/mathematical* intelligence involves the capacity to analyze problems logically, be good with numbers and investigate issues scientifically. These two types of intelligence dominate intelligence tests.

Three other multiple intelligences are arts-based: *musical* intelligence, which refers to skill in the performance, composition and appreciation of musical patterns; *bodily kinaesthetic* which is based on the use of the whole or parts of the body to solve problems or to fashion products; and *spatial* intelligence which is the ability to recognize and manipulate patterns in space.

There are also two personal intelligences: *interpersonal* intelligence, which is the capacity to understand the intentions, motivations and desires of other people and to work effectively

> There are many successful business people who never went to, or dropped out of university. Amongst whom are:
>
> Bill Gates
>
> Steve Jobs
>
> Alan Sugar
>
> Richard Branson
>
> Simon Cowell
>
> It would be foolhardy (and wrong) to suggest they lack intelligence.

with them and *intrapersonal* intelligence which is the capacity to understand oneself and to use this information effectively in regulating one's life. People have all of the above to varying degrees.

Academic debate continues regarding whether intelligence distinctions of this kind can be made. There is also continued business interest in Gardner's work and related, and widely published research and theories, suggesting they answer a need for detailed assessment of an individual's strengths and weaknesses in order, amongst other things, to avoid costly recruitment mistakes and executive derailments.

Below we look at further theories and approaches to intelligence and intelligence assessment and propose our own list of intelligences, designed to complement data collected in relation to the other elements included in this book.

Triarchic theory of intelligence

The Triarchic Theory of Intelligence (2003) developed by Robert Sternberg posits that human intelligence comprises three aspects – *componential, experiential and contextual*. The componential aspect refers to a person's ability to learn new things, to think analytically and to solve problems. This aspect of intelligence is reflected in higher standard intelligence test scores, which require general knowledge and ability in areas such as arithmetic and vocabulary. The experiential aspect refers to a person's ability to combine different experiences in unique and creative ways. It concerns original thinking and creativity in both the arts and the sciences. Finally, the contextual aspect refers to a person's ability to deal with practical aspects of their environment and to adapt to new and changing contexts. This aspect of intelligence resembles what lay people sometimes refer to as 'being street smart'.

Leader intelligence

Leaders are likely to have above average intelligence, with senior positions in business normally filled by individuals in the top 10 to 20 per cent IQ range. IQ testing is rarely carried out as part of recruitment or in later professional life for three main reasons. Firstly, ignorance and prejudice of their relevance on the part of human resource managers and others involved in the process of staff selection; secondly, the belief that educational achievement, self-confidence or social class are a proxy for intelligence; and thirdly, particularly at senior levels, a fear of embarrassment or litigation if an executive is told they are not bright enough for the job.

Ask recruiters what is required of senior executives and the range and level of the skills and knowledge seems boundless. The two approaches described below highlight some of the key attributes they habitually seek.

Menkes' executive intelligence

Menkes (2005) writing in the *Harvard Business Review* described what he called 'executive intelligence'. The gist of his argument is in the subtitle. 'It's all very well to be kind, compassionate and charismatic. But the most crucial predictor of executive success has nothing to do with personality or style.'

He points out that most of us have come across academically brilliant executives whose poor decision-making renders them ineffective. He argues that all managerial work falls under three headings: tasks, people and self. His approach is very similar to Adair's (2002) three-circle model: task, team and individual.

Menkes lists various things that intelligent leaders do. These include:

1. Accomplishing tasks: (cognitive skills)
- Critically examine underlying assumptions
- Identify probable unintended consequences
- Distinguish primary goals from less relevant concerns
- Anticipate probable outcomes

2. Working with, and through, others: (people skills)
- Recognize the underlying agendas of others
- Consider the probable effects of one's actions
- Acknowledge personal biases or limitations in one's perspectives
- Pursue feedback that may reveal an error in judgment and make appropriate judgments

3. Judging one's self and adapting one's behavior accordingly: (self-awareness)
- Seek out and use feedback
- Recognize when it is appropriate to stand one's ground and resist the arguments of others
- Acknowledge personal errors and mistakes

In terms of formal assessment, Menkes agrees that IQ testing is the best overall indicator of competence or success, but points out that some methods can be expensive and unreliable. He recommends that assessments are conducted face-to-face, rather than using paper or computers, and also that they do not follow a standard interview format. Usual methods tend to assess what people have learned and their confidence and articulateness rather than uncover abilities. He favors presenting executives with typical business problems and asking them to analyze them. He states 'The business world's reluctance to use intelligence testing of any kind … has robbed companies of a powerful tool for evaluating candidates for employment or promotion'. Menkes (2005).

Hogan's Business Reasoning Test

Hogan et al. (2009) takes a similar approach to Menkes. His Business Reasoning Test assesses business problem-solving ability – reasoning which he breaks down as follows:

Strategic Reasoning: concerns being able to evaluate current business practices from a strategic perspective and to understand how recent trends and technological innovations may impact future business development. High scorers focus on long-term issues and find solutions that integrate the needs of different business units. They quickly recognize fresh problems and appear innovative, curious, tolerant of ambiguity and interested in feedback.

Tactical Reasoning: concerns being able to reach sound, defensible conclusions using available information and data. High scorers focus on short-term issues, solving them one at a time. They excel at anticipating the consequences of decisions and the obstacles to their implementation. They bring discipline to the decision-making process and seem steady, precise, detail-oriented and professional.

Critical Thinking: concerns being able to define and solve complex problems. High scorers can balance short- and long-term goals, can link innovation with implementation, are able to recognize assumptions, understand agendas and evaluate arguments. The Critical Thinking score is composed of Tactical and Strategic Reasoning scales. Critical thinking predicts overall performance across many jobs.

Those that really don't have the horsepower to do what their job requires of them appear most in old established change-resistant or monopolistic organizations and in corrupt societies. Those who struggle to take over their father's firm but whose position in society or in the family prevents them from acknowledging and addressing the problem. In organizations where more competition exists, change is more prevalent and standard selection procedures used, they often don't get through the net (although a surprising number do).

A tendency to work hard and acquire knowledge and skills (crystallized intelligence) may be reflected in a strong CV or standard assessments, but if an individual does not also have good analytical or problem-solving skills (fluid intelligence), they may struggle, or at least take time, to complete unfamiliar tasks or to adjust to new challenges and roles. Equally, in this day and age when a premium is put on being quick-witted and agile, it is easy to underestimate the value of acquired intelligence. The Internet provides unprecedented and rapidly growing levels of information which leaders and managers are expected to seek out and absorb. The mantra of stakeholder engagement and the importance of research and development highlight the need to continue to accumulate knowledge and information.

The 'intelligences' outlined above have narrower (or unknown) applicability or 'transferability' across tasks and settings compared with general intelligence but acknowledge that certain personality traits, special talents, aptitudes, physical capabilities, experience and the like are important (sometimes

TABLE 4.1   Intelligence types

1.	Overall intelligence (the ability to think fast and solve problems)
2.	Verbal or linguistic intelligence (ability to use words)
3.	Logical or mathematical intelligence (the ability to reason logically, solve a number of problems)
4.	Spatial intelligence (the ability to find your way around the environment and form mental images)
5.	Musical intelligence (the ability to perceive and create pitch and rhythm)
6.	Body kinesthetic intelligence (the ability to use bodily functions or motor movements)
7.	Inter-personal intelligence (the ability to understand other people)
8.	Intra-personal intelligence (the ability to understand yourself and develop a sense of your own identity)
9.	Existential intelligence (the ability to understand the significance of life, the meaning of death and the experience of love)
10.	Spiritual intelligence (the ability to engage in thinking about cosmic issues, the achievement of a state of being and the ability to have spiritual effects on others)
11.	Naturalistic intelligence (the ability to identify and employ many distinctions in the natural world, e.g. classifying animals, plants)
12.	Emotional intelligence (the ability to understand and manage your own and others' emotions)
13.	Creative intelligence (the ability to go beyond what is given to generate novel and interesting ideas)
14.	Practical intelligence (the ability to find the best fit between yourself and the demands of the environment)

essential) for successful performance in many jobs. Many of them, and the 14 intelligences we propose below, would support the comprehensive assessment approach taken in this book (see Table 4.1).

Strengths

There has been a great deal of interest by Positive Psychologists on what are termed 'strengths' (also thought of as gifts), of which 24 have been identified. These are not determined by multiple intelligences or personality traits but are related to both (see Table 4.2). They are:

Of course, people's judgment of their own strengths and others' varies hugely. But the remote profiler can be alert to whether any of these strengths are consistently attributed to the subject being assessed and also whether they would be valued in dealing with them.

TABLE 4.2   Personal strengths

1.	**Curiosity**: interest in, intrigued by many things
2.	**Love of learning**: knowing more, reading, understanding
3.	**Good judgment**: critical thinking, rationality, open-mindedness
4.	**Ingenuity**: originality, practical intelligence, street smart
5.	**Social intelligence**: emotional/personal intelligence, good with feelings
6.	**Wisdom**: seeing the big picture, having perspective
7.	**Bravery**: courage, valor, fearlessness
8.	**Persistence**: perseverance, diligence, industriousness
9.	**Integrity:** honesty, genuineness, truthful
10.	**Kindness**: generosity, empathic, helpful
11.	**Loving**: able to love and be loved, having deep sustained feelings
12.	**Citizenship**: team worker, loyalty, duty to others
13.	**Fairness**: moral valuing, equality and equity
14.	**Leadership**: able to motivate groups, inclusive, focused
15.	**Self-control**: able to regulate emotions, non-impulsive
16.	**Prudence**: cautious, far-sighted, deliberative, discreet
17.	**Humility**: modesty, unpretentious, humble
18.	**Appreciative of beauty**: seeking excellence, experience of awe/wonder
19.	**Gratitude**: thankful, grateful
20.	**Optimism**: hopefulness, future-mindedness, positive
21.	**Spirituality**: faith, philosophy, sense of purpose/calling
22.	**Forgiveness**: mercy, benevolent, kind
23.	**Playfulness**: humor, funny, childlike
24.	**Enthusiasm**: passion, zest, infectious, engaged

Source: Furnham, A. & Lester, D. (2012) 'The development of a short measure of character strength'. *European Journal of Psychological Assessment*, 28, 95–101.

> ### *No-one wants this over more than I do. I want my life back*
>
> Tony Hayward, former CEO of BP speaking about the Deepwater Horizon oil spill. Tony Haywood was an experienced and well-qualified geologist when, having impressed at a leadership conference, his predecessor as CEO of BP, Lord Browne, hand-picked him to be his Executive Secretary. His stepping down prematurely could be attributed to many factors, but perhaps at the root it could stem from a weak selection process. Despite a stellar career, he is widely considered to have grossly mishandled the Deepwater Horizon crisis.

Our approach

Assessing intelligence

Many tests based on the multiple or executive intelligences are deployed in a professional context and are available online to self-administer. As previously noted, however, often they are not used in relation to senior-level appointments, when sensitivities and a focus on past performance and perhaps an attitude of 'better the devil you know' or 'who you know' have a tendency to predominate.

In RPP the assumption is that we are unable to access results of such tests or more general IQ scores, even if they have been administered. The models and concepts above, however, can still be of value in terms of clarifying the needs of a particular role and matching them to a subject's recorded (where available) or observed strengths and abilities.

No matter the context, an assessment of general intelligence is also useful. A lack of general intelligence is clearly likely to be more of a problem than being super-bright, although that can result in frustration with, or even contempt for, those who are slower or dimmer. Low intelligence tends to manifest itself in the following ways:

- *Speed*: Dim managers are poor at 'sizing up the situation', picking things up, seeing the big picture. Some are impulsive, acting rashly, but they are slow to see patterns, solve problems, and to see threats and opportunities. They are inefficient processors of data.
- *Accuracy*: Dim managers are often wrong. They make mistakes. Their analysis is simple-minded, superficial and full of illogical inferences. They are often intolerant of ambiguity, unable to see subtle or nuanced issues. They overlook, downplay or ignore important issues because they are too difficult to process.
- *Learning*: Dim managers are less trainable and benefit less from experience. They are slow learners and rarely pursue cognitively challenging or competitive activities in their spare time. In the workplace many eschew any form of learning or training because it shows them up as 'below par'.
- *Change/Risk*: Because they have difficulty in learning they don't like new things – ideas, technology, the unknown. They find it difficult trying to master them. Fear of change and risk can make them inflexible, but also easy to manipulate or intimidate if arguments are presented by others more clever or savvy.
- *Expression*: Dim leaders are often poor at articulation and use a more restricted vocabulary. Generally this is most apparent in relation to the written word. Whilst they may master motivational scripts and can inspire

support with passion, once the issues become more complex their powers of persuasion decline.

• *Wit*: Funny ('ha ha' or peculiar) is different from witty; it can be learned, wit can't. Few, if any, dim people possess the latter.

There are two further aspects of intelligence worthy of consideration: learning quotient, or how able and willing an individual is to learn; and thinking style, which considers how they prefer to problem-solve.

Learning quotient

When choosing a new colleague or business partner, key considerations will be, not only how much they have learnt, but how well they learn and how likely they are to be both able and willing to continue to learn in the future. In other words, what is their learning potential or Learning Quotient (LQ)?

Taylor and Furnham (2005) identify nine factors that influence an individual's LQ (see Table 4.3). These are:

TABLE 4.3 Influences on learning

Positive experience of learning	A child's experience at school has a major impact on how they view learning later on in life. But it is not just how the teachers encouraged the child but also how they felt they did compared to their peers.
Positive family and social environment	The atmosphere at home or amongst friends also has a major impact on the child. Was the child encouraged to read, how clever are the parents, was success acknowledged?
Age	Easy enough to measure. Many believe that the older we are the harder it is to learn, but this is often used as an excuse and its impact is less than many believe.
Intelligence	IQ which as we have discussed is easy enough to measure, but the real question is whether the individual is bright enough for the task.
Conscientiousness	The more conscientious the person the more likely they are to take learning seriously and do the necessary work.
Stability	Neurotics are easily distracted and find it hard to concentrate.
Openness	Openness is about being ready to have new experiences and open the mind to new possibilities – an essential quality for the learner.
Self-esteem	Confidence helps people learn. Someone nervous of water is going to find a swimming lesson hard. If you believe you can do something you are more likely to learn.
Motivation	Malcolm Knowles (1998) identified the need for adults to know why they were learning something as an important factor in their learning potential.

An overall assessment of an individual's LQ can be useful, for example, when assessing whether, as they move up an organization, they are likely to continue to acquire the skills and knowledge necessary to take on new roles and challenges. The over-promotion of managers is a common problem, known as 'the Peter Principle'. This states that, based on past success and achievement, 'employees tend to rise to their level of incompetence'. Most of us have experience of bosses who would fall into this category.

Breaking down LQ into its components also indicates learning preferences. On the basis of this knowledge, development plans can be drawn up or a broader assessment made regarding whether the general environment would provide suitable learning opportunities for the individual.

A discussion of learning styles, as put forward by Kolb (1984) and later Honey and Mumford (2000) and others, is beyond the scope of this book but are discussed in depth in *Learning at Work* (Taylor and Furnham 2005). For the purposes of RPP, knowing that someone is open to experience and possesses high self-esteem would suggest certain learning preferences – perhaps that they are more 'activist' to use Honey and Mumford's term. Someone conscientious and more reserved is likely to favor more reflective methods.

> Kevin McCullough, COO of RWE npower
>
> '... I know through first-hand experience that we've got some amazing staff, but equally I know that we don't always get everything right. Being approached by Channel 4 presented a unique opportunity to go undercover and really reacquaint myself firsthand about what life is now like at the sharp end of our business.'

People's learning preferences can often easily be observed. As an extreme example, not every CEO would willingly agree to participate in the TV series *Undercover Boss*, much less integrate any learning or concrete suggestions into future strategy. Some would prefer to canvas opinions through surveys or provide suggestion boxes, rather than mix with staff or temporarily take on a junior role. Yet others will just assume that they know it all. If so, as outlined earlier in this chapter, it might not only raise questions concerning their LQ but indeed their broader intelligence.

Thinking styles

The term 'thinking' or 'cognitive style' refers to how we process information. We have a degree of control over our way of thinking, meaning it is considered a preference rather than ability. As such, it is more likely to change and adapt, affected by any number of factors of which we may or may not be aware.

Here we present four categorizations of thinking style: divergent versus convergent and empathizing versus systemizing. Few of us are at an extreme, rather tending toward one or other style. Assessing which thinking style is most conducive to success in relation to a particular role, organization or task, and whether other individuals or teams with complementary styles can contribute, is valuable. Careful observation and data collection will give us an advantage in staff selection but also in choosing appropriate influencing techniques.

Convergent versus divergent thinkers

Does an individual enjoy brainstorming and 'thinking outside the box' or rather base decisions primarily on forensic evidence? Do they present using structured and rounded data-dependent arguments or a looser, more inspirational, visionary approach? When James Dyson set out to improve on existing vacuum cleaner designs, he made 5,127 prototypes before he was satisfied. Steve Jobs, on the other hand, created the Apple enterprise on the basis of his passion for a concept that many considered whacky at the time and found technicians to convert his idea into reality. Impatient with the process, he just wanted to see results and used his strength as a divergent thinker to inspire others to success. Both visionaries in their way, they employed different methods to reach their goals.

In his 1959 lecture entitled *The Two Cultures*, C P Snow was one of the first to draw psychologists' and educationalists' attention to the field, observing the differences in styles between those concerned with the sciences and the humanities, and the poor communication that often ensued.

Liam Hudson's work (1966) further stimulated research in this area. In his book *Contrary Imaginations* he argued that personality counts for as much as ability in an individual's choice of, and academic success in, different subjects. Based on his studies of English schoolboys, Hudson concluded that conventional approaches to assessment might be seriously under-valuing the talent of a section of the school population. He argued that education was geared too much toward promoting what he termed 'convergent thinking' which is particularly appropriate in the sciences and maths. Convergent thinkers bring material from a variety of sources to bear on a problem in such a way as to produce the 'correct' answer.

'Divergent thinkers' are more suited to artistic pursuits and study of the humanities. They elaborate a broad spectrum of ideas on the basis of some stimulus or need and are generally thought of as creative.

In the 1970s researchers came to similar categorizations based on their observations of very simple processes. They noted, for example, that if people were given a text to read and believed they would be examined, some tried to understand, contextualize and comprehend the 'big picture', while others focused on remembering what they believed to be the essential 'facts'. These two very different approaches have been called *deep* versus *surface* approaches.

Examples of tests to identify which sort of thinking comes more naturally to an individual are:

- In two minutes (only) write down as *quickly as possible* as *many as possible*, and as *unusual as possible*, things you could do with a paper clip (or hot water bottle, wooden barrel).
- In five minutes write down all the possible major and minor consequences if we never had to eat again (or if everyone went blind).

Another example is manifest in traditional brainstorming. By piggy-backing on the suggestions of others and no criticism allowed for daft, impractical ideas, the hope is that you open wide your mind and let your imagination run wild. You soon notice serious and significant differences between people. Clearly some people really enjoy the whole brainstorming experience and enter into the fun and games approach. They seem cognitively disinhibited. They happily come up with many and strange ideas. They would be more divergent thinkers. Others find the process uncomfortable and neither fun nor natural. They would tend to be convergent thinkers. The combination of both types of thinkers can be powerful and assessment useful. Teams might benefit from including both types of thinkers. When preparing a business pitch the decision on whether to depend on hard facts, logic and relate to experience or rather appeal to future possibilities and the excitement of the new and unknown should relate to the preferences of the target audience.

Empathizing–systemizing theory

In his book *The Essential Difference* (2011) Baron-Cohen, best known for his work on autism, argues that male and female brains tend to be wired differently. A greater percentage of women (44 per cent as opposed to 17 per cent) can be categorized as Empathizing (E) Types who recognize what another person may be feeling or thinking and respond to those feelings with an appropriate emotion of their own. Men more often have strengths in Systemizing (S) (54 per cent/17 per cent). S-Types seek to identify the laws that govern how a system works. Knowing the system they can then control it and predict its behavior. Baron-Cohen categorizes those with an interest in both systemizing and empathizing as B-Types. Which type you are depends predominantly, he argues, on biology – the amount of testosterone present in the womb, for example, or whether your grandfather was an engineer and your mother and father showed, when completing questionnaires or in their brain scans, systemizing tendencies. However, nurture also plays a role.

In its more extreme forms, Baron-Cohen states that S-Type is associated with autism and other conditions on the autism spectrum, such as Aspergers. Currently it is estimated that 1/200 are on the Autism/Aspergers spectrum with at least ten males to every female. Extreme S Types typically tolerate badly unpredictable or uncontrollable situations, including social occasions, becoming anxious or disinterested. Repetitive or obsessive behaviors would be symptomatic, as would difficulties in friendships and intimate relationships. They may also have 'islets' of ability, for example, in maths, drawing, music, their concern with detail being an advantage in these fields.

Baron-Cohen suggests that this S-Type interest in analysis and exploring and constructing systems would account for the greater uptake amongst men of Science, Technology, Engineering and Mathematics (STEM) study and careers. Typical S-Types would show an interest and aptitude in systems, collecting, classification, attention to relevant detail, rule-based and factual information. They are also better at map reading! It would also explain why they might be less comfortable with open systems and the lack of control often experienced when dealing with people. Some might even term them 'mind-blind' in that they are unable to detect others' thinking and so likely reactions. E-Type are able to 'mind read', show far greater strengths in interpreting body language, making eye contact, communication and expressing feelings. They also tend to put greater value on friendships.

Influencing different intelligences

The seventh of our influencers, logic or reason, is likely to play a more significant role for the generally more intelligent person. The intelligent person may still be swayed by non-logical arguments, but if there are logical lacunae in the argument they are more likely to pick up on them. An individual's thinking style or preference is also worth bearing in mind when deciding on how arguments are presented, and particularly as concerns the degree to which they are likely to look for facts and evidence, rather than vision and promise.

Key risks

What then are the risks for the negotiator, the recruiter, the team builder of ignoring or having insufficient insights into intelligence? We identify the following:

1. Attributing too much importance to formal qualifications when other achievements, interests and pursuits may indicate broader intelligence. A good degree might mean that the individual spent every waking hour working hard in the library. A lesser degree might reflect the fact that a very clever person led a rich life playing sport, acting in the university theatre group or pursuing their own intellectual fascinations rather than the set curriculum. This may say more about the individual's motivations, but that should be a separate consideration.
2. Similarly, a lack of investment in intelligence assessment may result in overlooking those who may bring invaluable intelligence, willingness to learn and a thinking style that fits the demands of a particular role or situation. It may cost more effort to find out exactly how intelligent a person is but it could be worth it; a bright individual without formal qualifications is going to be grateful and therefore more loyal to the employer who picks up on their intelligence.
3. Assuming there is one kind of intelligence – the brain is wired differently and different intelligences suit different roles. We value a lawyer or accountant's precision and eye for detail and a marketing director's ability to anticipate future trends.
4. Underestimating, particularly in senior roles, the importance of flexibility in using different 'intelligences', of self-awareness and of a willingness to learn.

Conclusion

In today's fast-moving work environment, general and specific forms of intelligence and the ability to learn are increasingly important factors in success. However, rather than test intelligence empirically we continue to rely on qualifications, experience, status and overall impressions when assessing individuals, particularly for senior roles. Widely accepted as the best overall predictor of success, more rigorous testing or consideration of general intelligence, or what type of intelligence is required for a particular role, is perhaps the single most important factor in avoiding derailment and Peter Principle casualties. Charisma, connections and education are no substitute, and being fearsomely but narrowly bright, with poor people skills and limited self-awareness and willingness to learn, can be a recipe for disaster.

RPP is effective because it supplements the usual, and sometimes misleading, indicators of intelligence with other, often readily available, recorded and observational data. It breaks intelligence down into its different components and assesses how they relate to the needs of a specific role or task. Coupled with an assessment of broader strengths, LQ and thinking style – a willingness to learn and an individual's preferred ways of absorbing and processing information – it goes a long way toward compensating for current more limited and limiting assessment approaches.

Recommended reading

Cattell, R. (1987) *Intelligence*. New York: Springer.
Deary, I. (2005) *Intelligence: A Very Short Introduction*. Oxford: Oxford University Press.
Gardner, H. (1999) *Intelligence Reframed*. New York: Basic Books.
Knowles, M. (1998) *The Adult Learner*. Woburn: Butterworth.
Mackintosh, N. (1998) *IQ and Human Intelligence*. Oxford: Oxford University Press.
Taylor, J. and Furnham, A. (2005) *Learning at Work*. Basingstoke: Palgrave.

5

chapter

Personality

In the English language there are almost 30,000 words and countless more expressions to describe personality traits. Hearing someone described as cold, callous, kind, tender-hearted, lazy, diligent, likeable or anti-social gives us clues to their character and preferences, whether we will like them and how they might respond to a variety of roles and situations.

The importance of person-job fit within organizations is so apparent that formal personality assessment, categorizing individuals on the basis of traits and behavior – how they interact with others, respond to deadlines, spend their leisure time or approach a task – is often routine as part of recruitment or team-building. It enables us to make judgments regarding how comfortable a colleague is likely to feel in a particular environment, how effective they will be under pressure and how well they will relate to colleagues, clients or other organizational stakeholders (see Figure 5.1).

Before meeting a potential client or business partner, collecting data on their preferences and behavioral characteristics – a pen picture of what they are like – is also useful. What would be a good venue for a meeting, a quiet café or noisy bar? Are they likely to worry about a new venture? Would they feel confident networking on our behalf or being in the spotlight? How easy will it be to establish rapport with them? Will it require a toning down or other form of adaptation on our part to fit their personal style?

When recruiting an external board member or someone at a senior level, personality assessment is not routine. As with intelligence testing it may be deemed inappropriate – they have, after all, got this far, they must be

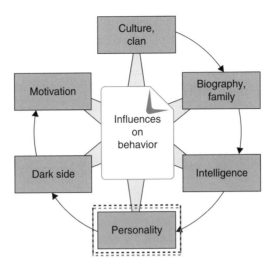

FIG 5.1 The six dimensions: personality

competent. However, as indicated elsewhere, when attaining more senior levels some form of assessment of a subject's natural preferences, and whether they are aware and able to manage them appropriately, is often critical.

Extreme personalities are explored in greater depth in Chapter 6 – The Dark Side Traits. The behavior associated with personality extremes can on occasions be admired and valued and may account for a subject doing well in business. Tough and decisive at a time of crisis, conscientious in the face of heavy workloads. Most of us are 'ambiverts' but will exhibit more extreme behavior when under stress, perhaps due to an unaccustomed level of responsibility or when our personality preferences are not catered for. Identifying these tendencies early on helps avoid potential problems.

In this chapter, having expanded on internationally recognized trait definitions, we highlight where even milder personality preferences might be incompatible with certain roles and activities. We also explore the linked concept of 'emotional intelligence', useful in that it relates to an individual's degree of awareness and management of behavioral tendencies, enabling, for example, a motivated introvert to learn to become more extraverted. We also highlight the importance of

Most of us are 'ambiverts' but will exhibit more extreme behavior when under stress.

integrity, an essential element in building trust, and how we must allow for different interpretations of it according to background and context.

Defining personality

Hall and Lindzey (1957) term personality 'the essence of a human being'. It is what makes you unique and once formed, usually by late adolescence, it remains fairly constant throughout adult life.

Many early attempts at determining personality could be classified as 'type theories' with distinct and discontinuous categories of membership. Individuals are either classified as one or the other. 'Trait theories' are favored by academics these days. Type theories proved to be too arbitrary and unreliable. Trait theories place individuals along a continuum of traits based on quantitative rather than qualitative assessment. Both theories classify individuals and associate specific behavior with these classifications. However, as outlined in Table 5.1, their approach to categorization varies in a number of respects.

Personality theories, like psychology in general, have a long history but a short past. The ancient Greeks, and before them the Chinese, both had clear theories of personality. Most people are familiar with Galen's theory (AD 170) of humors or bodily fluids leading to four temperaments – choleric, melancholic, phlegmatic and sanguine. Building on these, nineteenth-century thinkers pondered personality in terms of the strength and speed of emotional reaction to other people and events. Those of quick and strong reactions were thought of as choleric and those of slow and strong as melancholic. Equally those reacting quickly and weakly might be described as sanguine, while those slowly and weakly were phlegmatic (see Figure 5.2).

TABLE 5.1 Differences between traits and types

Trait theory	Type theory
Concerned with universals possessed in different amounts	Concerned with preferences which are perhaps inborn or learnt
Involves measuring	Involves sorting
Extreme scores are important for discrimination	Midpoint is crucial for discrimination
Normally distributed	Skewed distribution
Scores mean amount of trait possessed	Scores indicate confidence that sorting is correct

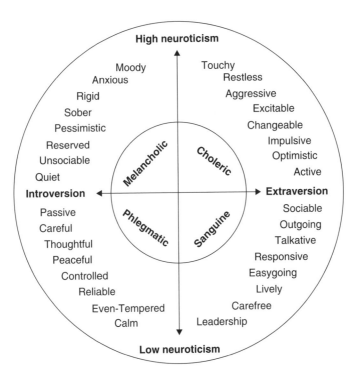

FIG 5.2 The two-dimensional description of personality

Source: Based on Galen's original work (170 ad), Lamera (1938).

Clear dimensions of extraversion–introversion and neuroticism–stability can be traced through many philosophical speculators until the turn of this century, being found in the writings of Hippocrates and Galen, Wundt and Jung, and Eysenck and Cattell. Of these, perhaps the most celebrated of all traits is extraversion. This construct can be measured by self-report (questionnaire), ratings by others, and indirect or objective measures such as salivation after receiving 'lemon drops' in the mouth, color preference or speed of reaction.

Personality theories, like psychology in general, have a long history but a short past.

Even amongst trait theories, which now predominate, there has been considerable argument about the nature and structure of personality. There is now broad consensus however, that:

• You can pretty well (parsimoniously and accurately) describe an individual's personality by describing where they stand on a limited number of dimensions, sometimes termed super-factors like introversion–extraversion. Some people are very strongly extraverted, others just averagely so. Some are very stable, others very neurotic.

- The normal distribution amongst the population in relation to all five commonly used dimensions (or super-factors – see below) is along the 'Bell Curve'. Those individuals that tend toward the extremes on one or more dimension are of particular interest in personality testing as they have stronger drives and preferences, are more inflexible and can even tend to mental illness.
- These dimensions are unrelated to each other; how high or low you score on one factor has little or no influence on how high you score on another. So, for example, warmth can be attributed to an individual being high on both extraversion and agreeableness.
- Associated traits, sometimes termed primary factors (Costa & McCrae listed six related to extraversion – warmth, gregariousness, assertiveness, activity, excitement-seeking and positive emotions) permit some overlap between super-factors, i.e. some behaviors, needs and preferences are shared.
- Each category can be related to characteristic social behavior: high extraversion to, for example, sport and social contacts, neuroticism to drug taking, disagreeableness to delinquency and conscientiousness to educational success. Personality traits can also be used to predict marital success, health and longevity.
- Personality is part accounted for by nature and part nurture (60/40). It remains fairly constant throughout adult life but with some scope for alteration through trauma, training and other influences (such as culture).
- Individuals cannot easily change their personality but can learn new and different behavioral repertoires – i.e. manage them better for particular purposes; introverts can learn to behave like an extravert and become a 'socialized extravert'. Similarly someone who is neurotic can learn to cope with anxiety better without actually changing their underlying personality.
- Personality testing offers great potential as, unlike moods, it is not influenced by exposure to film, music or drugs.

Personality assessment

Given it is now widely accepted that individuals will have certain preferences, and based on these adopt characteristic behaviors, accurate identification of which can be a powerful tool. In some cultures psychological analysis is less prevalent, but in many we read articles on the subject, for fun self-administer personality tests freely available on the Internet, and accept they are part of routine assessment for employment.

This knowledge and the results generated shape our self-perceptions and enable us to select and give feedback to colleagues, team members and others. Often we demonstrate a high awareness of our own and general personality types. However, it is also not unusual to encounter people who express surprise, dismay and often anger when given (accurate) feedback on their personality. The Five Factor Model described below lends itself well to assessment, as most people are able to recognize their own behavior and observe them in other people.

Five-Factor Model

There have been vigorous critiques of the 'five factor approach' or 'Five-Factor Model' (FFM) of personality, on which Americans Costa and McCrae (1992) based their NEO Personality Inventory. This was developed in 1985 and has subsequently been updated several times. The model has become familiar to many, certainly those working in human resources, and is now generally considered to have universal validity. The model identifies five orthogonal, that is, unrelated, personality traits and states that it is possible to measure individuals against each on a spectrum from high, to average, to low. The terms most used in relation to each trait, along with typical behavior, are given in Table 5.2 below, but sometimes other terms are also employed. Neuroticism is also referred to as emotionality, emotional control, affect; extraversion is also related to social adaptability, surgency, assertiveness, power; openness to experience can be enquiring intellect, culture, intelligence, intellect; agreeableness is referred to sometimes as conformity, love, likeability, friendly compliance; and conscientiousness can be described as will to achieve, responsibility, work.

Below, for the purposes of RPP, we describe the different traits in more detail, as well as commenting on the advantages and disadvantages of being an extreme personality type with reduced behavioral flexibility.

Neuroticism

Neurotics are likely to be anxious, depressed, guilt-ridden, phobic and sick. They don't tend to enjoy good long-standing and satisfying personal relationships and jobs. Neuroticism's benefits are generally not immediately apparent, though Nettle (2006) notes that their heightened vigilance,

TABLE 5.2   The Big Five traits

High	Average	Low
1. Neuroticism		
Sensitive, emotional, and prone to experience feelings that are upsetting	Generally calm and able to deal with stress, but you sometimes experience feelings of guilt, anger or sadness	Secure, hardy and generally relaxed, even under stressful conditions
2. Extraversion		
Extraverted, outgoing, active and high-spirited. You prefer to be around people most of the time	Moderate in activity and enthusiasm. You enjoy the company of others but you also value privacy	Introverted, reserved and serious. You prefer to be alone or with few close friends
3. Openness to experience		
Open to new experiences. You have broad interests and are very imaginative	Practical but willing to consider new ways of doing things. You seek a balance between the old and the new	Down-to-earth, practical, traditional and pretty much set in your ways
4. Agreeableness		
Compassionate, good-natured and eager to cooperate and avoid conflict	Generally warm, trusting and agreeable but you can sometimes be stubborn and competitive	Hard-headed, skeptical, proud and competitive. You tend to express your anger directly
5. Conscientiousness		
Conscientious and well organized. You have high standards and always strive to achieve your goals	Dependable and moderately well organized. You generally have clear goals but are able to set your work aside	Easy-going, not very well organized, and sometimes careless. You prefer not to make plans

wariness and risk aversion can be assets. Neurotics are very aware of subtle (and possibly threatening) social changes, which can be a strong survival mechanism in certain environments. Further, combined with other factors such as intelligence and conscientiousness, Neuroticism (at optimal levels) can act as a very efficient source of achievement and competitiveness. At the other extreme, those very low in Neuroticism, who are 'stable' or 'highly adjusted', while generally better able to cope, can bring some disadvantages. They may be too trusting and eager to avoid social and physical hazards; they may underperform and strive less hard because they are afraid of failure. They may also be socially insensitive to the anxieties and worries of those around them and, therefore, have a small social support network.

A typical neurotic would be Woody Allen; at the other end of the scale the epitome of stability might be Vladimir Putin, the President of Russia.

Extraversion

Extraverts are sociable, sensation-seeking and have more social support. Their attitude to, interest in and experience of sex means they tend to have more sexual partners, 'mating success' and offspring. However, it also means they are more prone to infidelity (Nettle, 2005), which may impact their children by, for example, exposing them to step-parents, an established risk factor in their development. Extraverts tend also to be more active and exploratory, therefore more likely to be involved in accidents. Their sensation-seeking and risk-taking disposition, particularly if it is combined with other traits like Neuroticism and Psychoticism, mean extreme extraverts are highly likely to get involved in anti-social and general criminal behavior. Introverts are less sociable but safer; they run the risk of a lower likelihood of finding mates and social support networks, but lead a more secure lifestyle, which is better for child rearing.

There are many extraverts in the public world, perhaps one of the most iconoclastic being Bill Clinton. Finding an introvert well known in public life is impossible because a true introvert would avoid publicity like the plague.

Openness to experience

Openness to experience is marked by creativity and cognitive complexity. It is also associated with intelligence and a 'life of the mind': open individuals are attracted to the unusual and the unconventional. Openness is a good predictor of artistic and scientific achievement, as well as innovation (Furnham, 2008). However, it is also associated with schizophrenia and schizotypy (which is defined as less severe than schizophrenia but on the same dimension), with mental breakdown and (very) poor personal relationships. The flipside of novel thinking is delusions and supernatural and paranormal ideas. Creative individuals, when emotionally stable and particularly in the arts, are highly attractive to others and therefore have many different mates and a wide relationship network. However, those with 'unusual' beliefs can easily be described as 'mad' and rejected by society. With all these traits, it is situational variables that really determine the adaptiveness of the trait. This is probably more the case with Openness than with any of the other Big Five trait factors.

Gosling (2009) nominates Leonardo Da Vinci, a prolific inventor, as his most open personality, citing his brilliance as an artist and sculptor combined with his fascination with science, astrology and philosophy. A contemporary example might be Stephen Fry who combines a love of classical works of literature, theatre and TV with a passion for modern technology. Finding a typical closed personality is less easy in real life. Ebenezer Scrooge in

Charles Dickens' novel *A Christmas Carol* is pretty closed minded until his transformation late in the novel.

Agreeableness

Agreeable people are empathic, trusting and kind. They are well-liked, respected and valued as friends. They are conflict-averse, always seeking and attempting to create harmony and concord. The trait is highly valued and being sensitive (emotionally intelligent) to others' moods is clearly advantageous. However, being too trusting, particularly of anti-social individuals, could be counter-productive. Being excessively attentive to the needs of others rather than self may also be problematic. Agreeable people may be easy to exploit and unable or unwilling to assert their rights. Paradoxically, it appears that people who are called tough-minded, critical and skeptical often do better in the professions and business than those with high Agreeableness scores.

Finding a genuinely agreeable person in public life is surprisingly difficult. Many would like us to think they are so, but we hesitate to nominate a truly agreeable personality other than in fiction; perhaps Phoebe in the TV series 'Friends' comes close to it.

Conscientiousness

Conscientious individuals are hardworking, dutiful and orderly. They show self-control and tend to be moral. They seek out and follow good advice – such as that of health practitioners – and therefore tend to live longer. They may be achievement-oriented and highly diligent. It is no surprise that this trait is one of the clearest markers of success in educational and occupational life. If matched with cognitive ability and social intelligence, it is a very important marker of adaptive success. Conscientious people plan for the future and are happy to work constantly for desirable long-term payoffs. An antipathy to all sorts of opportunities, however, may mean that they fail to exploit certain chances that come their way. The major downside of high conscientiousness is associated with perfectionism, rigidity and social dogmatism. Conscientiousness may also be thought of as a reaction to low ability in competitive settings. That is, students learn to be competitive to compensate or 'make up' for lack of ability. This trait is rarely associated with creativity. However, bright, Open, Conscientious people can, and do, become very successful entrepreneurs.

Bankers, lawyers, accountants and air-traffic controllers are, we would all hope, conscientious. Ben Bernanke (Chairman of US Federal Reserve) and Mervyn

King (former Chairman Bank of England) are high on conscientiousness. At the other end of the scale Oscar Wilde and other artists and writers might feature.

You can often get very good clues to a subject's personality and where they are on personality scales by observation or asking colleagues and others very specific questions about how they typically behave or react. In social situations the extreme extravert, like the extreme introvert, is particularly easy to spot because their drives and needs are so strongly and constantly manifest. But learning someone routinely stays late in the office or counters criticism with attack can, along with other evidence, give us clues to their level of conscientiousness and neuroticism and enable us to assess whether, and when, this could make them uncomfortable or vulnerable in some way.

Emotional intelligence

Despite its popularity, and the fact that most people claim to have heard of it, very few can accurately define emotional intelligence, often referred to as EQ. Goleman's (1996) book of the same name played a huge role in the popularization of the concept and chimed with the zeitgeist. Some make dramatic claims concerning its value. One such claim is that cognitive ability or traditional academic intelligence contributes only about 20 per cent to general life success (academic, personal and work), while the remaining 80 per cent is directly attributable to emotional intelligence. Coupled with the contention that there is a critical period to acquire the basis of emotional intelligence – probably during early to late adolescence – and that, as an adult it is comparatively more straightforward to acquire technical competencies in a job than soft skills, the concept of emotional intelligence has spawned a huge training industry.

Skeptics claim that 'charm and influence' became 'social and interpersonal skills' which have become 'emotional intelligence'. Often business people prefer to talk about emotional competencies (rather than traits or abilities). These are essentially learned capabilities rather than tendencies formed early and difficult to change. If one is to include older related concepts, it is possible to find a literature dating back 30 years showing such skills predict occupational effectiveness and success. There is also convincing empirical literature that suggests they can be improved and learnt.

The emotionally intelligent or competent person is held to be aware of, sensitive to and perceptive about their own and others' emotions.

They are emotionally literate. Another important aspect is that they know how to manage – change, moderate and control – their own and others' emotion. They know what to do when they or others are 'down', frightened or aggressive. Below is a simple two-by-two way of conceiving emotional intelligence: self versus other, emotional awareness versus management.

A characterization of a non-emotionally intelligent subject would be the young male who experiences social anxiety, discomfort and rejection while attempting to interact with and influence others (specifically those they are attracted to, which is most often people of the opposite sex). Hence over time they find solace in computers and other activities with a high skills/ low contact basis. Thus, in early adulthood, they appear to be technically competent in certain areas (IT, engineering) but still rather undeveloped in people skills and more specifically emotional awareness and regulation. They may even be 'phobic' about emotional issues and resistant to social skills and other training. Such an individual would not only be less able to pick up emotional intelligence 'skills' but also less willing to try. To acquire technical skills often requires considerable dedication, so reducing opportunities to acquire other social/emotional skills. In preference, a person with low emotional intelligence would continue to choose technology rather than people for fun, comfort and as a source of ideas.

Understanding and using emotions/feelings are at the heart of business and indeed being human. As such those adults who are rigid, with poor self-control, poor social skills and who are weak at building bonds are at a disadvantage in most, although not all, jobs.

Those with high levels of emotional intelligence:

- Are better at communicating their ideas, intentions and goals. They are more articulate, assertive and sensitive.
- Have better team-work social skills and create collaborative climates, so increasing organizational commitment, a key factor in success.
- Identify their own and their teams' strengths and weaknesses, enabling them to leverage the former and compensate for the latter.
- Possess effective and efficient coping skills and so cope better with demands, pressure and stress.
- Accurately identify what followers feel and need and are able to provide support and inspiration.
- Generate more excitement, enthusiasm and optimism and are less prone to negative, defensive and destructive coping and decision-making styles.

The importance of emotional intelligence at work is illustrated by non-scientific sampling suggesting that approximately 70 per cent, and a considerably higher proportion of women, would choose a boss with high emotional intelligence over one with a high IQ. Asked to justify their choice, most people explain having worked for 'brainy boffins' who were hopeless at the fundamental rubrics of management: setting challenging goals, giving support and feedback and looking after the team. Curiously, one rarely hears about the warm and fuzzy manager who 'lost the plot', failed to see opportunities, lacked a strategic plan and could not quite tumble the numbers. Emotional sensitivity, rather than analytic power, is thought of as the more valuable management skill. If asked a further question – which is easier to train/improve? – approximately 80 per cent believe emotional intelligence can be acquired much more easily than broader intelligence.

In this context, understanding the distinctions drawn in the previous chapter regarding intelligence types is useful, as is relating them to a specific role or task. In some roles social skills are of paramount importance, but intellectual analysis (fluid intelligence) or technical knowledge (crystallized) is absent; it can lead to poor, even disastrous business performance. In all areas, ideally a subject should demonstrate awareness and willingness to improve or at least manage their softer skills.

Naturally, most individuals are somewhere in the middle on the personality trait dimensions and rarely tend toward more extreme behavior. When we do, depending on our level of awareness and willingness to change given constructive and authoritative feedback, we are often able to manage effectively potentially damaging aspects of our personality. With awareness, the natural introvert can learn to be more outgoing and socially confident, and the extravert manager focus not only on PR but also on all-important strategy and number crunching. As we have seen above, emotional intelligence - self-awareness and awareness of how others perceive us and our circumstances, and having related softer skills - are amongst the competences most valued in the workplace. They are therefore a reliable indicator of management success.

Trust and integrity

Nobody wants to work or associate with someone who is untrustworthy, yet often our judgment of whether they are or not just comes down to gut feeling and a predisposition to believe what they say, perhaps due to their general likeability.

Hope-Hailey (2012) suggests trust can be broken down into four components particularly relevant to the workplace:

- Ability – demonstrable competence at doing their job.
- Benevolence – a concern for others beyond their own needs and having benign motives.
- Integrity – adherence to a set of principles acceptable to others. These encompass fairness and honesty.
- Predictability – a regularity of behavior over time.

Hope-Hailey talks of an employee's 'trust fund', that is, the level of trust built up in an organization and over the course of a career. Most employees would claim to put a high value on trust and integrity. Most would also claim to act according to established standards and rules. Talking to previous colleagues and reports might undermine these claims.

Rules and standards may be unwritten – loyalty to a family member in the Middle East for example, and/or recorded in company manuals and contracts. Transgressions are by no means rare, as illustrated by a long catalogue of well-publicized infringements. Examples might be British MPs lying about their expenses or speeding, priests violating young boys. Whistle-blowers such as Edward Snowden and Chelsea/Bradley Manning appear to have put their own interests above those of the organizations they represented or, in the case of Snowden and Manning, justify undermining them for ideological or political reasons.

Furnham identifies the five factors most associated with lack of integrity at work as:

- Perception of corporate deceit, that the organization is not everything that it professes to be.
- Perceived inequity in treatment – one set of rules for one employee, quite another for another.
- Bullying and mistreatment of the employee or acceptance of it on the part of managers and colleagues.
- A low-trust environment where expectations are low, both on the part of management and employees.
- Broken promises – often at the recruitment stage but also later on in a career.

Breaches of trust often result in some form of punishment, humiliation and loss of status. Nonetheless some are still willing to engage in damaging behavior, both within organizations and beyond.

A lack of integrity can be related to personality. A subject exhibiting conscientiousness (related to dependability, perseverance and achievement oriented toward specified, and therefore usually acceptable, goals) would tend to be resistant. Others low on agreeableness and conscientiousness would be more prone to underhand activities. Young people who engage in vandalism, fraud, violence and theft are typical examples. Low arousal levels amongst extraverts mean individuals seek higher levels of stimulation, in turn prompting risk-taking and excitement-seeking behavior that may not be socially acceptable or legal. The opposite is true for introverts, who display stimulus-avoidance tendencies. Studies by Eysenck and others back this up, finding that criminals and those partaking in deviant behavior at work of any sort tend to be high on Extraversion, Neuroticism and psychosis (aggressiveness and interpersonal hostility). They lack guilt, empathy or sensitivity to the feelings of others.

Personality 'misfits'

We can perhaps think of personalities who might do well in dangerous or morbid jobs such as a steeplejack, pathologist or forensic dentist. The emotionally unintelligent computer geek might give a company significant technological and competitive edge. More often than not, however, it is difficult to fit the oddest or more extreme personalities to jobs. Those at any extreme of the personality

> Individuals high in neuroticism are prone to distress and dissatisfaction regardless of their life situation. They will always be best suited to low stress positions requiring little emotional control and a different job is unlikely to resolve completely problems that derive from their more extreme basic emotional make-up.

dimensions – a neurotic demonstrating obsessive compulsive tendencies or someone far too easy going – generally present more of a risk than opportunity and are of less appeal than those demonstrating greater flexibility. A psychologist might baulk at the concept of 'personality incompetence' or 'personality misfit', and yet these are seen at all organizational levels and are usually most dangerous when accompanied with power and authority. Even temporary lapses in control can have disastrous repercussions.

In Table 5.3 we choose to identify potential job 'incompetencies' and those situations or environments likely to cause individuals at one or other extreme of the personality dimensions discomfort. So, for example, assigning an introvert to a sales or marketing position is likely not only to cause them stress

TABLE 5.3   Emotional competencies

Self-Awareness	Social Awareness
• Emotional self-awareness	• Empathy
• Self-confidence	• Organizational awareness
• Accurate self-awareness	• Service orientation
Self-Management	**Relationship Management**
• Emotional self-control	• Influence
• Adaptability	• Conflict management
• Achievement orientation	• Leadership
• Optimism	• Change catalyst
• Initiative	• Developing others
• Transparency	• Team work and collaboration

but also prove unsuccessful. Meeting them in a busy bar with music will also not put them at ease.

Costa, McRae and Kay (1995) note that, by taking into account personality traits and their associated strengths and weaknesses, many problems in relation to career, job changes and job promotion could be avoided. Inappropriate promotion wherein an individual reaches a level and position not at all suited to their profiles can have serious repercussions. They may lack the ability, tenacity or even courage to do managerial jobs. As a result they undergo stress and perform badly to the detriment of their organization and those around them. Changing the job to fit their particular preferences may not be possible and, even if it is, it may mean the job is inefficiently and ineffectively executed. The organization itself can change relatively rapidly in terms of its values, also resulting in misfit. A crisis in the industry, a buy-out, a merger or acquisition can relatively easily lead to a new culture and different behavioral requirements by management. A perfect fit between personal and organizational values and behavior can be very easily broken.

Unsuitability for a particular role can be overcome to a degree, of course, if the individual perceives a need to manage the behavior arising from their personality traits. At work they may, for example, seek out training opportunities, mentors or take other steps to adapt. Equally, naturally ebullient businessmen might find it difficult to establish rapport with a serious and revered statesman-like figure. Once again awareness of the natural differences in approach is key to success.

In terms of broadly desirable personality traits and related 'qualities', our research leads us to conclude the following regarding indicators of success in employment, particularly at more senior levels (although the points made can be applied in other contexts also):

- Emotional stability: Derailed people are frequently emotionally vulnerable. Failure at work may increase neurosis, but neurosis is certainly more likely to cause it. One needs to be hardy, resilient, and even stoical to succeed in business. This does not mean being emotionally illiterate: far from it.
- Conscientiousness: They work smart and hard. They tend to follow instructions and are orderly. They are diligent and prudent. Unsuccessful working people don't have the work ethic and tend to be clock-watchers. Occasionally excessive conscientiousness is the undoing of a manager. Fanatic workaholics are as much associated with derailment as those very low in conscientiousness. There is a period in all managers' careers when they simply have to work very hard, be well-organized and diligent. On the other hand slavish, obsessional dedication to work is a recipe for disaster. There is an optimal amount of conscientiousness required at work. People often do not make it to senior positions if they do not have enough. At any stage in their career bitterness over a broken psychological contract or some other 'organizational mishap' may lead them to clock-watch and be ineffective.
- Openness: Successful people usually anticipate and embrace change. They need to be original and creative but also practical. Few people make it to senior management with low openness scores. They tend to be too dull, conventional and traditional to lead with imagination. But very high scores can easily derail managers. They may be dreamers and impractical. They may be prone to waste large amounts of time and money on 'white elephants', namely projects that go badly wrong. They may err too frequently on the side of aesthetic appeal rather than practical function.
- Extraversion: Successful people need to learn to behave as if they were extraverted even if they are not. They need to be socially confident and interpersonally skilled and relaxed. The higher you go in organizations the more you rely on other people to complete tasks. Extreme introverts do not enjoy many of the responsibilities of senior management: running interminable meetings, PR appearances, hosting parties. Good leaders know it has to be done and do it. Equally very extraverted managers need backup and to temper their natural ways of behaving. Whilst they may enjoy the social aspects of the job they may well neglect the serious strategy and number-crunching that is of equal importance.
- Agreeableness: Do successful people need to be agreeable? At times but to do well in business, a manager also has to be tough: competitive,

egocentric, arrogant and devious. Probably what characterizes the successful manager is that they can act agreeably with their own staff, but as necessary disagreeably with the competition. Successful managers are, in short, very stable, medium or high in conscientiousness and openness; average in extraversion and medium to low in agreeableness.

- Emotional intelligence: They understand emotions and are able to change their, and often others', behavior appropriately. They are sensitive; derailed ones over-sensitive. They worry, get depressed, become anxious ... but only occasionally and appropriate to the circumstances. They also have healthily adaptive coping strategies. Unsuccessful people worry all the time. Their moodiness, fickleness and prickliness cause real problems at work.
- Integrity: If someone is untrustworthy and duplicitous, they always pose a risk and of then being found out and punished. Best avoided in all but the basest professions.

Careful assessment of personality traits, along with levels of integrity and emotional intelligence, can help identify early on potential problems or limitations when considering an individual for a position. It can also suggest appropriate remedial action. Costa, McRae and Kay (1995) note that, of the personality dimensions, neuroticism and conscientiousness are of particular relevance to all jobs because of how they influence an individual's ability to adapt.

As noted elsewhere, competence or 'fit' in a particular role is not just a matter of personality. Indeed the whole premise of this book is that we have to build a rounded picture of an individual to predict accurately and manage behavior and performance.

The business advantage

In Howard and Howard's work *The Owner's Manual for Personality at Work* (2010), they break down the Big Five and describe how to identify and manage each trait. Understanding the significance of an individual's profile is valuable, but we need to know what impact it has in the workplace. We described in Table 5.2 the traits of the Big Five personality factors. In Table 5.4 we identify work situations likely to be of discomfort. In Table 5.5 we combine Howard and Howards' research with our own findings to look at factors to be borne in mind by, for example, a businessperson embarking on a negotiation or the head-hunter who wants to relax his interviewee and elicit maximum information from them.

TABLE 5.4 Extremes or misfits

Extraverts	Introverts
• Assertive/sociable • Overtly self-confident • Active/energetic • Accident-prone • Impulsive/spontaneous • Optimistic	• Reserved/self-contained • Serious • Reflective and analytical • Observant of rules and procedures
Situations of discomfort/incompetency	
• Solitude • Under-stimulation • Monotonous tasks • Having to criticize or deliver bad news • Tasks involving accuracy and care • Reflection and deep analysis	• Quick-fire brainstorming • Customer handling • High-stimulus environments, e.g. noisy bars, open-plan offices • Big groups • Speaking up
Openness	**Closedness**
• Innovative/questioning • Curious and insightful • Versatile problem-solvers • Quirky/mischievous • Idealistic/dreamers • Appreciative of arts	• Conventional/cautious • Practical • Low on EQ • Not intellectually curious
Situations of discomfort/incompetency	
• Administrative tasks • Quality-control and monitoring • Situations of conformity	• Where few rules/traditions • Thinking outside the box • Empathizing with others
Stable	**Unstable**
• Calm and even-tempered • Optimistic and contented • Good self-control • Self-reliant and stress-resistant • Confident • Analytical	• Anxiety-prone • Moody and unpredictable • Pessimists • Impulsive • Respond emotionally • Prone to stress/absenteeism
Situations of discomfort/incompetency	
• Where requirement for sympathy/compassion	• Unsafe/insecure environments • Sound, unemotional decision-making • Customer handling • Leadership • Where subject to frequent criticism
Agreeable	**Disagreeable**
• Co-operative/compliant • Sympathetic/warm • Courteous and generous • Trusting • Self-effacing • Straight-talking/candid	• Suspicious/wary • Hard-headed • Outspoken • Showy • Self-centered • Shrewd/charming • Complicated

(continued)

TABLE 5.4   Continued

Situations of discomfort/incompetency	
• Competition to raise standards • Bargaining and selling • PR/advertising/self-promotion • Counseling	• Team-working/cooperation • Caring for others • Boosting morale

Conscientious	Non-conscientious
• Non-spontaneous • Self-disciplined • Organized/thorough/persistent • Resourceful • Dutiful	• Low work ethic • Disorganized • Hedonistic • Lacking in ambition

Situations of discomfort / incompetence	
• High workload • Carpe diem	• Working to deadlines • Planning

TABLE 5.5   Taking advantage

	Stable	Neurotic
Environment	Relaxed, even in hostile places, wears more sober clothing	Likes to keep their distance, don't sit too closely, values tranquility
Content	Speaks in a measured manner, rational	Tendency to interrupt
Timeframe	Keeps to schedule but not stressed by delays or uncertainty	Poor timekeepers, crises will distract
Discomfort zone	Working with people who are emotional and irrational	People who invade their personal territory and people who show little empathy with their own situation
	Extraverts	Introverts
Environment	More lively meeting places, perhaps a restaurant or bar, with people around but focus on them, office door open, sits facing the door	More formal office, with limited number of (expert) people present with whom subject feels at ease, stays in background, prefers more subdued lighting
Content	Engage in enthusiastic and exploratory discussion emphasizing possibilities, tends to take others at their word, talks loudly and fast, tactful	Good data-based arguments using familiar written formats, highlighting reliability and downplaying risk and uncertainty
Timeframe	Demonstrate flexibility in taking discussions/consultation further but also feel able to push for a quick decision	Allow subject time to reflect and request further information but also try and establish mutually agreeable timeframe

Discomfort zone	Solitude, under-stimulation, monotonous tasks, having to criticize or deliver bad news, tasks involving accuracy and care, reflection and deep analysis	Quick-fire brainstorming, customer handling, high-stimulus environments, big groups, speaking up
	Open	**Closed**
Environment	Creative, arty, informal, appears busy	Organized, formal, traditional, wall hangings depict action, plants
Content	Encourages debate, allows questions, enjoys change for change sake, will generate new ideas, not bound by rules, forward looking	Few options, conclusions and solutions easily identified, conservative views, prefers the status quo
Timeframe	Open ended is OK, will have difficulty being on time	Punctual, clearly defined timeframe, commits to one career
Discomfort zone	Administrative tasks, quality-control, monitoring, situations of conformity	Little process, few rules or traditions, thinking outside the box, empathizing with others
	Agreeable	**Tough**
Environment	Loads of family memorabilia, follows office dress code	Pleasure-seeking, shows pride in accomplishments, office and dress can be daring
Content	Tends to agree, dislikes argument or confrontation	Can be an aggressive questioner, argumentative, uses expressive language, does not always feel the need to agree
Timeframe	Likes to be on time, but will be forgiving of others who are late	Will keep to their own time table and ignore others' diary requirements
Discomfort zone	Having to say no, aggressive behavior	Decisions based on the politically correct, weakness in leadership
	Conscientious	**Disorganized**
Environment	Neat, everything in its place, looks professional	Cluttered desk, allows interruptions, casual dresser
Content	Enjoys clarity, likes to have an agenda	Happy to open old issues even if others think they are settled, little structure to papers or presentations
Timeframe	Punctual, meetings will end on time, prefers to finish one task before embarking on another	Late and will allow meetings to drift
Discomfort zone	Untidy, disorganized environments, people who are poorly prepared	Strongly regimented environments where they have to conform

Influencing different personality types

Taking as a basis the influencers identified in Chapter 1 – Introduction, we identify those tending to be most effective with the five main personality types.

Neurotic/stable

Neurotics are likely to respond well to all six Cialdini influencers. In addition, they will listen to logic but are more likely to follow their heart than their minds. Clearly stable characters are in general less influenced by the emotional and respond to authority and a more logical approach.

Extravert/introvert

Introverts are likely to respond to each of the influencers, but they will want to see the arguments justifying what is being proposed and will be less emotional in their response. On the other hand authority, social proof and logic have lesser influence over extraverts. They have sufficient confidence and desire to challenge leading them to resist the kind of pressure such influencers produce. Liking the other person and reciprocation are more likely to have some impact.

Open/closed

Open-minded people are inherently more susceptible to influence; they will want to think about the new experience offered and will be attracted to something unusual or scarce. There is a correlation between open-minded people and higher levels of intelligence and it would be wise to ensure the logic is sound. Closed-minded people will not share the curiosity offered by a new situation or proposition and will be harder to move to the change they are being asked to undergo. They will respond but will need to be able to explain it to themselves through reason as well as emotion. Doing what they have always done is comfortable for them, particularly if bolstered by the knowledge that others also do similar things – social proof.

Agreeable/tough

Agreeable people do not like to say no, so reciprocity, liking, social conformity, authority and logic will be powerful influencers. Tough people on the other hand will be much harder to influence. A combination of reciprocity, liking and logic are likely to have most impact.

Conscientious/disorganized

Conscientious people will respond to all the influencers, though scarcity will probably be less effective as an influencer. The disorganized soul may want to respond positively but needs to be kept up to the mark. Reciprocation, authority and commitment are likely to have some impact.

Key risks

What risks do the negotiator, recruiter or team builder face if they ignore or have insufficient insights into personality? We identify the following:

- Seeing personality in black and white terms. Most of us are part extravert, part introvert, part neurotic, part stable, etc. We need to be alert to people's preferences and these may incorporate preferences at both ends of the spectrum.
- While our personalities are largely fixed by the time we get our first job, it is possible to change our behavior. So an introvert can learn how to be a social animal, a disorganized person can become tidy and keep to a schedule. Training will help people change their behavior but discomfort will increase the more people are placed in roles which do not 'fit' their natural preferences.
- Lack of perspective and self-awareness coupled with inability or unwillingness to manage behavioral preferences, particularly in relation to people, but also situations and tasks.
- Not managing and monitoring the factors that lead to disaffection at work and that may result in lapses in integrity.

Conclusion

Personality is a broadly reliable predictor of individual performance in a role or situation and as such is often measured by business.

More successful leaders will generally learn to manage their personality preferences, particularly as regards softer 'people skills' or emotional intelligence. However, as discussed in greater scope and detail in the next chapter – Dark Side Traits, personality extremes become less manageable when responsibilities and pressure increase. The signs that related behavior could be problematic will often be there early on but cleverly masked or unnoticed in the context of wider contributions and abilities. At all levels, the willingness to control negative behavior can be eroded by perceived dissonance between personal integrity and wider organizational or societal values and goals. For leaders, early identification reduces the likelihood of derailment. In any role unnoticed and unaddressed by management personality misfits and extremes have the potential to undermine performance and cause problems to others.

Recommended reading

Cooper, C. (2010) *Individual Differences and Personality*. London: Hodder Education.
Furnham, A. (2008) *Personality and Intelligence at Work*. London: Routledge.
Goleman, D. (1995) *Emotional Intelligence*. New York: Bantam Books.
Haslam, N. (2007) *Introduction to Personality and Intelligence*. London: Sage.
Howard, P. and Howard, J. (2010) *The Owner's Manual for Personality at Work*. Austin: Bard Press.
Nettle, D. (2007) *Personality: What Makes You the Way You Are*. Oxford: Oxford University Press.

6
chapter

The Dark Side Traits

As outlined in the previous chapter, each of us has a personality profile that can be accurately mapped, and which sometimes reveals extreme, and often problematic, tendencies. Psychologists talk of Bright Side and Dark Side traits, both of which are powerful predictors of behavior. Psychologists are interested in our personality *traits*; psychiatrists in personality *disorders*. In this chapter we talk about the meeting ground of psychology and psychiatry – the dark side of our personality, the mud at the bottom of the pool (see Figure 6.1).

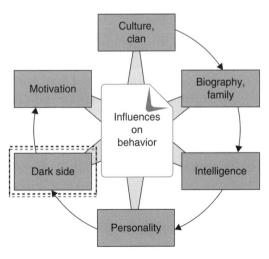

FIG 6.1 The six dimensions: Dark side

We all have a profile of Dark Side traits that may, or may not, cause us and those around us problems. Each of us is at risk of manifesting our dark side when stressed, bored, frightened and distracted. Some people become very emotional and others the precise opposite. Some clam up and others talk a great deal. Some people have more 'darkness' than others and it shapes all of their behavior. Others' Dark Side behaviors may remain hidden and only emerge under stress. When they do they become vulnerable and their behaviors can have a catastrophic impact on the organizations they represent or serve.

Dark Side traits all have a long history and have an onset no later than early adulthood. They influence the sense of self – the way people think and feel about themselves, and how other people see them. There are some gender differences. Anti-social disorder is more likely to be diagnosed in men, while the borderline, histrionic and dependent personality in women. One of the most important ways to differentiate personal style from the Dark Side traits is flexibility. There are lots of difficult people at work but relatively few whose rigid, maladaptive behaviors mean they continually have disruptive, troubled lives. It is their inflexible, repetitive, poor stress-coping responses that are the marks of disorder.

The disorders often powerfully influence interpersonal relations at work. Oldham and Morris (1991) state that they reveal themselves in how people 'complete tasks, take and/or give orders, make decisions, plan, handle external and internal demands, take or give criticism, obey rules, take and delegate responsibility, and co-operate with people'. The anti-social, obsessive-compulsive, passive-aggressive and dependent types are particularly problematic in the workplace. People with Dark Side traits have difficulty expressing and understanding emotions. It is the intensity with which they express them and their variability that makes them odd. More importantly they often have serious problems with self-control.

Furnham (2010) examined the paradox of personality pathology at work and noted that three categories, or types, are most commonly implicated in management derailment. They are, in order of frequency, anti-social (psychopath), narcissistic and histrionic, otherwise referred to as the Dark Triad. In lay terms, psychopaths are selfish, callous, superficially charming, lacking in empathy and remorse; narcissists are attention-seeking, vain, self-focused and exploitative; while histrionics are dramatic, attention-seeking and lack the ability to focus over any length of time.

These same disorders often prove an asset in acquiring and temporarily holding down senior management positions. The charm of the psychopath, the self-confidence of the narcissist and the emotional openness of the histrionic are, in many instances, useful business traits. When candidates are physically attractive, well-educated, intelligent and have a Dark Triad profile, it is not difficult to see why they are selected for senior management positions. In this sense, assessors and selectors must bear part of the blame for not selecting out those who so spectacularly derail.

Kets de Vries (2006), like others in this area, recognizes the double-edged sword of self-belief, self-confidence or narcissism in the business world. He noted: 'a solid dose of narcissism is a prerequisite for anyone who hopes to rise to the top of an organization. Narcissism offers leaders a foundation for conviction about the righteousness of their cause. The narcissistic leader's conviction that their group, organization, or country has a special mission inspires loyalty and group identification; the strength (and even inflexibility) of a narcissistic leader's worldview gives followers something to identify with and hold on to. Narcissism is a toxic drug however. Although it is a key ingredient for success, it does not take much before a leader suffers from an overdose.'

So how do we uncover someone's dark side?

As stated above, high or moderately malfunctioning personality-disordered behavior can remain under control most of the time and only really become an issue when a subject reaches a senior position and is subject to more sustained frustration and stress. Because of this, potential problems are often not picked up on until it is too late.

Perhaps the most insightful and useful approach to identifying Dark Side behaviors has been that of Hogan and Hogan (2001). They have developed a self-report questionnaire, called the Hogan Development Survey, which, using accessible language, quite specifically measures 11 of the personality disorders.

Hogan and Hogan (2001) say that this 'view from the dark side' gives an excellent understanding of the causes of management derailment.

They argue it is probably easier to define incompetence than competence, that there are obviously many 'mad' managers in organizations, and that helping people to identify potentially bad managers or managers at risk of derailing can alleviate a great deal of suffering. They also note from their reading of the literature, that derailment is more about having undesirable qualities than not having desirable ones. The two are related, as outlined in Table 6.1.

Hogan's Development Survey measures have alerted many researchers and managers to the fact that understanding and looking out for evidence of personality disorders is crucial if serious selection errors are to be avoided. Their research in the area has led them to these conclusions:

- Many derailed managers have impressive social skills: this is why their disorders are not spotted at selection but only later by their subordinates.
- Bad managers are a major cause of misbehavior (theft, absenteeism, turnover) by staff: it is poor treatment that often makes them resentful.
- It is important to take the observer's view in personality: that is the descriptions of the personality disorders given by those that deal with them.

For the remote personality profiler, one option might be to conduct interviews with a subject's peers, direct reports, internal customers or successor two or three months after they have moved on from a role or organization. In *Understanding the Talent Wave* Clutterbuck (2012) terms such investigations 'legacy audits'. Useful questions which he lists and which would serve to highlight Dark Side behaviors include:

- Did people feel that there were hidden agendas?
- Were people able to give the manager critical feedback?
- What negative pressures, if any, have now been removed?
- Were creative ideas stifled or encouraged?
- Did the manager spend more time managing up, or managing down?
- Which was more important: team reputation or the manager's reputation?
- What can you now talk about openly that you couldn't before?
- What problems, if any, had been buried but are now beginning to surface?
- Is there a sense of relief that the manager has gone, or a sense of loss?
- Is there a sense that the manager was fair and equitable in how they treated members of the team?

Much of this can, of course, be summarized with the question, would the team like the manager to come back?

TABLE 6.1   Dark Side characteristics

DSM-IV personality disorder (dark side) descriptions		Hogan & Hogan (1997) HDS themes		Bright side descriptions
Borderline	Inappropriate anger; unstable and intense relationships alternating between idealization and devaluation	Excitable	Moody and hard to please; intense but short-lived enthusiasm for people, projects or things	Very high neurotic; low agreeableness; low conscientiousness
Paranoid	Distrustful and suspicious of others; motives are interpreted as malevolent	Skeptical	Cynical, distrustful and doubting others' true intentions	High neurotic; low openness; low agreeableness
Avoidant	Social inhibition; feelings of inadequacy and hypersensitivity to criticism or rejection	Cautious	Reluctant to take risks for fear of being rejected or negative evaluation	Very high neurotic; very low extraversion
Schizoid	Emotional coldness and detachment from social relationships; indifferent to praise and criticism	Reserved	Aloof, detached and uncommunicative; lacking interest in or awareness of the feelings of others	Very low extraversion; low openness
Passive-Aggressive	Passive resistance to adequate social and occupational performance; irritated when asked to do something he/she does not want to	Leisurely	Independent; ignoring people's requests and becoming irritated or argumentative if they persist	Very low agreeableness; low conscientiousness
Narcissistic	Arrogant and haughty behaviors or attitudes, grandiose sense of self-importance and entitlement	Bold	Unusually self-confident; feelings of grandiosity and entitlement; over valuation of their capabilities	Very high neurotic; high extraversion; very low agreeableness
Antisocial	Disregard for the truth; impulsivity and failure to plan ahead; failure to conform	Mischievous	Enjoying risk taking and testing the limits; needing excitement; manipulative, deceitful, cunning and exploitative	Very low agreeableness; very low conscientiousness

(continued)

TABLE 6.1 **Continued**

Histrionic	Excessive emotionality and attention seeking, self-dramatizing, theatrical and exaggerated emotional expression	Colorful	Expressive, animated and dramatic; wanting to be noticed; needing to be the centre of attention	Very high neuroticism; very high extraversion; very high agreeableness
Schizotypal	Odd beliefs or magical thinking; behavior or speech that is odd, eccentric or peculiar	Imaginative	Acting and thinking in creative and sometimes odd or unusual ways	Very high neuroticism; very low extraversion; very high openness
Obsessive-Compulsive	Preoccupation with orderliness; rules, perfectionism and control; over-conscientious and inflexible	Diligent	Meticulous, precise and perfectionist, inflexible about rules and procedures; critical of others	Low openness; very high conscientiousness
Dependent	Difficulty making everyday decisions without excessive advice and reassurance; difficulty expressing disagreement out of fear of loss of support	Dutiful	Eager to please and reliant on others for support and guidance; reluctant to take independent action or go against popular opinion	Very high extraversion; very high agreeableness

The Dark Side traits

As with other areas of assessment, it is possible to identify Dark Side tendencies amongst business contacts and others without formal testing. Below we describe those behaviors indicative of the 11 Dark Side behaviors identified by Hogan and Hogan. To these we have added a twelfth – manipulative or Machiavellian.

Argumentative and vigilant

These people are super-vigilant: nothing escapes their notice. They seem tuned into mixed messages, hidden motives and secret groups. They are particularly sensitive to authority and power, and obsessed with maintaining their own independence and freedom. In its extreme clinical form these people are paranoid.

Distrust and suspiciousness of others at work is their abiding characteristic. Their colleagues' and boss's motives are interpreted as malevolent, all the time. The 'enemy' is both without and within. Naturally they are often found thriving in security organizations where their suspiciousness is not only normal but frequently praised.

They suspect, on the basis of limited evidence, that others are exploiting, harming or deceiving them about almost everything both at work and at home. They are preoccupied with unjustified doubts about the loyalty or trustworthiness of subordinates, customers, bosses, shareholders, etc., on both big and small matters. They are reluctant to confide in others (peers at work) because of the fear that the information will be used against them – kept on file, used to sack them.

Vigilant types are slow to commit and trust, but once they do so are loyal friends. They are very interested in others' motives and prefer 'watch-dog' jobs. They are not compromisers and often attack attackers. Many of their characteristics make them excellent managers: alert, careful, observant and tactical.

Some jobs suit these people well: security, the military, perhaps insurance. But the hyper-vigilant, argumentative, wary manager can be very difficult to live with. Often those with paranoia are not particularly problematic but buckle under stress and it is then that this disorder is noticeable. Skepticism turns into cynicism and then full-blown paranoia.

Solitary and reserved

These are the cold fish of the personality-disordered world: distant, aloof and emotionally flat, often preferring the affection of animals to that of people. These are the loners. They are very self-contained: they do not need others to admire, entertain, guide or amuse them. And yet they report being free of loneliness. They seem completely dispassionate. They are doers and observers, not feelers. They seem stoical in the face of pain and passion. Relationships? They can take them or leave them. They don't really understand emotions. They are, in the psychiatrist dictionary, schizoid.

These people are not team players, nor are they sensitive or diplomatic. They are oblivious to office politics. Hence they may be more successful in solitary careers. They are not anti-social but asocial. They are the 'hollow man': empty, flat, emotionally unmovable. They may have a rich fantasy life but a very poor emotional life.

They can be very tough in the face of political adversity; they have a hard surface and they can take criticism and rejection. They can also stay focused and on task, and not be distracted by tumult, emotional upheavals and stressful meetings. Through it all, they will continue to do their jobs. When the pressure is really on, they retreat into their office, begin handling matters themselves and stop communicating. This leaves others at a loss to know what they want or need.

Again, there are jobs where detached, solitary ways of behaving can be somewhat advantageous. The R & D scientists, the meteorologists on an uninhabited island and the artistic crafts person may work very well alone. It is when they are promoted to the position of managing teams that the problem arises.

Imaginative and idiosyncratic

These creative types have a rich inner life and often seek emotional experience. Hence they are often drawn to religion and pharmacological techniques that promise to test the limits. They seek rapture and nirvana. They may be marked by acute discomfort with, and reduced capacity for, close relationships. They show many eccentricities of behavior. They may look odd and have a reputation for being peculiar. In its clinical form they are described as Schizotypal. Others call them eccentric.

They often have very odd ideas about business: how to succeed, whom to hire, what controls what. They can also have very strange beliefs or magical thinking that influences behavior and is inconsistent with business norms. Examples would be superstitions or beliefs in clairvoyance and telepathy. They can seem other-worldly and may be very difficult to follow.

Many organizations do not tolerate these idiosyncratic types. They dress oddly and work strange hours. They are not very loyal to their companies and do not enjoy the corporate world. They do not connect with staff, customers and their bosses. Their quirky quasi-religious beliefs estrange them yet more from the normal world of those around them. They are often loners. Under stress and heavy workloads, they can become upset, lose focus, lapse into eccentric behavior and not communicate clearly. They can be moody and tend to get too excited by success and too despondent over failure. However, they do want attention, approval, and applause, which explains the lengths that they are willing to go to in order to elicit them.

The imaginative, idiosyncratic person is unlikely to reach a very high position in organizations though they may be promoted in advertising or academia. The absent-minded, nutty professor and the creative advertising genius share many schizotypal behaviors. If talented they may do well but rarely as people managers. Steve Jobs had many talents and qualities, and he was certainly successful, but he showed some eccentric and difficult behaviors.

Mischievous and adventurous

This Dark Side factor is associated with being amoral or asocial, impulsive and lacking in remorse and shame. The most defining characteristic is their lack of conscience, empowering them to be ruthless excitement-seekers. It is indeed, perhaps for obvious reasons, the most studied of all the Dark Side traits and probably the most important for those interested in individual differences at work. Once called 'moral insanity' it is found more commonly among lower socio-economic groups, no doubt because of the downward drift of these types. Since the 1940s it has been shown that the characteristics defining this Dark Side trait – self-centeredness, irresponsibility, impulsivity and insensitivity to the needs of others – are found in many professions. They are the stuff of the sociopath, or psychopath in old language.

These people show a disregard for, and violation of, the rights of others. They often have a history of being difficult, delinquent or dangerous. They show a failure to conform to social norms with respect to lawful behaviors including lying, stealing and cheating. They are often nasty, aggressive, con artists, the sort who get profiled on business crime programs. They are massively impulsive and fail to plan ahead. They live only in, and for, the present. Most frustrating of all they lack remorse. They are indifferent to, or rationalize, having hurt, mistreated or stolen from another. They never learn from their mistakes. Where they are concerned, the anti-social label might seem a serious understatement.

Many show very consistent behaviors – superficial charm and intelligence, absence of anxiety in stressful situations. They are not risk-adverse; indeed, they love the thrill of adventure, putting others' lives in danger as well as their own. They tend to appear self-confident and not overly concerned with the approval of others. They live for the moment.

These individuals do not hide their feelings and they do not experience stress unless confined or frustrated. They are, in a sense, adolescents all their life: careless, irresponsible, hedonistic, forever sowing wild oats. They need excitement all the time and are very easily bored. They can be successful entrepreneurs, journalists, bouncers, lifeguards and managers.

They make very bad bosses and bad partners because they are egocentric, continuing a relationship only as long as it is good for them. As a result their relationships are rarely long-lasting and meaningful. They have two pretty crucial human ingredients missing: conscience and compassion. Hence they can be cruel, destructive, malicious and criminal.

It is difficult to estimate the number of successful 'industrial' psychopaths, or what Babiak and Hare (2006) call 'Snakes in Suits'. It is also sometimes difficult to explain why they get away with it for so long. However, it is no surprise when enquiring from those who are or have worked with a successful psychopath to learn how much misery they bring to the workplace.

Psychopaths can easily look like ideal leaders: smooth, polished and charming. They can quite easily mesh these aspects with their dark side as an amoral and manipulative bully. In the past it may have been politics, policing, law, media and religion that attracted psychopaths, but more and more it is the fast-paced, exciting and glamorous world of business.

Excitable and mercurial

People like Marilyn Monroe, Adolf Hitler and Lawrence of Arabia have been diagnosed with this disorder. They were impulsive, unpredictable and reckless. Most of all excitable and mercurial types tend to have problems with their self-image, often split in their positive and negative views of themselves. They can vacillate between self-idealization and self-abhorrence. They are, in the psychiatric world, borderline personalities.

They can become dependent and clinging. They often show a pattern of unstable and intense interpersonal relationships characterized by alternating between extremes of love and hate, worship and detestation. Most have identity disturbance – a markedly and persistently unstable self-image or sense of self. They are not really sure who they are and their assumed identity can easily change. They are impulsive with money, sex, booze, driving, etc., and, in every sense of the word, accident-prone.

At work they can be passionately involved with others. They can really admire their bosses when praised but this can just be a phase. They insist on being treated well and have a keen sense of entitlement. They can easily see themselves as more important than others do. As managers they get very involved with their staff and expect total dedication. When their unrealistic expectations are not met they can get very moody and churlish. They can have great difficulty concentrating.

Some experts believe that the term 'personality disorganization' is best suited to this disorder because they seem midway between the functional and dysfunctional.

They do not handle stress or heavy workloads very well, and they tend to explode rather easily. Also they are hard people to talk to and to maintain a relationship with. Consequently they change jobs frequently and they have a large number of failed relationships. They are so easily disappointed, and their first instinct is to withdraw and leave. They are all self-centered – information and experience is evaluated in terms of what it means for them personally – and they take the reaction of others personally. They personalize everything, but they do so privately. What others see are emotional outbursts and a tendency to withdraw.

Colorful and dramatic

These 'drama queens' are attracted to limelight jobs and strive for attention and praise. Setbacks can lead easily to serious inner doubts and depression. They are certainly emotionally literate and open with all their emotions. But these emotions can change very quickly. As managers they exhibit excessive emotionality and attention-seeking behaviors. They are, in its clinical condition, histrionic.

Most are uncomfortable in situations in which they are not the centre of attention and try always to be so. They delight in making a drama out of a crisis. Their interaction with others is often characterized by inappropriate sexually seductive or provocative behavior. Typically this causes more of a reaction in women than men. They display rapidly shifting and shallow expression of emotions. They are difficult to read. Most use physical appearance (clothes) to draw attention to self but may also have body piercing or tattoos.

They are easily influenced by others or circumstances and therefore are both unpredictable and persuadable. Many consider relationships to be more intimate than they actually are. Being rather dramatic they feel humdrum working relationships more intensely than others.

They get impatient with, and anxious about, details and routine administrative functions. They prefer gossip to analysis and tend not to be good at detail. They are highly sociable and have intense relationships. They live to win friends and influence people and can do so by being very generous with compliments, flattery and appreciation. They hate being bored and life with them is never staid and dull. They dislike being alone.

At work they can be persuasive and insightful. They enjoy the world of advertising, PR, sales and marketing but need strong backup for things like plans, budgets and details. They are also known for being volatile and moody. They can be effusive with both praise and blame.

At their best, they are bright, colorful, entertaining, fun, flirtatious, and the life and soul of the party. At their worst, they don't listen, they don't plan, they self-nominate and self-promote, and they ignore negative feedback.

This Dark Side type deals with stress and heavy workloads by becoming very busy, enjoying high-pressure situations when they can then be the star. Breathless with excitement, they confuse activity with productivity and evaluate themselves in terms of how many meetings they attend rather than how much they actually get done. A key feature of these people that others may not appreciate is how much they need and feed off approval, and how hard they are willing to work for it. This explains why they persist in trying to be a star after their lustre has faded.

Arrogant and self-confident

These Dark Side characters have a grandiose sense of self-importance. They exaggerate achievements and talents and expect to be recognized as superior without proof. Most are preoccupied with fantasies of unlimited success, power, brilliance and money. They believe that they are special and unique and can only be understood by, or should associate with, other special or high-status people (or institutions). They may try to buy themselves into exclusive circles. Always they require excessive admiration and respect from everyone at work. Often they have a sense of entitlement, that is, unreasonable expectations of especially favorable treatment or automatic compliance with their manifest needs. Worse, they take advantage of others to achieve their own ends, which makes them terrible managers. They lack empathy. All are unwilling to recognize or identify with the feelings and needs of others. They have desperately low emotional intelligence. Curiously they are often envious of others and believe that others are envious of them. They show arrogant, haughty behaviors or attitudes all the time and everywhere, at work and at home. At times this can be amusing but is mostly simply frustrating.

They are essentially narcissists who are super self-confident and express considerable self-certainty. They are 'self-people' – self-asserting, self-possessed, self-aggrandizing, self-preoccupied, self-loving and, ultimately, self-destructive. They really believe in themselves and that they were born lucky. At work they are outgoing, highly energetic, competitive and very political. They can make good leaders as long as they are not criticized, or made to share glory. They seem to have an insatiable need to be admired, loved and needed. They are often the epitome of success – ambitious, driven, possessing high self-esteem, self-disciplined, socially networked. The world is their stage.

But narcissism is a disorder of self-esteem. It is, in a sense, a cover-up. They self-destruct because their self-aggrandizement limits their personal and business judgment and perception. At work they exploit others to get ahead, yet they demand special treatment. Their reaction to any sort of criticism is extreme: shame, rage and tantrums. They aim to destroy that criticism, however well intentioned and constructive. They are poor empathizers and thus have low emotional intelligence. They can be consumed with envy and disdain of others and prone to depression. Manipulative, demanding and self-centered, even therapists don't like them.

What is most distinctive about narcissists is their self-assurance, which often, paradoxically, gives them charisma. They so completely expect to succeed, take more credit for success than is warranted or fair, and they refuse to acknowledge failure, errors or mistakes. When things go right, it is because of their efforts; when things go wrong, it is someone else's fault. This leads to some problems with truth telling because they always rationalize and reinterpret their failures and mistakes, usually by blaming them on others.

Narcissists can be energetic, charismatic, leader-like and willing to take the initiative to get projects moving. They can be successful in management, sales and entrepreneurship. However, they are arrogant, vain, overbearing, demanding, self-deceived and pompous. They are so colorful and engaging that they often attract followers.

Narcissists handle stress and heavy workloads with ease; they are also quite persistent under pressure and they refuse to acknowledge failure. As a result of this inability to acknowledge failure, or even mistakes, and of the way they resist coaching and ignore negative feedback, they are unable to learn from experience.

The business world often calls for and rewards arrogant, self-confident and self-important people. They seek out power and abuse it. They thrive in selling jobs and those where they have to work the media. But, as anyone who works with and for them knows, they can destabilize and destroy working groups by their deeply inconsiderate behavior.

Cautious and sensitive

These are social-phobics. They are socially isolated and withdrawn. Feelings of possible rejection drive them to situations where they are likely to be shunned. Nonetheless, they seek acceptance, approval and affection. Clinically, they are described as avoidant.

These individuals show social inhibition, feelings of inadequacy and hypersensitivity to negative evaluation. They are super-sensitive, delicate flowers. They are therefore unlikely to reach high levels in management or be particularly successful at work.

They seek safety, to be with people and in environments they know and trust. But they can easily become anxious, guarded and worried. Beneath a polite and cool facade they can feel very uneasy. They cope with their anxiety by being prepared for everything. They like life, their friends and work to be safe, secure and predictable. They can be effective, reliable and steady and show little need for variety and challenge. They like bureaucracy and standard procedures and are pleased to help their seniors. They do well in technical fields that require routine, repetition and habit.

The avoidants are so afraid of rejection that they live impoverished social lives. The paradox is that they avoid close relationships that could bring them exactly what they want, acceptance and approval. Because they feel isolated, unwanted and incompetent, they are sure others will reject them. Often they are rejected because of their cold, detached behavior.

Under stress, avoidants begin to adhere to established procedures, and will rely on the tried and true rather than on any new technology or other procedures. They may try to control their staff, for fear that someone will make a mistake and embarrass them, especially with their seniors. They do exactly what their seniors tell them, and they enforce standard rules and procedures with reports and others over whom they have power. They hate to be criticized. What others see is cautiousness, rigidity, adherence to standardized procedures and resistance to innovation and change.

Dutiful and devoted

People with this disorder are more heavily reliant on other people for support or guidance than most. Like young children they can be clingy, submissive and subservient in all relationships, fearing separation. Dutiful types are carers – most happy helping others to be happy. Others give meaning to their lives. They worry about others and need others. They find contentment in attachment and define themselves by others. They are not good at giving (or receiving) criticism and negative feedback. At work they are co-operative, supportive, caring and encouraging. They do brilliantly in jobs like nursing, social work and voluntary organizations but rarely take on senior positions that require managerial duties. As managers they have a pervasive and excessive need to be taken care of by others. This leads to submissive and clingy behavior and fears of separation. Psychiatrists call them dependent.

They all have difficulty initiating projects or doing things on their own (because of a lack of self-confidence in judgment or abilities rather than a lack of motivation or energy). So they resist change, particularly where it leads to them being isolated or threatened. Some go to excessive lengths to obtain support from others, often humiliating themselves in the process. All feel uncomfortable or helpless when alone because of exaggerated fears of being unable to care for themselves at work (and home).

They do not make good managers because they are too quick to be apologetic, submissive and self-deprecating. They attach themselves to others who may all too easily take advantage of them. Kind, gentle, generous and full of humility they do not believe in themselves. They have very low self-confidence in all aspects of life and acquire self-esteem through their attachments to others.

They respond to stress by freezing and becoming passive and by hoping that someone else will take the initiative, step up, make a decision, assign responsibility and get things moving. They are too reliant on the initiative of others and can become a bottleneck for productivity and a source of delay and lost time.

This personality disorder is nearly always associated with being a number two rather than a number one in any relationship. If they have staff almost inevitably they do not manage them well.

Leisurely

This Dark Side type is very concerned about 'doing their own thing'. They demand the 'right to be me' and believe nobody should deprive them of that right, that at work and in private relationships nobody should own them. They like the companionship of others but need strong defenses against being ill-used. They are particularly sensitive to fairness. They are passive-aggressive.

They do not find the workplace of great importance. They can be good managers and workers. But they do not work overtime, take it home or worry much about it. They certainly will not do any more than their contract specifies. They do not work to please their boss or to feel better about themselves. They are often heard saying 'It's not my job' and they tend to be suspicious of workplace authority. If their boss asks them to work harder, faster and more accurately they feel unfairly treated, even abused. They are super sensitive to their rights, fairness and the need to avoid exploitation. They seem leisurely.

For them success is not everything. They tend not to rise above middle-management levels because they are not ambitious or thrusting enough. For them the game is not worth the candle.

They don't generally appear stressed. They sulk, procrastinate and forget when asked to do things they think are not fair. They are rarely openly defiant, yet they are often angry. They snipe rather than confront. And they are often furious. They can be needy but resentful about those moods. They are in essence oppositional rather than assertive. They often have downward job mobility.

They are frequently late for meetings, they procrastinate, they work at around 80 per cent of their capacity, and they are very stubborn and hard to coach. They will rarely directly confront others. Their prickly sensitivity, subtle cooperativeness, stubbornness and deep absorption make them both unpredictable and unrewarding to deal with. As a result, they have trouble building and maintaining a team.

They handle stress and heavy workloads by slowing down, by simply ignoring requests for greater output and by finding ways to get out of work. Because they are overtly co-operative and agreeable, it takes a long time to realize how unproductive and refractory they actually can be. They are self-centered, they focus on their own agendas and they believe deeply in their own superior natural talent and right to leisure.

People need to be aware that they are not nearly as co-operative as they seem, and that they merely pretend to agree with you about work and performance issues. They also need to get them to commit to performance goals in public, in front of witnesses, so that a community of people can hold them accountable. Social pressure won't change their views of the world, but it will serve to make their performance deficits less easily deniable.

There are many senior managers with this rather unattractive profile. In fact this personality disorder is so pervasive that it has disappeared from some disorder categorizations. Their pathology may serve them, but the burden of it frequently rests heavily on their long-suffering staff.

Diligent and conscientious

They are frequently known for their zealous perfectionism, for their attention to detail, for their rigidity and for their formality. They are also often the workaholics – those who really 'live' the work ethic. They are competent, organized, thorough, and loyal. Even when on holiday or at 'leisure' they are intense, detailed, goal-orientated and active. They are familiar to many as obsessive-compulsive.

These managers show a preoccupation with orderliness, perfectionism, and mental and interpersonal control. This comes at the expense of flexibility, openness and efficiency. They make for the most anal of bureaucrats. They are always preoccupied with details, rules, lists, order, organization or schedules to the extent that the major point of the business activity is lost and forgotten. All show perfectionism that interferes with task or project completion. They worry their own, overly strict, standards will not be met. And of course they demand perfection in others. Seriously driven workaholics to the exclusion of leisure activities and friendships, they have a well-deserved reputation for being over-conscientious, scrupulous and inflexible about matters of morality, ethics or values.

Curiously they are unable to discard worn-out or worthless objects even when they have no sentimental value. They hoard rubbish at home and in the workplace. They are reluctant to delegate tasks or to work with others unless they submit exactly to their way of doing things. They do not let go and so pay the price. They are misers toward both self and others. Money is viewed as something to be hoarded for future catastrophes. Because they never fully spend their budget they never get it increased. In short they show rigidity and stubbornness and are thus really unpleasant to work for.

Conscientious, obsessive-compulsives rise through the ranks through hard work. But at certain levels they start to derail because they have problems making quick decisions, setting priorities and delegating. They tend to want to check the details again and again. They function best as right-hand men to leaders with strong conceptual skills and visions. They are very self-disciplined and put work first. They are often not very emotionally literate and can be fanatical and fundamentalist about moral, political and religious issues. They can find it difficult to relax and to throw things away. Their relationships are marked by conventionality and coolness. They are faithful, responsible but unromantic and unemotional. They can be seen as mean, over-cautious.

Diligent and obsessional, they tend to become stressed by heavy or increased workloads. They respond to them by working longer and harder (not smarter) and they fall further and further behind, something they find intolerable. They often become a bottleneck to productivity because everything must pass through, be checked, revised and approved by them. They will not let go anything that is not completed according to their standards. They closely supervise their staff. Suggesting how they can prioritize work, putting tasks into context and prompting them to reflect on the big picture can help.

The diligent, conscientious type can do very well in business. Certain jobs, for example related to health and safety and quality control, demand a degree of obsessive-compulsive checking. But, like all the other disorders, it is too much of this trait that can lead to serious problems, both for the individual and their staff. It often produces phobias and other stress-related illnesses. Just as in all the other disorders there is a curvilinear relationship between the disorder and success at work. Too little diligence and dutifulness is as detrimental as too much.

Manipulative/Machiavellian

Machiavelli, arguably the first political scientist, wrote *The Prince* in 1532. The author's name is leant to a style of leadership and management associated with cynicism, deceit and guile. *The Prince* argued it is better for leaders to have a win-at-all-costs philosophy. Machiavelli was interested in political power. Large companies are like mini-states in both size and governance. It could be argued that, despite all claims to the contrary, leaders essentially achieve, exercise and maintain power by behaving as Machiavelli suggested.

Machiavellianism is not strictly speaking a personality disorder. It is not included in the APA DSM-V list. Nor is it included in Hogan's list, nor in Dotlich and Cairo's *Why CEOs Fail* (2003). There is, however, sufficient literature attributing it to leaders to justify including it here.

To be described as Machiavellian is to be insulted. It means being duplicitous, egocentric and manipulative. Machiavellians are low in empathy and have little concern with conventional morality. They are often amoral as well as immoral with a utilitarian perspective. Low ideological commitment: short-term, tactical goal achievement is their major task. Machiavellians share many similarities with Mischievous and Adventurous types but are not as clinically disturbed. They are cynical but do have a conscience that they try to over-ride. They behave according to a set of beliefs and values, rather than because of a personality disorder. Among students Machiavellians are the anti-religious, hedonistic, radical and tough-minded.

Psychological study in the area goes back to the work of Christie and Geis (1970). They argue, amongst many other things, that society encourages Machiavellian leadership – high scorers win, low scorers lose. It is Machiavellians' extreme emotional detachment and goal orientation that makes them better leaders, even more so if they can 'fake' empathy. An interesting study by Austin et al. (2007) looked at the possible relationship between Machiavellians and emotional intelligence. They suggested that they had low EQ, being disagreeable and low on conscientiousness. Machiavellians are manipulative yet not empathic.

Over the years there has been a lot of work on Machiavellianism and where it is 'located' in relation to personality. It has been found that Machiavellianism is associated with four of the personality disorders – borderline, paranoid, negativistic and anti-social.

In the 1960s Christie and Geis developed a test for measuring a person's level of Machiavellianism. Their *Mach – IV* test, a twenty-statement personality survey, became the standard Machiavellianism self-assessment tool. The questions they ask indicate what we should be looking for in such manipulative people. Statements with which Machiavellians might agree are: 'Never tell anyone the real reason you did something unless it is useful to do so', 'The best way to handle people is to tell them what they want to hear', 'It is hard to get ahead without cutting corners here and there' and 'It is wise to flatter important people'.

Machiavellians do well when work environments are loose flowing and unstructured. The fewer the rules, constraints, checks and balances the better. They also do well in situations where the norm is face-to-face communication. They can turn on their superficial charm.

Co-workers and subordinates, but not always bosses, know the selfish, misanthropic self-serving nature of Machiavellians. This becomes very apparent when multi-source (360°) rater feedback is gathered. Bizarrely Machiavellians often believe that they (really) are good citizens of the organization.

One recent study by Al-Khatib et al. (2008) looked at the negotiation tactics of Machiavellians. They focused on things like competitive bargaining, inappropriate information gathering, attacking opponents' networks, making false promises and misrepresenting information during a negotiation process. They believe that Machiavellianism may be situational and highly contingent on the magnitude of the issues at stake. That is, that particular business situations trigger Machiavellian behaviors.

The Dark Triad

According to Paulhus and Williams (2002) there are in fact only three kinds of bad character: Machiavellians, Narcissists and Psychopaths – manipulator, arrogant and mischievous in our language. They are the hardest to manage, mostly because they do not see any problem with what they do and because they possess considerable charm and many leadership qualities valued in the modern Western business world.

There have been a number of research papers grouping these three together. Furnham, Richards and Paulhus (2013) have reviewed and evaluated them. They conclude that dictators such as Ghaddafi or Saddam Hussein likely possess more than one of the Dark Side traits, as would terrorists such as Osama Bin Laden and Norwegian Anders Breivik, whose court case provoked long debates regarding what kind of disorder he might be suffering from. According to Paulhus and Buckels (2011) their psychopathy provoked extreme brutality and their Machiavellianism facilitated strategic manipulation. Finally their narcissistic sense of superiority and entitlement readily justified such behavior in their own eyes.

To date, research shows that Dark Triad types tend to:

- Show aggression in controlled laboratory studies.
- Cheat in academic settings.
- Get even – they seek and get revenge on those who have offended them.
- Stalk – male psychopaths stalk romantic targets.
- If given the opportunity, claim to have won a lottery.
- Acquire various types of body modification – notably, body piercings and tattoos.
- They also show an extreme retaliative reaction to terrorism.
- They act on their sexually deviant fantasies.

Influencing Dark Side types

As previously stated, the strength of the influencers listed in Chapter 1 – Introduction is that they can be used with most people and adapted to most circumstances. Below we suggest those which will tend to be most effective with specific Dark Side types, although some will remain impervious to most influencing techniques, unless they see compliance as clearly being in their own selfish interests. We provide brief notes here for each Dark Side trait but describe how to manage them in much more detail in Chapter 9 – Managing Extremes.

Argumentative and vigilant (habitual distrust)

Masters of conspiracy theories these people will find fault with most persuasion tactics, but they may respond to people they like, trust and, in the end, logic will have some impact.

Solitary and reserved (aloof)

These people find it hard to form relationships. It follows that if they do find someone they can communicate with they will respond well to them. The challenge is developing that relationship over time. Appeal to logic rather than emotional argument.

Idiosyncratic (eccentric)

They will like the scarce, something that is different. They also work best when they like and trust someone and that person shows interest in what they do.

Mischievous and adventurous (sociopaths)

Perhaps these are the most difficult to influence as they have set their own agenda and will deflect most influencing techniques which are contrary to their own selfish interests. They will enjoy the risks associated with pursuing the scarce or exclusive.

Excitable and mercurial (volatile)

The challenge with these people isn't so much influencing them in the short term – they will follow an idea or project quite easily – but to maintain their interest over a longer period. They will respond well to people they like but, in its most extreme manifestation, even friends will be abandoned.

Colorful and dramatic (melodramatic)

These people enjoy company and particularly those they are comfortable with; they will be happy doing what most others do, so social proof and liking are most likely to work best. They enjoy being the centre of attention.

Arrogant and self-confident (narcissistic)

Vain people are in fact insecure and need a lot of reassurance and to be told they are right. They will respond best to people they like and feel they can trust. Flattery is going to have most impact.

Cautious and sensitive (excessive caution)

They will be uncomfortable with new or risky projects, preferring situations supported by many others and where there is already a track record. Consistency and social proof will work with these people.

Dutiful and devoted (eagerness to please)

These people will respond well to authority and to people they like.

Leisurely (passive resistant)

Persistence and patience is needed with these types; they need to be gently reminded of their earlier promises, using all of the persuasion techniques identified. Give them plenty of affection – they revel in it.

Diligent and conscientious (perfectionist/obsessive-compulsive)

They will have an appreciation of order and consistency; events or projects taking them out of their comfort zone will make them uncomfortable.

Manipulative and Machiavellian

Like mischievous types they are impervious to most forms of persuasion, unless of course, it suits their own selfish aims. Have a manipulator on your side to match their 'dirty' tricks.

Risks

- It is easy to be taken in by people with Dark Side traits – they are often practiced in concealing their extreme tendencies. This is particularly true in the case of narcissists, sociopaths or Machiavellians. They frequently exhibit high levels of charm and attractiveness which distract from their more destructive tendencies.
- Dark Side behaviors can contribute to success but, particularly at senior levels where pressures are greater, can prove unmanageable. Early diagnosis is key to avoiding derailment and the need for costly replacements.
- If we don't identify Dark Side types, there is a risk of inadvertently triggering a negative and possibly extreme reaction in our dealings with them.
- Dark Side traits are difficult to live with and, if unmanaged, can have hidden costs in terms of impact on colleagues and associates.

Conclusion

Of all the elements studied in *Revealed*, the Dark Side probably arouses the most interest. Most of the traits described in this chapter have positive characteristics. The sociopath possesses charm and determination, the narcissist confidence and the obsessive-compulsive subject will make sure detail is attended to. This makes them come over as attractive and makes identification of their dark side much harder.

However the problems they cause through their, at times, deeply unpleasant and, in the main, socially unacceptable behaviors can outweigh the benefits. On discovering their dark side, a typical response is to get rid of them. This too has a potential cost in terms of loss of the valuable skills, experience and knowledge they may possess. The trick is therefore to identify their dark side early and put measures in place to manage them before they cause the subject to derail or otherwise cause damage to the organization.

Recommended reading

Babiak, P. and Hare, R. (2006) *Snakes in Suits: When Psychopaths Go to Work*. New York: Regan Books.
Dotlich, D. and Cairo, P. (2003) *Why CEOs Fail*. New York: Jossey Bass.
DSM-IV: American Psychiatric Association. (2000) *Diagnostic and Statistical Manual of Mental Disorders* (4th edition Revised). Washington, DC: APA.
Furnham, A. (2010) *The Elephant in the Boardroom*. Basingstoke: Palgrave Macmillan.
Ronson, J. (2011) *The Psychopath Test*. London: Picador.

chapter 7

Motivation

Most of us are curious about what motivates others. What drives them, why they do the silly, odd, at times clearly mad things they do? What accounts for their addictions, tastes and reactions to others? Why do they spend so much time and effort in certain activities? Why do they crave power or recognition to such a degree? (see Figure 7.1)

Motivation is the starting point and backdrop to explaining or anticipating a subject's behavior. It is what activates and drives behavior. The word comes from the same Latin root as motion: it literally means *to move people*. A subject's

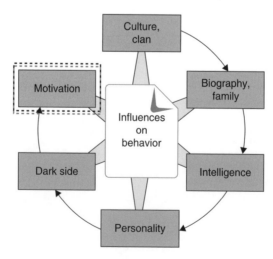

FIG 7.1 The six dimensions: motivation

underlying motivation is most accurately identified and understood when we take into account all the factors that make them who they are – the elements covered in earlier chapters of this book. In relation to some subjects strong themes or motives will emerge and dominate behaviors. To understand what really motivates us and others is often particularly difficult, but extremely important if you want to predict behavior.

Motivation is the starting point and backdrop to explaining or anticipating a subject's behavior.

People themselves often cannot tell you what their motivation is, and sometimes don't want to admit it to themselves or share it with others. The unknowable has more power. Short-term more superficial motives are relatively easy to identify. The candidate needs a job, the negotiating partner wants a good deal. But there is real benefit in trying to unearth deeper motives. A job applicant may have demonstrated in earlier roles that they have the drive to win new business, reduce costs and make profits. But we may also judge their attitude to be 'anything for the sake of short-term recognition and financial reward'. This may not sit well with the culture of our organization. Dissatisfied with management's failure to acknowledge their efforts, they may quickly become disgruntled and punish the organization. A subject may be lured by the promise of a high salary, but not really enjoy the cut and thrust of business. Unlikely to admit at interview that they are unwilling to work hard, they may consistently prioritize home life over work, complaining of unfair expectations, exaggerating stress-related symptoms.

In the same way that current recruitment procedures fail to give sufficient importance to long-term motivation and goals, research into valued business contacts or negotiating partners is also often overlooked. Well-researched data and carefully crafted presentations don't guarantee that a negotiating partner will advocate internally on our behalf. With increasingly rigorous anti-bribery and corruption legislation and internal company guidelines, gifts and wining and dining may not be an option. We need to be more creative, assessing, for example, whether the promise of information, status and contacts might be of personal value to them and add weight to our cause.

To date, motivation has defied the common definition that personality theory and the other elements in this book now enjoy. Theories abound and psychologists, management and leadership specialists have no shared language to describe it. In this chapter we review some of the research and most widely used models and definitions, providing our own list by way of summary.

Finally, we prompt the reader to identify clearly the scope for matching a subject's motivation with a specific role or organization.

Five questions in search of an answer

Motivation is a fascinating but complex topic to understand. Here we answer five commonly asked questions and so provide a backdrop to the motivation theories described later in the chapter.

1. *Where do drivers/needs/motives come from?*
   The answer is biology and biography – inherited abilities and temperament and, in particular, early shared and personal experiences. The more extreme these factors or experiences are the more likely they are to influence motives. A very extravert individual is likely to be motivated by social interaction. Experiences, such as losing a parent at a young age, being constantly bullied at school, growing up in a very poor or religious community, being one of many siblings can all be significant. Attributing motives to such factors is not straightforward. Their impact often only comes to light through counseling.

2. *Do drivers (motives) change (much) over time?*
   Autobiographical studies of individuals seem to imply that motivational patterns established early in life never change very dramatically. Thus, the drive to accumulate wealth, to find excitement or even fame is likely to be fairly constant, it being a question of degree. Others disagree. In our view it is probable that there is some constancy but the strength of particular motivational forces may alter over time.

Millionaire Howard Hughes was the son of the founder of the Hughes Tool Company, which revolutionized oil well drilling. Hughes inherited 75 per cent of the company in 1924, following the death of his father. Progressively he bought out relatives' shares in the business, eventually becoming the company's sole owner.

Aged 23 Hughes moved to Hollywood and embarked on a series of new business ventures, all of which were successful. As a film producer he won academy awards and achieved success at the box office. In 1932, he followed another passion, setting up the Hughes Aircraft Company. Two years later he built and test-piloted the H1, at the time the world's most advanced plane. In 1935, he set a new air speed record. He subsequently moved to Las Vegas, where he purchased four hotels and six casinos.

Hughes is mostly remembered, however, for his eccentric behavior and reclusive lifestyle in later life, caused in part by an obsessive–compulsive disorder. He spent his last 20 years out of the public eye living in hotel penthouses around the world.

Hughes was described as never being the same after suffering a fiery plane crash in 1946. That year he threw out his golf clubs and clothes, convinced they were contaminated with syphilis. He avoided socializing and his germ obsession began to spiral out of control. Hughes hired three guards to work in eight-hour shifts at the bungalow where he lived, to intercept flies to which he developed an overwhelming fear.

Over the next 20 years, Hughes became increasingly reclusive, a shell of the man he was before. He wore tissue boxes for shoes, began to store his bodily waste in glass jars and drafted lengthy memos on the proper way to open tin cans without touching them. X-rays taken at autopsy revealed broken hypodermic needles lodged in his arms, and his six-foot-four frame weighed less than 90lb (41kg). So few people had seen him during his later years that the Treasury Department had to use fingerprints to identify his body. On his death in 1976, Hughes left an estate estimated at US$2 billion. A sad psychiatric case where high sums of money seemed to have left him worse rather than better off.

3. *Do people have mixed (even contradictory) motives/drivers?*
   As described above, behavior is determined by multiple, and frequently complex factors, sometimes termed 'push' (*approach*) and 'pull' (*avoidance*). These are rarely easily described or targeted at one specific goal. Even the simplest motive such as hunger relief can be very complex: what, how and when you eat differs considerably from one person to another. Most behavior also has a mix of benefits and drawbacks that are difficult to juxtapose rationally. Lester Piggott's tax avoidance brought him shame and imprisonment when clearly he had no need to expose himself to that risk.

Lester Piggott remains the most famous jockey in British racing history. Known affectionately as 'The Long Fellow', he won the Derby nine times, his first victory at 18 in the well-known Epsom race of 1954. He won more than 5,300 races worldwide during 47 years in the saddle.

Piggott, who was infamously mean, despite an estimated fortune of £20 million, was jailed for a year in 1987 for tax fraud, having failed to declare income of £3.25m to the Inland Revenue. It was the biggest tax-evasion case of its time.

4. Are motives/drivers conscious or unconscious?

There are two aspects to motivation: what will and what can people tell you about what motivates them. We all tend to disguise motives we believe are less socially acceptable than others – hedonism, greed and deep competitiveness being examples. We are self-evidently more willing to be frank about socially approved motives, such as a concern for others.

Freud argued that the two great drivers of all action are sex and aggression, but that these two very powerful and primitive motives are deeply sanctioned by society. So, even if people are willing to tell you their motives, more often than not they are preconscious or subconscious. Their origins are hidden in the dark, inner theatre of our past, and they are neither obvious to others nor to ourselves.

Freudians further argue that people characteristically adopt defense mechanisms to protect themselves from anxiety. Patients with psychosomatic illnesses often attribute their problems to physical not mental causes. They may also explain their ill-founded and erratic behaviors by calling into question, not their own, but others' attitudes and behaviors.

Some defense mechanisms are healthier than others and are used both to explain and obscure an individual's motivation (see Table 7.1).

5. What is the difference between intrinsic and extrinsic motivation?

Intrinsic motivation is to do something for its own sake: because of the sheer joy of the activity. Extrinsic motivation is based on the rewards and punishments that the act may bring. Most activities have a combination of the two: artists paint out of creative joy and instinct (intrinsic) but also for profit

TABLE 7.1   Defense levels and mechanisms

Defense level	Defense mechanism	Definition
Pathological	Denial	Refusal to accept unpleasant aspects of an external situation because one finds it too threatening
	Distortion	Changing and reshaping reality as one sees fit
	Projection	Lessening anxiety by unconsciously expressing undesirable wishes; shifting these undesirable thoughts, feelings and impulses to someone else
Immature	Acting out	Unconscious expressions/impulses without registering the emotion behind them
	Fantasy	Tendency to escape reality to resolve internal and external conflicts e.g. excessive daydreaming
	Idealization	Perceiving individuals to possess more positive qualities than they actually have
	Passive aggression	Expressing anger or frustration through indirect methods onto other people
	Identification	Role modeling; taking on another's behavioral patterns
Neurotic	Displacement	Shifting emotions onto another target considered more acceptable or less threatening
	Hypochondriasis	Perceptions of an unknown illness as a reaction to negative feelings toward others
	Intellectualization	Using logic and intellectual components of a situation to distance oneself
	Isolation	Separating emotions from events i.e. talking about a situation without displaying any feelings
	Rationalization	Convincing oneself that things are fine through false rationale i.e. making excuses
	Reaction formation	Behaving in a manner that is the reverse of how one truly feels to avoid anxiety
	Regression	Reverting to an earlier stage of development rather than handling the unpleasant situation consistent with one's current developmental stage
	Repression	Blocking uncomfortable thoughts
Mature	Altruism	Behavior that brings both internal satisfaction and pleasure to others
	Anticipation	Knowing and accepting that future discomfort may occur
	Humor	Using humor when expressing unpleasant thoughts i.e. making fun of uncomfortable situations

	Introjection	Identifying with a person or object to the degree that they become part of the individual
	Sublimation	Transferring negative emotions into more positive actions, behavior or feelings
	Thought suppression	Consciously pushing thoughts into the unconscious i.e. not paying attention to an emotion in order to cope with the present situation

Source: Adapted from Valliant

> Benny Hill, international star of the show of that name, earned millions over the course of his career. Nonetheless, *The Daily Star*, a popular British newspaper, referred to him as 'Mr. Mean', after regular sightings in his local area of a distinctly un-showbizzy-looking Benny poring over tins of food in a supermarket, and trudging home with plastic bags.
>
> He lived in a small apartment, of which he never used the second floor, and his friends say he usually had an unmade bed, dirty dishes and heaps of paper everywhere. He kept the many awards he had won throughout his career hidden in a large box.
>
> In 1992 Benny Hill died aged 68, alone and undiscovered for many days in his apartment, leaving an estate worth over £7 million.

(extrinsic). When starting out on his career, Benny Hill changed his name in homage to his favorite comedian, Jack Benny. This, along with his seeming disregard for his wealth, might indicate that his motivation was intrinsic rather than extrinsic and that money was rather a by-product of his success.

Money

Money for many is the most powerful and simple motivator. People have murdered for money. Employers sometimes feel it is the only motivator that ensures consistent results. This, as indicated below, is only one of three quite distinct positions with regard to whether, in the workplace at any rate, money is an effective motivator. The three positions are:

- **Money is motivational:** Money motivates people, and extra money motivates people to work extra. Employees compete when rewarded to raise productivity or standards. It is not always possible to promote people, so money is a simple, effective, equitable way to reward workers. Money is accepted by all workers, at all times, everywhere.

- **Not sure:** If employees are highly paid, money may be insufficient reward. Beyond a certain level it has no effect. Monetary reward may set employees against each other, leading to conflict in the office. It is often difficult to determine the standard or basis for the decision to award the employee money and openness can lead to conflict.
- **Money is not motivational:** Money trivializes work. Work for many professional employees should be its own reward. The amount received may not bear any relation to what the employee does. If the employer believes awarding money motivates, perhaps the salaries are too low. Paradoxically it can reduce intrinsic motivation. There are many other ways to motivate employees.

Furnham (2014) argues that there are four reasons why people are not simply motivated by money:

- They adapt to the changes in levels of money very quickly so any effect wears off quickly.
- It is not the absolute amount of money that people are paid but rather the amount comparative to those in the work group.
- Perceptions of fairness are ultimately important, which is why issues around executive pay and pay secrecy are so important.
- Other things such as job security, work–life balance and time off can be more important than money. There are many subtly different pay schemes, which can have different effects on performance.

Kohn (1999) also offers six reasons why this, perhaps surprising, conclusion is valid:

- **Pay is Not a Motivator**: Whilst the reduction of a salary is a demotivator, there is little evidence that increasing salary has anything but a transitory impact on motivation. This was pointed out 50 years ago. Just because too little money can irritate and demotivate does not mean that more money will bring about increased satisfaction, much less increased motivation.
- **Rewards Punish:** Rewards can have a punitive effect because they, like out-right punishment, are manipulative. A reward may be highly desired but, by making a bonus contingent on certain behaviors, managers manipulate their subordinates. This experience of being controlled is likely to assume a punitive quality over time. Thus, the withholding of an expected reward feels very much like punishment.

- **Rewards Rupture Relationships:** Incentive programs tend to pit one person against another, which can lead to all kinds of negative repercussions as people undermine each other. This threatens good teamwork.
- **Rewards Ignore Reasons** – Managers sometimes use incentive systems as a substitute for giving workers what they need to do a good job. This might be constructive feedback, social support or autonomy. Offering a bonus to employees and waiting for the results requires much less input and effort.
- **Rewards Discourage Risk Taking:** People working for a reward generally try to minimize challenge and tend to lower their sights when they are encouraged to think about what they are going to get for their efforts.
- **Rewards Undermine Interest**: Extrinsic motivators are a poor substitute for genuine interest in one's job. The more a manager stresses what an employee can earn for good work, the less interested that employee will be in the work itself. If people feel they need to be 'bribed' to do something, it is not something they would ordinarily want to do.

Motivation theories

Numerous theories have been developed to explain the complexities of motivation. We outline some of the most notable below.

Need theories

According to need theories we are all driven by basic and other, rather different, 'higher order' needs. Non-satisfied needs generate tension and a drive to act and the stronger the need, the stronger the motivation to meet it. Need theories describe rather than explain the origin of needs or precisely how an individual can fulfill them.

The most sophisticated theories attempt to describe all needs. Murray (1938) came up with 16 needs that we list below, along with the typical behaviors associated with them (see Table 7.2).

McClelland

One of the most oft-cited motivation theorists is McClelland (1983). He identified three major motives or drivers:

1. The need for affiliation: needing to be liked, included and accepted by others. An individual with a high need for affiliation is likely to be a team player, good at customer services and to have a wide circle of friends. They

TABLE 7.2   Murray's original taxonomy of needs

Need	Description
Abasement	To submit passively to external force; to accept blame, surrender, admit inferiority or error
Achievement	To accomplish something difficult; to master, manipulate, surpass others
Affiliation	To draw near and enjoyably cooperate or reciprocate with liked others; to win their affection, loyalty
Aggression	To overcome opposition forcefully to fight, avenge an injury, oppose or attack others
Autonomy	To get free of confinement or restraint; to resist coercion, be independent
Counteraction	To master or make up for a failure by striving; to overcome weakness
Defendance	To defend oneself against assault, criticism, blame; to vindicate the ego
Deference	To admire and support a superior; to praise, be subordinate, conform
Dominance	To control one's human environment; to influence, persuade, command others
Exhibition	To make an impression, be seen and heard; to excite, amaze, fascinate, shock others
Harm avoidance	To avoid pain, physical injury, illness, and death; to escape danger, take precautions
Infavoidance	To avoid humiliation; to quit or avoid embarrassing situations, refrain from acting because of the fear of failure
Nurturance	To give sympathy and gratify the needs of someone helpless; to console, support others
Order	To put things in order, to achieve nearness, organization, cleanliness
Play	To act humorously without further purpose; to like to laugh and make jokes
Rejection	To separate oneself from disliked others; to exclude, expel, snub others
Sentience	To seek and enjoy sensuous impressions
Sex	To form and further an erotic relationship; to have sexual intercourse
Succorance	To have one's needs gratified by someone sympathetic; to be nursed, supported, protected, consoled
Understanding	To ask or answer general questions. An interest in theory, analyzing events, logic, reason

like to co-operate. A strong need for affiliation and the drive to be liked can affect a person's behaviors adversely, prompting them to make unwise decisions to increase their popularity. They crave acceptance and are very susceptible to flattery. They may also react badly if they perceive themselves to have been excluded or under-valued.

2. The need for power: needing to influence, lead and dominate others and make an impact in society as a whole. Some people have a need for personal power or power over others. This is a need for control and domination. Others have a need for institutional power. Power can be intoxicating: it is a major driver in politicians and business people.
3. The need for achievement: needing to achieve, excel and succeed at everything. Usually those with a high need for achievement set challenging but realistic goals for themselves. This type of person prefers to work alone or with other high achievers. They do not need praise or recognition. Achievement of the task is their reward. Competitive sportsmen and successful businessmen are often driven by this motive.

Equity theory

This is entirely concerned with perceived fairness. Individuals wish to be treated justly, by other people (boss, spouse) and institutions. They would tend to respond well to performance-related pay measures but react badly to discriminatory or unfair treatment. If wronged, they often seek revenge or retribution, possibly through propaganda, force, punishment, or simply by challenging the status quo. The unfairly privileged may also act, perhaps citing the cause of justice, honor, rights or reconciliation.

Furnham and Taylor developed some of these ideas further in *Bad Apples* (2011). It explores, amongst other things, employees' motives when they engage in counter work behaviors (CWBs). The causes and motivation behind fraud, sabotage, theft, whistle-blowing and other forms of punishment or retribution, such as disloyalty and resignation, were found to be complex but usually a mix of personality, the influence of other outside forces, and a breakdown in the relationship between employer and employee. When expectations are disappointed, hurt is felt. The employee seeks to redress the balance or becomes increasingly alienated. Employers are well advised to invest in understanding the level and nature of workers' concerns to avoid such behaviors.

Values

In Chapter 2 – Culture, we spoke of different cultures having common or similar values that arise from shared experiences, sustain common interests and define expected behaviors and norms. Within the wider cultural context a subject will develop their own individual value system, largely formed by their family upbringing, personality and education, as discussed in Chapter 3 – Biographical Information.

Rokeach (1973) distinguished two types of values – terminal (or end-states to be achieved) and instrumental (ways of achieving them). Examples of each are given below in Table 7.3.

While the list is fairly comprehensive it focuses more on what might be considered positive virtues.

Furnham (2015) has devised a Work Values questionnaire. Though designed for self-assessment, it can also be used to assess what a particular position offers and, based on evidence collected by the remote personality profiler, whether the subject is likely therefore to find fulfillment in a specific role (see Table 7.4).

TABLE 7.3   Terminal and instrumental values from the Rokeach value survey

Terminal Values	Instrumental Values
A comfortable life (a prosperous life)	**Ambitious** (hardworking, aspiring)
An exciting life (stimulating, active life)	**Broad-minded** (open-minded)
A sense of accomplishment (lasting contribution)	**Capable** (competent, effective)
A world at peace (free of war and conflict)	**Cheerful** (light-hearted, joyful)
A world of beauty (beauty of nature and the arts)	**Clean** (neat, tidy)
Equality (brotherhood, equal opportunity for all)	**Courageous** (standing up for your beliefs)
Family security (taking care of loved ones)	**Forgiving** (willing to pardon others)
Freedom (independence, free choice)	**Helpful** (working for the welfare of others)
Happiness (contentedness)	**Honest** (sincere, truthful)
Inner harmony (freedom from inner conflict)	**Imaginative** (daring, creative)
Mature love (Sexual and spiritual intimacy)	**Independent** (self-reliant, self-sufficient)
National security (protection from attack)	**Intellectual** (intelligent, reflective)
Pleasure (an enjoyable, leisurely life)	**Logical** (consistent, rational)
Salvation (saved, eternal life)	**Loving** (affectionate, tender)
Self-respect (self-esteem)	**Obedient** (dutiful, respectful)
Social recognition (respect, admiration)	**Polite** (courteous, well-mannered)
True friendship (close companionship)	**Responsible** (dependable, reliable)
Wisdom (a mature understanding of life)	**Self-controlled** (restrained, self-disciplined)

Instructions: Below are listed 37 different work-related factors that may be important to you when you look for or change jobs. Please indicate how much you personally value each one of them by circling the appropriate number. Give higher ratings to factors that are more important to you and lower ratings to factors that are less important to you. There are no right or wrong answers – we are interested in your personal opinions.

TABLE 7.4 Furnham's work values questionnaire

	Unimportant Important					
1. **Balance** – a job that allows me to lead a balanced life	1	2	3	4	5	6
2. **Benefits** – a job that provides many features additional to pay (e.g. pension top-ups, extra holidays)	1	2	3	4	5	6
3. **Bonuses** – a job that provides many opportunities for topping up the basic salary	1	2	3	4	5	6
4. **Clarity** – a job with clear and well-defined roles and responsibilities	1	2	3	4	5	6
5. **Comfort** – a job that can be carried out in physically comfortable conditions	1	2	3	4	5	6
6. **Competition** – a job that provides me with opportunities to compete with others	1	2	3	4	5	6
7. **Conditions** – a job that can be carried out in conditions that are safe, modern, and clean	1	2	3	4	5	6
8. **Contribution to society** – a job that allows me to work for a good cause	1	2	3	4	5	6
9. **Effortlessness** – a job that is relatively easy and does not require excessive effort	1	2	3	4	5	6
10. **Equipment** – a job that can be carried out with up-to-date equipment and technology	1	2	3	4	5	6
11. **Flexibility** – a job that allows me to work flexible hours to suit my personal needs	1	2	3	4	5	6
12. **Independence** – a job that allows me to work autonomously without much supervision	1	2	3	4	5	6
13. **Insurance** – a job that provides health and life insurance	1	2	3	4	5	6
14. **Intellectuality** – a job that is challenging and involves a lot of thinking and analysis	1	2	3	4	5	6
15. **Location** – a job that is conveniently located and easily accessible	1	2	3	4	5	6
16. **Organizational image** – a job within an organization that is widely recognized and respected	1	2	3	4	5	6

17. **Pay** – a job that is very well paid.	1	2	3	4	5	6
18. **Perks** – a job that provides many extras (e.g., company car, discounts on goods, etc.)	1	2	3	4	5	6
19. **Personal growth** – a job that provides opportunities for self-improvement	1	2	3	4	5	6
20. **Personal relevance** – a job that provides me with opportunities to use my personal talents, education, and training	1	2	3	4	5	6
21. **Power** – a job that allows me to control my destiny and be influential	1	2	3	4	5	6
22. **Promotion** – a job that provides opportunities for rapid advancement	1	2	3	4	5	6
23. **Recognition** – a job that leads to clear and wide recognition of my achievements	1	2	3	4	5	6
24. **Regularity** – a job that can be performed in a standard, stable, and controlled manner	1	2	3	4	5	6
25. **Responsibility** – a job with many appropriate responsibilities	1	2	3	4	5	6
26. **Safety** – a job that can be carried out in safe and secure conditions	1	2	3	4	5	6
27. **Security** – a job that is secure and permanent	1	2	3	4	5	6
28. **Simplicity** – a job that is not overly complicated	1	2	3	4	5	6
29. **Social interaction** – a job that provides many good opportunities for social contact with others	1	2	3	4	5	6
30. **Status** – a job that is generally recognized as 'high-status' in our society	1	2	3	4	5	6
31. **Stimulation** – a job that I personally find very interesting	1	2	3	4	5	6
32. **Supervision** – a boss who is fair and considerate	1	2	3	4	5	6
33. **Teaching** – a job that allows me to train others and to pass on my expertise	1	2	3	4	5	6
34. **Teamwork** – a job that provides me with opportunities to cooperate with others	1	2	3	4	5	6
35. **Tranquility** – a job that is not particularly stressful	1	2	3	4	5	6
36. **Variety** – a job that allows me to get involved in many different kinds of activities	1	2	3	4	5	6
37. **Visibility** – a job that gives me a fair amount of publicity	1	2	3	4	5	6

Organizations often have very distinct cultures and it can also be useful, particularly at senior levels or when recruiting a board member, to assess whether, as a visible representative of an organization, a subject would identify personally with its goals and way of doing things.

The Hofstede Centre provides an interesting set of cultural dimensions related to organizations that could be used to assess organizational fit. These are:

- Means versus goal oriented – we identify with the 'how' versus we identify with the 'what'
- Internally versus externally driven – we know what is best for the client or we don't need to care about them versus we do whatever the client wants
- Loose versus tight work control – easy-going versus tight work discipline
- Local versus professional – we identify with our direct boss and/or with our work group versus we identify with our profession and/or the content of our work (work life is a dangerous affair versus we love to find out what is happening in the rest of the world)
- Open versus closed systems – newcomers are welcome versus they first have to prove themselves
- Employee versus work-oriented – management takes co-responsibility for the welfare of their people versus management believes that if they don't put their people under pressure nothing will happen
- Degree of leadership acceptance – from low to high
  Degree to which people identify with their organization – from low to high

If for example, a subject is moving from the private to public sector, perhaps they will be frustrated by a more bureaucratic, slow-moving organization and a relative lack of visible accountability. Would a company at the forefront of technology fit with the subject's need for excitement, or would they prefer to safeguard the welfare and security of staff through more meticulous planning? As a senior manager do they want to be challenged internally or respected as the expert?

For a subject to undertake a senior role convincingly and without undue stress, we need to assess their degree of comfort with and buy-in to what the organization is all about.

Reinforcement theories

This approach is the most straightforward. It emphasizes the consequences of activity. If the outcome is positive an individual will continue the activity. If negative they will not. For every action there are essentially four possible outcomes: positive reinforcement (praise, money, fame); negative reinforcement (threats to do better, try harder); punishment (physical, verbal) and ignoring the behavior. The latter two would naturally tend to prompt the individual to desist from it.

The theory recognizes that any complex behavior has multiple outcomes, some positive, others not, some anticipated, some unforeseen. To understand why an individual starts, but more importantly continues, to take part in any activity, we need to look at the balance sheet of outcomes for the individual. Observing which activities they pursue most avidly over time gives a clearer picture of their motivation.

Expectancy theory

This theory focuses on the rational side of motivation, specifically people's expectations of the outcomes of their activity. The theory suggests that people will only take part in an activity if:

- They believe their efforts will result in the desired outcome
- That a particular outcome will be rewarded
- That the rewards are valuable to them personally.

If any of these three beliefs are not held then motivation will weaken or cease. To motivate others, the theory suggests that leaders need to clarify expectations, link rewards very clearly to performance and give the rewards that are most positively valued.

Bringing it all together

After a review of the many issues and studies in the area we believe we can determine an individual's behavioral profile using nine different motives. These are most relevant to the workplace, but may also be applied to other areas of life.

For each motivation we describe typical normal and extreme behaviors. Readers will notice that many have similar profiles to those described in previous chapters: the Dark Side narcissist, extravert fun lover, the super bright high achiever.

Achievement

The civil service, Secret Service and other professions requiring a degree of confidentiality are examples of those attracting people for whom satisfaction in doing a job or task well is motivation enough. Doctors derive their satisfaction from saving or improving the quality of patients' lives, an IT specialist from solving a particularly tricky software problem. They feel no need to shout about it – job well done.

At its extreme, however, determination to achieve a result can have unfortunate side effects – a blinkered approach, failing to see the bigger picture, self-absorption, treading on or ignoring people's feelings. Delivery is important, but not at any price.

Recognition and vanity

For people with this profile, the positive attention of others spurs them on and makes them work harder. It helps their self-esteem and satisfies a desire or need to feel valued. For them fame, visibility and publicity are important.

At its extreme this tips over into exhibitionism and narcissism. The quiet approval of their peers does not suffice; they are peacocks, want constant adulation, acknowledgment, praise and prizes, often outside their immediate work environment. Without them they can become angry and disruptive.

Power and influence

People driven by this motive tend to like to be thought of as leader-like, assertive, competitive and ambitious for success. They enjoy being influential and wielding power. They like to think they 'get things done'. They talk about challenges and have a lifestyle that shows off their worldly success. If taken to extremes their behaviors can make them unlikeable and difficult colleagues.

Pleasure and hedonism

This is the fun, pleasure, excitement and variety motive. Many have a work-hard, play-hard philosophy. They can be seen as very entertaining, with a great sense of fun. Employees with this profile might joke at work, exhibit a relaxed attitude to lunch hours, frequent office parties or social events, use office gyms and enjoy taking the air in nearby parks or gardens.

Hardcore hedonists though are often seen as flirtatious, dramatic and impulsive. Bored with details, they are considered frivolous and lacking in seriousness, expressing their desires without reservation. They might get involved rather too much with drink, drugs and sex and disparage 'party-poopers'.

Beliefs and creeds

These are people who really care about what they do. They can be seen as courageous exemplars of a creed, prepared to make sacrifices for their beliefs. Often they are passionate about what they do and want others to share in that passion.

Some take their creed very seriously and it can dominate their lives. They can see people in terms of 'us and them', 'believers and non-believers', those who are onside and those who are not. As such they might be thought of as over-zealous, narrow or closed-minded.

Steve Jobs is reputed to have been like that in the early days. Anita Roddick built her Body Shop empire on an ethical approach to work and she attracted people who cared about similar things. For some a company's creed or values can be an important factor in deciding whether they will use their products and services or work for them.

Acceptance and inclusiveness

These people don't like being alone and can have a strong need for varied social contacts, striving to be considered friends, confidants and co-workers. They join groups, societies and clubs and spend a lot of time learning the rules and cultural norms so that they are seen as 'one of us', adopting beliefs and behaviors as necessary to gain acceptance.

Most work environments can accommodate such people, but if their desire to be with people, chat or gossip is too strong they can be disruptive. For many people work is their social life and they are lost without it – as evinced by the number of people who become depressed or lost when they retire.

Risk and excitement

Who doesn't occasionally crave a bit of excitement? Where we find it, however, varies. It could be in the challenge of a negotiation, an away-day go-carting, meeting well-known or influential personalities. The extravert will perhaps seek out a greater degree of stimulus, but most of us look for at least some interest and variety in our lives.

At extremes, people's fear of boredom can be so intense that they lead their lives on the edge, doing things that others may consider dangerous. They talk about 'feeling really alive' when taking often great physical risks. They take risks with money and even the law for the thrill it gives them. Risk and the drug-like endorphins it generates become addictive, and while their behaviors might in some contexts appear courageous and heroic, all too often they veer toward being foolhardy, untrustworthy and dangerous.

Materialism and possessions

Material goods and possessions are important to most of us and drive us to do certain things, whether it is working hard to earn an above-average salary or paying regularly into a pension plan to secure our long-term future. People motivated by materialism and possessions tend to seek out others like them, all the while being sensitive to social comparisons. They tend to flaunt what they have.

At the extreme a desire 'to keep up with the Jones's' may result in irrational behaviors, the philosophy of 'he who dies with most prizes/toys wins' regardless of the consequences. Others hoard possessions, even if they are of little material value, believing that it gives them some protection. All tend to have simple belief systems, 'to have' being more important than 'to be'.

Safety and security

These people seek stability, certainty, predictability and safety in the form of structure, organization and order. They enjoy daily routines, prefer regular income and would put some savings by.

Their fear or dislike of ambiguity and risk can make them seem overly cautious and conformist, slow to make decisions and scared of making mistakes. They seek out jobs and groups that 'follow rules' and 'do things according to the book' and would show discomfort in a more dynamic environment.

Influencers

By attributing one or more of the nine motivators specified above to a subject, we create a backdrop to developing appropriate strategies of influence. It is a useful exercise in that it can keep us focused on what is likely to be the *underlying*, and perhaps concealed, basis of their actions. However, if we do not examine them in more detail, as the previous chapters in *Revealed* guide us to do, we are unlikely to find attributing broad motives to be of any real benefit. Our approach will be unsubtle, paying insufficient heed to the myriad cultural, biographical, biological and personality factors and constraints that will come to the fore in a specific role or situation. So while 'knowing someone' is driven by the need to achieve, what achievement means to that individual can only be understood if we take the time to know them better in a particular context. Annex 2 provides a template to help keep us focused on the matter at hand.

Key risks

There are two main risks in relation to motivation.

- The first and principal risk is assuming unquestioningly that the other person shares your motivation and values and judging them accordingly.

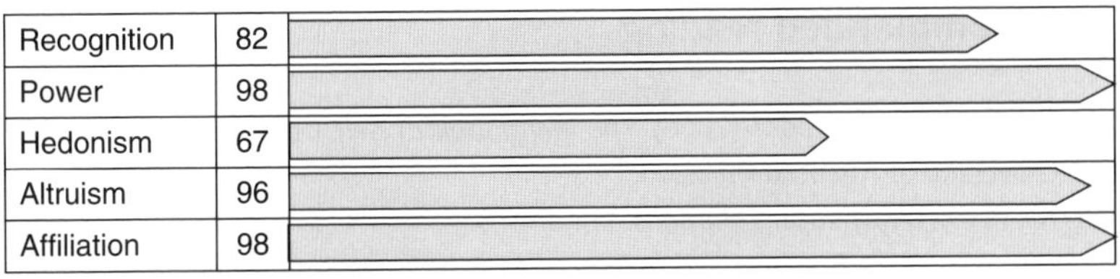

Recognition	82	
Power	98	
Hedonism	67	
Altruism	96	
Affiliation	98	

FIG 7.2 / **Motivation as a combination of factors**

A patriot finds it hard to believe good of someone who does not share their own passion; a financially motivated person assumes everyone is motivated by money; and those highly motivated by power are often denigrated by others as over ambitious, Machiavellian or even ruthless.

- The second risk is that we look for only one motivator. There is always a combination of motivators, with varying strengths. This is perhaps best illustrated by looking at the Hogan assessment of an individual in Figure 7.2. In this particular case we can see that the person being assessed is high on power and affiliation, altruism, with recognition and hedonism following up strongly.

/ Conclusion

Through the preceding chapters we have seen how to build up a picture of a subject. We have looked at the influences to which they have been exposed, their natural abilities and preferences, and how these are likely to affect their behaviors. This behavioral profile gives us vital clues as to what drives them and whether they have hidden predominant or extreme behaviors that might undermine their performance or otherwise cause conflict. Without this research it is easy to be taken in or judge behaviors erroneously, based purely on the situation at hand, the information they choose to share with us, and our own subjective views and approach.

Motivation is the final and key element in our cycle of six because it is a product of all the other factors. The other elements contribute to our assessment and give us confidence in our judgment, but as we approach the negotiation, recruitment or management of the individual, above all clarity about their motivation will determine our success.

Recommended reading

Deci, E. and Ryan, R. (eds) (2006) *The Handbook of Self-Determination Research*. University of Rochester Press.

Ford, M. (1992) *Motivating Humans*. London: Sage.

Furnham, A. (2014) *The New Psychology of Money*. London: Routledge.

Furnham, A. (2015) *The Work Values Questionnaire: A Motivational Measure*. London: ABRA.

Furnham, A. and Taylor, J. (2011) *Bad Apples*. Basingstoke: Palgrave Macmillan.

Kanfer, R., Chen, G. and Pritchard, R. (eds) (2008) *Work Motivation*. London: Routledge.

Kohn, A. (1999) *Punished by Rewards*. Boston: Houghton Mifflin.

McClelland, D. (1983) *Human Motivation*. Cambridge: Cambridge University Press.

Remote Personality Profiling

In the previous chapters we have given an overview of what we consider the most critical influences on how individuals think and behave. In this chapter we look at where we can find the evidence for a personality profile and begin to look at how we can use it.

In many business situations we cannot ask our target person to complete a series of psychometric tests nor come to personal interview. It is difficult to call into question the abilities of a senior manager, and yet we may not be convinced that they will cope with the additional responsibilities and intellectual challenges of leadership.

We can commission 'due diligence' enquiries to ensure the subject has no criminal record, nor is he in financial trouble. Without much digging, we can usually find out about their qualifications and experience and decide whether they match job specifications. But often this tells us very little about the individual. What values do they hold and how do they view the world? How do they behave in teams and manage workloads? How do they react under stress? How can you get their attention and most effectively encourage them to collaborate, negotiate or invest in a cause?

In this chapter, we help the researcher and analyst to draw conclusions regarding the target person's behavior, mind-set and motivations based on generally accessible data. Often the more information, the more complete the picture, but even with gaps – perhaps we cannot pinpoint key childhood influences or find someone who can comment on how they handle tricky meetings – we will gain insights which give us advantage. For instance we may know they may prefer smaller gatherings, are quick to make accusations, expect a degree of respect due to status rather than achievement, seem to have a tendency not to see the big picture and have a passion for golf. Individually all these snippets of information can be useful. Together they build a person's behavioral profile and can be used to identify risks and develop suitable strategies for managing, negotiating with, motivating and in other ways influencing the subject. The strategies we can deploy are outlined and recommendations made in relation to our different elements in Chapter 9 – Managing Extremes.

Potential sources of information

No assessment can, of course, be made without access to information regarding at least some of the six elements. With diligence and guidance much can be gleaned from open sources: LinkedIn; biographies; self-reports; commentaries on the Internet and posts on social media. Direct observations from, for example, TV appearances; presentations; and, of course, interviews with past and present colleagues, friends, family members and business associates, all help build up a clear profile. Another source that may be available and should not be overlooked is company records incorporating historical test results and appraisals. We comment on some of the most widely applied tests below. As discussed in earlier chapters, factors such as personality, intelligence, motivation and Dark Side behaviors remain fairly constant throughout life and so, assuming the tests were professionally and sensitively administered in different cultural contexts, insights are likely to remain valid, though summary reports may need to be reviewed in the light of current requirements.

Scope and reliability of data

Online and other recorded information

Timesaving software exists to help analyze the, at times, vast amounts of information available on the Internet – a search on the name of Richard Branson on Google in April 2013 produced over 40 million hits. However, it is often expensive and requires specialist researchers to interpret it.

Sometimes a person may have a very low Internet profile, be previously unknown to the organization, and the nature of our enquiry may be too sensitive to allow us to approach third parties. Clearly, in such cases we have to assess the scope of the data collected and whether it is sufficient for us to reach reliable conclusions. In addition we should be wary of an excess of data relating to one element blinding us to important deficits in others. The quality and interpretation of data collected is also obviously of concern. In organizations computer-generated and written psychometric test scores are favored as they are empirically verified.

Using remote assessment methods has the advantage often of distancing the assessor from the subject and forces him to seek evidence, but it is still possible to fall victim to carefully presented or spun information. Well-known figures and celebrities in particular spend a lot of time and money molding their image, and we should also be wary. Twitter accounts might not be written by the individual themselves, and websites obscure or highlight particular aspects of their background or personality as befits the image they wish to create.

Even less prominent individuals select what information they make available to others. This may distort our views.

Human sources

Companies frequently seek to verify or supplement findings about individuals through interviews with the subjects themselves. Paul Ekman explains in *'Emotions Revealed: Understanding Faces and Feelings'* (2004) how people give away their true feelings through small gestures over which few have any control. Interviews can therefore be very revealing. However, few are tuned into the subtleties of body language and so are still unable to detect lies or interpret emotional responses to particular issues.

The remote personality profiler relies on an alternative methodology, also often used by business – multi-rater feedback (MRF). MRF, or 360-degree feedback, is a way to collect data on an individual or group from a range of stakeholders, particularly boss, peers, subordinates and clients. In business circles it is popular and routinely deployed for a range of purposes. These include development, appraisal, teambuilding, validation of training, organizational development and remuneration. Its strength lies particularly in building self-awareness and gaining additional, often unexpected, insights into performance issues.

Participants can assess themselves or be confidentially assessed by their boss, their staff, team members, internal/external customers, suppliers, family and friends. Raters or 'respondents' judge perceived behavior, not the intentions behind it.

Psychologists are interested in how individuals combine, discount or emphasize certain information in order to come up with a particular impression. They also consider the extent to which rater differences are a function of the varying type and scope of information each has on a subject. Both these questions highlight the usefulness of identifying a range of good sources to make a proper assessment.

In this regard, what Ghorpade (2000) terms the 'paradoxes' of 360-degree feedback can usefully be taken into account. His five considerations are:

- *Employee Development Paradox*: Is feedback primarily to develop or appraise? The extent to which people are willing to provide accurate, differentiating ratings is a function of purpose.
- *Multiple Constituents Paradox*: Having different perspectives does not necessarily mean having better feedback.
- *Anonymous Ratings Paradox:* Anonymous ratings may lead to more honest, but not necessarily to more valid, ratings.
- *Structured Feedback Paradox:* The generic feedback may have little relevance to a specific workplace.
- *Managerial Involvement Paradox:* Managerial involvement may legitimate the process but it may also taint it.

But when selecting and presenting feedback data, these additional considerations, outlined by Bracken and Timmreck (2001), are even more relevant to the remote personality profiler. They specify eight characteristics of 'good' feedback.

- *Credibility*: The feedback should come from credible sources, in this case individuals who have had sufficient opportunity to observe job-relevant behavior and are motivated to present the feedback honestly.
- *Timeliness*: The feedback should, to the extent possible, occur without significant delay that might reduce its accuracy. Timeliness speaks to the need, at a minimum, to inform the rater as to the specific time frame that is relevant (for example, the last year).
- *Fairness*: In this context, the perception (and reality) that the feedback is fair begins with the common standard that is applied to all participants as defined by the content of the instrument and consistent administration.
- *Clarity*: Ambiguity regarding feedback causes hesitation and misdirected actions. Clear, behavioral items presented (in feedback reports) in a manner to promote full understanding of the feedback and help advance acceptance.

- *Relevance*: The feedback should be restricted to behaviors that are job-relevant and clearly communicated as being important to individual and ultimately organizational effectiveness.
- *Consensus*: A major rationale for multi-source feedback (MSF) as a cause of behavior change is in the power found in consistent feedback from multiple sources. It is certainly difficult to discount feedback that sends a common message from many reliable observers.
- *Actionability*: The feedback must indicate behaviors that the participant can address through constructive actions.
- *Specificity*: The MSF process should encourage specific behavioral feedback from raters, supported both by behavioral items and by training raters to write in comments that offer insight as to the basis of the ratings.

In RPP, our assumption is that, initially at least, the purpose is not personnel development so much as screening-out or assessing the potential for development. It could also be to get a clearer picture of how someone is likely to behave in a given situation, such as a negotiation. As such, some of the above points are of less relevance to the remote personality profiler than others. Nonetheless, they do emphasize the importance of careful analysis, both of the source and of the quality of data provided.

We also need to allow for the interviewee's and our own prejudices or bias. As highlighted elsewhere, we all operate from a particular cultural or professional background and have preferences leading us to filter and interpret information through our own lens. This is a topic also touched upon in Chapter 2 – Culture, where we discuss national personality types and leadership styles.

Language and social media

There is an increasing body of research analyzing the use of language and how it correlates with world developments. Social media (e.g. Twitter and Facebook) have been used, for example, to predict national mood in relation to different seasons and fluctuations in stock market prices. Search patterns on Google have been proven to detect influenza epidemics weeks before the official data confirms them.

There is also research that demonstrates links with different human profiles. Schwartz et al. (2013) from Plos One looked at the use of language by 75,000 people on Facebook and found significant correlations with personality traits (as well as age and gender). So introverts often use the words Anime (an art form, specifically an animation, popular in Japan), Internet, sigh, computer and Pokemon, while extraverts use party, can't wait, love_you, Ya and baby.

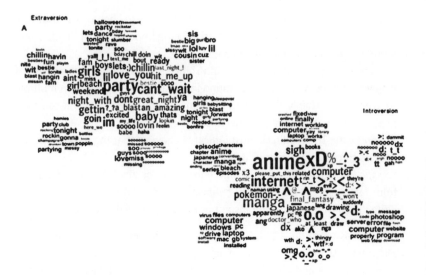

FIG 8.1 / A word map

Schwartz et al. (2013) produce word clouds such as that in Figure 8.1 to demonstrate their findings.

More research needs to be done in this field before it becomes sufficiently reliable to be used in RPP, but it is a promising area of study for these purposes.

Seeking the evidence

In the remainder of this chapter, for each of our six elements we:

- Give a brief overview of what we are assessing (the content of Chapters 2–7) and broadly what it can tell us about the subject;
- Outline some general considerations in research and analysis specific to this element;
- Illustrate using the case study of Alphafox.

The RPP Questionnaire on which we base our profiles is given in Annex 1. It is not necessary, nor likely possible, to answers all the questions. The research questions can be completed by a basic researcher and then passed to others for assessment based on the material provided in Chapters 2–7.

Our questionnaire is designed to reduce the scope for personal bias and misunderstanding. In addition the researcher should:

- take into account the purposes of assessment and focus on areas of particular interest;
- use open sources by preference;
- seek to substantiate conclusions with more than one piece of evidence, preferably from varied sources;
- identify gaps clearly;
- *not* slavishly follow this order of questions or feel they have to answer every question;
- look for the unusual;
- where the answers are not available from open sources, interview a third party who knows the subject well;
- conduct the interview using genuinely open questions in a cognitive interviewing style, encouraging the other person to describe the subject with minimal interruptions.

Introducing our case study: Alphafox

Alphafox is the real subject of a report commissioned to Remote Profiler with his identity disguised. The client was the Chairman and board member of a British company who requested a profile and assessment of his suitability as a prospective investor and board member. In addition to open research, primarily using the Internet, Members of the board who had met Alphafox were available for interview. There were, however, some significant information gaps concerning his private life. We were also unable to identify for comment a suitable individual of Spanish origin.

We highlight our main findings concerning Alphafox in relation to each element and, in relation to the brief, draw general conclusions and recommendations at the end of the chapter. We comment briefly on how to manage Alphafox but propose a more detailed strategy in Chapter 9– Managing Extremes.

Culture

In Chapter 2 we considered the many ways in which culture affects us and highlighted some academic sources that give us insights regarding values and behavioral norms. It is not possible in this book to cover all possible cultures, so independent additional research concerning the implications of, for example, adhering to a particular religion or of being brought up in an environment where it predominated, may be necessary. Given its present-day relevance, we explore in particular national culture and the differences that might arise in international business dealings. Chief amongst those providing useful guidance is Hofstede. His website www.geert-hofstede.com/countries.html allows a comparison of countries using bar charts. He also provides succinct descriptions of how countries are ranked against the four main value dimensions and what behaviors might be expected to arise from them. In reading, intuitively we register similarities and differences with our own country and are able to identify whether they are significant.

As noted in Chapter 2, however, it is only possible to describe the environment where an individual has been raised or to which they have been exposed. As Hofstede rightly warns there is no guarantee that an individual of a particular nationality will adhere to the behaviors, attitudes and beliefs that characterize it. Culture can also take other forms – religious, socio-economic, ethnic or even gender. Some of these and others are discussed in Chapter 2, along with factors that may weaken their cultural identity or at least make them more flexible. These include key relationships, being bilingual, periods of time spent abroad and work experience. The specific setting also plays a role, influencing their level of comfort and confidence in the expectations of those around them. Personality dimensions, as discussed in Chapter 4, are also relevant here.

A final consideration related to culture is time, discussed by a number of experts in cross-cultural management. Differing concepts of time, once identified, can go some way toward overcoming misunderstandings and explaining a subject's approach to business and other tasks.

A case study

It is proposed that Alphafox, of Spanish origins, is appointed as board member and investor in Omega, a British company. In this context it is useful to identify key value differences between the two cultures. These are shown diagrammatically below.

The most significant difference between Spanish and British citizens is the extent to which the Spanish can tolerate uncertainty. In the workplace this means that they change jobs fewer times and have an emotional need for rules, even if they do not work. They are motived by security

The most significant difference between Spanish and British citizens is the extent to which the Spanish can tolerate uncertainty.

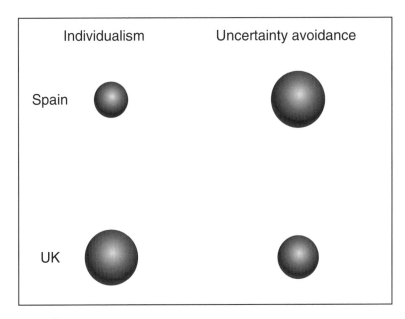

FIG 8.2 Alphafox: cross-cultural comparison, Spain and the UK

and esteem. The British have a much greater tolerance of ambiguity and are more concerned with strategy.

A second difference is the way in which people look after themselves, their immediate family and in-groups. In exchange they expect loyalty from members. Relationships are important; the employer/employee relationship is basically moral, like a family link. The British believe the employer/employee relationship is contractual, and for them the task is more important than the relationship.

Alphafox is of Spanish Catholic origin, both his parents having been born in Madrid. He has joint British and Spanish nationality. He was born and educated in London where his father set up his business, having decided to abandon Spain due to the harsh political and economic conditions.

Alphafox is a fluent Spanish and English speaker and has no discernable foreign accent in either. He is thought to be critical of his elder brother's management of his father's firm and to resent not having been asked to get involved in it. He now lives in Switzerland (for tax reasons) but travels extensively back and forth to Marbella where he has a house, London and elsewhere on business.

He is considered a good boss but does not welcome criticism and unsolicited suggestions or changes to agreed plans. He employs some family members in management roles and has remained loyal to a small circle of close advisors since setting up in business.

Spain is a 'time-blind', polychronic country and, indeed, Alphafox appears to have a relaxed attitude to time. He often takes unrelated calls during meetings and conducts them outside the office over lunch or dinner. His personal orientation seems to be more toward the past, as he often refers to the need to learn from past mistakes and can bear grudges.

Biographical information

As we have said elsewhere in the book, our six elements are all interwoven. The upbringing of a child can weaken their cultural ties if, for example, they travel a lot or go to school in a different country from their parental home. An individual's interest in learning is often dependent on parental attitudes to education or experiences at school.

In Chapter 3 – Biographical information we identified some of the key early influences on an individual and likely impacts. We must be wary of attaching too much importance to any one aspect or interpreting them too rigidly. It may be tempting to assume that trauma or misfortune will lead an individual to view the world in a particular way or act in such and such a manner. However, the range of possible variables is usually just too wide for us to say with any certainty. Psychoanalysts can go through months of deep therapy with a patient and only in the latter part of the treatment discover some more hidden explanation for certain behaviors.

What we can do is highlight important events – either in relation to the individual themselves, or in the broader context – which are likely to be of interest or significance. Knowing, for example, that an individual lived in an era of communism or was in Berlin when the wall came down may help establish points of common interest.

Equally, by identifying the norm for someone of a particular background or past, we can be alert to when our subject does not fulfill expectations and dig some more. The working class boy who has overcome the odds. The woman who operates comfortably in a male-dominated organization. Is there a negative aspect to their behavior? Have they suppressed a natural tendency in order to succeed which may emerge with negative repercussions under stress?

If a subject is in any way out of the ordinary this should arouse interest. As we have seen, factors such as physical attractiveness, can over-ride failings, leading to a more favorable assessment of a subject than is perhaps warranted. Men cope with being unusually small in different ways, as do gays with their sexual orientation. A woman may possess unusual perspectives of value to a male-dominated board.

Most of the information relating to the subject is factual and can often be found only if CVs exist or they have an unusually informative presence on the web. Friends or colleagues may also have some of the answers. The questionnaire covers basic biographical details, the subject's family and early years and later life.

Alphafox's biography

Alphafox was born in 1970 in London and has three siblings, an elder brother and two younger sisters. His father, who died in 2003, came from a working class family but went on to make his fortune in the international road transport industry. Alphafox's mother is alive and he visits her at least once a month, but little is known about her or indeed the rest of the family who have a remarkably low public profile. Alphafox's relations with his siblings are occasionally tense. His elder brother runs the family transport business. It continues to be successful.

Alphafox enjoyed a privileged upbringing due to his father's success and the family continue to enjoy the trappings of wealth. Alphafox has always spoken highly of his father's achievements and his humble beginnings. There is no evidence to suggest that he suffered any misfortunes in early or indeed later life.

He attended day school in London and then went to King's College, London, and afterwards studied for a Masters in Finance from Bath University. Both of these are prestigious universities with rigorous entry criteria. His results are unknown. In 1993, shortly after finishing his studies, he borrowed 3 million dollars from a cousin to build his telecoms company. He resigned as CEO in this first company but continues to hold 25 per cent of the shares. He has started other companies, mostly in the tourism industry and involving other family members, but without the success of his first company. He believes his greatest achievement is founding Omega. Alphafox has based all his companies in the UK but for tax reasons does not now live there.

Alphafox is unmarried and little is known about his private life. In business he maintains a strong network of contacts, centered in London.

Intelligence

Intelligence, as measured using IQ scores, has been proven to be a good overall predictor of success. An individual's educational achievements can also tell us a lot about someone's intelligence and, to a degree, learning potential. Willingness and ability to learn are important in most roles.

But qualifications and status do not tell the whole story. Sometimes being industrious, nepotism and even luck can mask a level of intelligence unequal to the responsibilities of a senior executive and manager. Poor performance may be compounded by a thinking style that holds back rather than inspires or does not suit a more creative environment. The same is true in negotiations or other business situations. When you pitch a hard-nosed donor for funds, wouldn't it help to tailor your approach to match their thinking style – presenting tight logical and evidential arguments rather perhaps than inspiring them with a looser vision of possibilities?

The RPP questionnaire is designed to establish their general level of intelligence (IQ), with analysis disaggregating crystallized from fluid intelligence, with the latter being more critical in senior, analytical roles. It will also help identify cognitive styles and learning quotient (LQ).

Alphafox – Intelligence

Alphafox frequently refers to the importance of further education and in his speeches urges young entrepreneurs to take their education seriously. He is a remarkably avid reader of magazines, journals and the Internet, but rarely reads a book. He is good with numbers and can absorb a spreadsheet quickly. One observer described him as an 'instinctive analyst'.

He founded and built his first company with financial support from his cousin. He has subsequently attempted a number of start-ups but most have failed, which others attribute to an over-reliance on 'gut' rather than investment in understanding the market.

The fact that Alphafox went to a good university and gained a degree (without nepotism) indicates a good all round intelligence. He is creative (many new business ideas) but he also spends time studying spreadsheets. He is therefore capable of both convergent and divergent thinking.

Figure 8.4 shows how Alphafox approaches learning (the length of the bar indicates the confidence of the report writer in making that judgment – the shorter the more confident)

	Low		Moderate		High
General intelligence				⟷	
Crystallised intelligence		⟷			
Fluid intelligence				⟷	
Convergent thinker		⟷			
Divergent thinker				⟷	

FIG 8.3 / Alphafox: intelligence and cognitive style

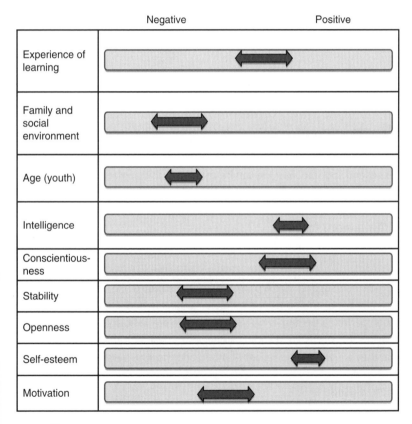

FIG 8.4 / Alphafox: learning profile

Personality

Costa and McCrae's Five Factor Model (FFM) is widely used to describe different personality types or preferences. Determining whether a subject is high, medium or low on the scales of Neuroticism, Extraversion, Openness, Agreeableness and Conscientiousness gives us clues as to the sorts of roles to which they are best suited and in which environments and company they would feel most comfortable. Most of us fall somewhere in the middle on all five dimensions and show flexibility – sometimes enjoying a noisy party (extravert) but at others preferring a walk alone in the woods (introvert). Some people, however, show a strong tendency toward an extreme, and this preference may, particularly at times of stress, tip over into disruptive or negative behaviors. At their most extreme, they may be considered personality disorders as discussed below and in Chapter 6 – Dark Side traits.

In researching a subject, caution should be applied in relying too heavily on adjectives or phrases used by those who know them. These may reflect personal bias. Conclusions should be drawn primarily from observed behaviors.

Alphafox – Personality

Extravert–introvert

Alphafox gives the appearance of being outgoing, gregarious, attention seeking and spontaneous. He can be charming, amusing and has a good sense of humor. He does however value his privacy and resents intrusions into his private life. Unlike most extraverts he discloses little about himself, particularly to close business friends.

Neurotic–stable

The indicators suggest that Alphafox is not well adjusted. He is irritated by others; he can be tense, emotional and temperamental. He frequently complains about others' performance and is not trustful. There are indicators of some neurotic behaviors. He needs good coping strategies to deal with this, but it is not clear what they are. He is very vigilant of others and those he feels he can't trust.

Open–closed

The set up of Omega was visionary and he is concerned with the big picture. This trait is closely associated with the individual's intellect, on which we have already commented. The fact that his other projects have not been so successful might suggest that Alphafox is operating out of his depth.

Agreeable–tough

There seem to be two sides to Alphafox in this aspect of his personality. His public persona suggests that he is easy-going, sensitive, caring and someone who likes others. In business it is almost the opposite – he will take and maintain unpopular positions; he will bulldozer his agenda and yet avoid confrontations, preferring to dismiss or confront colleagues by email or by sending proxies. He tends to form a view, dismiss others' opinions and adjust the facts to suit his argument. He can be very curt when dealing with staff.

Conscientious–disorganized

Alphafox prefers to set his own rules and is resistant to negative feedback. He appears to act spontaneously and can be impulsive. But he gives the impression he is hard working and even a workaholic. And while he is resistant to negative feedback in private, he is concerned about the public perception of him.

Alphafox does not enjoy working in teams and is more at ease telling people what to do than discussing ideas and distributing tasks. He prefers dealing with others one-to-one and is not a ready listener. He has had a high turnover of more junior staff. We do not consider him to have a particularly high level of emotional intelligence.

Alphafox does tend to favor certain trusted contacts and can be impatient with the rules, at times preferring to take things into his own hands. He is somewhat secretive and does not like to be called to account.

Extravert		←						Introvert
Neurotic	←							Stable
Open		←						Closed
Agreeable						←		Tough
Conscientious							←	Disorganised

FIG 8.5 Alphafox: personality assessment (Big Five)

Dark Side

When people are off their guard, tired or under pressure they can display counter-productive work behaviors (CWBs), sometimes called the Dark Side.

These can adversely affect their relationships with customers, colleagues and employees. Often people are unaware they are displaying these negative behaviors.

Detecting Dark Side traits can be challenging as many who possess them become adept at hiding them, at least from those whose opinion matters to them. The psychopath is known to be a charmer, the histrionic is entertaining and the narcissist can be a reassuringly confident leader.

For this reason also many of the questions in the RPP questionnaire will be difficult to answer and the researcher will only be able to form general impressions. However, given the importance of identifying such traits, we provide a comprehensive list.

Alphafox Dark Side

Excitable and mercurial: mood swings, overly optimistic about people and projects and then disappointed with them

Alphafox gives the impression of being a moderately high risk in this area. He is intense and energetic but volatile and sometimes explosive; he overreacts to criticism, can become easily frustrated and annoyed and tends to become disappointed with projects or people. People around him feel they have to 'hold back'.

Argumentative and vigilant: cynical and overly sensitive to criticism, lacks trust

Again Alphafox is close to, if not actually in, the high-risk zone. He is alert to signs of betrayal; he seems argumentative and easily offended and he expects to be mistreated and retaliates. He is a deeply suspicious person. Much of this suspicion comes from his father who often spoke of fraud and theft in the technology sector. Alphafox did suffer from bad management and probably fraud in some of his other start-ups.

Cautious and sensitive: overly worried about being criticized, resistant to change and reluctant to take chances

We judge Alphafox to be between low and moderate risk on this scale. He accepts new challenges, is confident and will speak up, but he does fret over staff mistakes. He can also obsess and get stuck in a view or opinion; he may need reassurance.

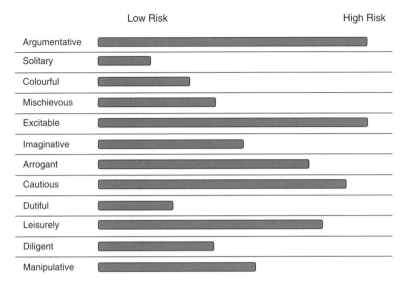

Low Risk   High Risk

- Argumentative
- Solitary
- Colourful
- Mischievous
- Excitable
- Imaginative
- Arrogant
- Cautious
- Dutiful
- Leisurely
- Diligent
- Manipulative

FIG 8.6 / **Alphafox: Dark Side profile**

Leisurely: says one thing and does another, seems stubborn, unco-operative and a procrastinator

Alphafox shows some high-risk and moderate-risk indicators – he has good social skills and makes a positive first impression, but covertly feels mistreated and challenges the competence of top management.

Arrogant and self-confident: over-confident, inflated view of own abilities

While there are some of these characteristics present, we do not see them as a high but rather moderate risk (see Figure 8.6).

/ Motivation

In Chapter 7 we identified nine motivations particularly relevant to the workplace. Most people will have more than one motivation in their make-up. Identifying their real motivations remotely is as challenging as identifying Dark Side behaviors. People are conscious of what is considered acceptable. Today's bankers, for example, are playing up their belief in doing good for the country – altruism and playing down their desire for large financial rewards. Identifying underlying motivation(s) and their strength is, of all the six elements, the most critical. Shaped by the other elements, it provides the clearest overall explanation of why a subject behaves the way they do.

Alphafox's motivations

Alphafox's most significant motivations are:

Recognition and vanity

Alphafox enjoys fame and his status as one of the big entrepreneurs. He regularly appears on TV and has all the trappings of a rich man. He is protective of his good name and reputation.

Power and influence

Alphafox wants to make things happen and outperform the competition. He leverages his reputation and the Omega brand to ensure the best deal and treatment by others. Even when he has formally passed control on to others, he seeks to reassert his influence.

Pleasure and hedonism

The society press would have Alphafox as high on hedonism: the pursuit of fun, pleasure and a lifestyle organized around eating, drinking and entertaining. In his appearances on TV he does little to disabuse this idea.

Beliefs and creed

Alphafox has established his own charity and donates to worthy causes, mostly in Spain. There are some indicators that this interest has tailed off recently and that it is not a very impressive operation. He would still want to be known as altruistic, but there is a question about whether this is him wishing to *be seen* to be altruistic or *genuinely* caring about others, society or the environment.

Materialism and possessions

This has a high score for Alphafox – he is interested in making money, realizing profits, finding new business opportunities and a lifestyle organized around investments and financial planning. He takes a great deal of interest in Omega's business matters. (see Figure 8.7)

Recognition	
Power	
Hedonism	
Beliefs	
Materialism	

FIG 8.7 / **Alphafox: motivations**

Pulling it all together

In RPP our aim is to gain insights into an individual's behavior, mind-set and motivation and, on the basis of those insights, decide whether their behaviors are, or are not, likely to be desirable and manageable in a particular context or role. In the case of a biographer, this could be in order to determine why they are remarkable in some way. In the more practical business environment, it could inform our decision regarding whether we wish to recruit someone to a role or how we should handle them in a delicate negotiation.

The weighting attached to each of the elements identified in *Revealed*, and sub-elements within them, will vary depending on the purpose of the assessment. If, for example, you are meeting a Saudi businessman, cultural difference is likely to be a strong area of focus. Agreeability could be an important consideration if you are asking the CEO of a bank to reinvent himself convincingly as the friendly, ethical face of banking. It's toughness that got him there. Can he be flexible and change?

Weighting increases the effectiveness of RPP but does not imply that the research process can be shortcut. In the case of Alphafox, for example, it is only through broader research that we discover that charity is more a means of social acceptance and aggrandisement than based on a genuine concern for others. We might over-estimate his persuasive powers if we don't take into account the generous seed funding from his cousin. Each area of research has the potential to contribute to other areas of assessment and none should be seen in isolation.

Conclusions

At the end of each of the sections above, we have presented the evidence contributing to our assessment of Alphafox, who has been proposed as a member of the board of a British company. Having both established and run successful companies, he is deemed to have relevant experience and knowledge. But is he personally suited to sit on the board alongside senior executives with backgrounds very dissimilar to his own? Will he make a contribution or, potentially, undermine the current harmonious relations and effective management of the company?

In discussion with the client, Remote Profiler established that the clear priority requirements of the job, additional to industry knowledge, were:

- Ease of working in a multicultural and, particularly, British environment;
- Strong analytical skills and flexibility in dealing with a rapidly changing and competitive market;
- Ability to keep calm under pressure, particularly in dealing with the media and other stakeholders;
- A genuine commitment to building a successful and dynamic company.

There were some significant gaps in our knowledge, but, nonetheless, we were able to conclude the following.

- Culture: He is comfortable operating in a multi-cultural environment and is well disposed toward the UK and familiar with all aspects of British culture. Vestiges of 'Spanishness' however are apparent in his behavior. He dislikes uncertainty and changes of plan and also has loyalty to, and expects loyalty from certain groups and, when disappointed, can react angrily. He also seems to expect to be treated with respect and, although understands the need to consult, does not enjoy team working. Nor does he encourage personal criticism – he can be sensitive if challenged on his arguments or reasoning when presenting a case – and does not expect those beneath him to take the initiative.
- Biography: Alphafox is used to privilege and though he is well known to the media, relatively little is known about his friendships and other aspects of his personal life. He has had few long-term relationships. He is well networked in business circles but does not socialize with work contacts.
- Intelligence: He is intelligent enough to operate at a high level but his judgment and planning have proved at times poor, indicating greater crystallized than fluid intelligence. He values formal education highly and shows a keen interest in keeping up with technology and other new developments. He at times is prone to let his enthusiasm and vision overtake logic and deeper understanding but shows a capacity for both divergent and convergent thinking. He is susceptible to praise for his intellect.
- Personality: Most significant amongst his traits are high neuroticism and impulsivity. He is quick to criticize and does not cope well with stress. While

he is assured in public, his personal confidence levels may not be so high. Winning him over will require considerable flattery and ego-boosting. He does not show a high degree of compassion or concern for others at work. Having suffered from suspected fraud himself, he is alert to it and places a high value on trust. While secretive in his own dealings he is always ready and able to defend his actions.

- His most significant Dark Side traits are volatility (excitable and mercurial) and deep skepticism (argumentative and vigilant). This suggests that he is prone to emotional outbursts and becomes easily upset with other people and projects. Others may describe him as critical and easily irritated and if he becomes disappointed with people, he may give up and/or not follow through on commitments. His very skeptical attitude suggests he may have a chip on his shoulder. He is likely to be cynical, mistrustful and easily angered. He will be suspicious of others' actions and intentions as well as fault-finding.
- Motivation: Alphafox is strongly motivated by external recognition of his achievements, a personal desire to make money and power. He is concerned about his financial security. He judges his achievements against his father and his cousin. He likes to win and gain approval. He does not need to be part of the 'club' either socially or in the workplace.

Recommendations: Alphafox has considerable funds available and useful contacts in the City. He also brings an international dimension, making him an attractive addition to the Board. He is bright enough for the job and is sociable when in public. He is highly driven and will win new business and drive a good bargain.

The degree of his volatility and skepticism is however worrying. He will be a difficult partner and member of the team. He will not socialize with other board members, nor let them into his private life, and yet he will appear relaxed and easy-going in public and in front of cameras. If he is wronged he is likely to turn against the company and will be quick to litigate. There may be skeletons in his cupboard.

Conclusion

We all make assessments of people and comment on their personality and what drives them. Most of these are based on instinct and too often on first impressions. Instinct is useful, but in this chapter we have tried to provide readers with an evidential basis for making assessments.

One piece of evidence is rarely enough to make a confident assessment – furthermore many of the criteria we have looked at have a cross reference to each other. So someone who is strongly motivated by excitement is likely to be an extravert, those who seek safety and security are more likely to be introverts and those who need recognition will be high on the narcissistic scale.

The subject is complex and requires expertise to make a rigorous and valid assessment of a subject. In this chapter we have given a brief description of the kind of evidence needed to make assessments. For more information on the subject or for an assessment of a particular person, please contact the authors by email to info@remoteprofiler.com.

Even given these caveats, research as outlined in this chapter can provide invaluable clues as to how to manage and influence the subject, with techniques discussed in the next chapter.

Recommended reading

Dotlich, D. and Cairo, P. (2003) *Why CEOs Fail*. New York: Jossey Bass.
Ekman, P. (2004) *Emotions Revealed*. New York: Phoenix.
Goffman, E. (1981) *Forms of Talk*, Philadelphia: University of Pennsylvania Press.
Hogan, R., Hogan, J. and Warrenfeltz, R. (2007) *The Hogan Guide*. Tulsa: Hogan Press.
Howard, P. and Howard, J. (2010) *The Owner's Manual for Personality at Work*. Austin: Bard Press.

9

Managing Extremes

Let's return to our starting point, Dale Carnegie's sage advice, given back in 1936:

> *When dealing with people, remember we are not dealing with creatures of logic; we are dealing with creatures of emotion, creatures bristling with prejudices and motivated by pride and vanity.*

People are complex, but throughout *Revealed* we contend that, by analyzing the six elements that influence a person's behavior, we can understand them, if not completely, at least better, and have greater confidence in predicting their behaviors and how to influence them (see Figure 9.1). RPP offers the potential to operate from a basis of full, or at least fuller, knowledge and so manage risks.

The journey so far has been about identifying the factors that influence behavior coupled, in the previous chapter, with more detailed guidance on what research will help us compile, remotely, a profile of a subject of interest. But we also promised a *practical* book. This means that we need to be selective and focus on those areas where a subject can be considered extreme, either (or both) in terms of being unusual or very different from our outlook or approach. In this chapter we provide further guidance and present the RPP framework, which will assist the reader focus on the most significant elements.

In describing traits or behaviors we have made frequent mention of the 'normal distribution curve' and the value of first understanding the norm and then identifying where our subject is on it (see Figure 9.2).

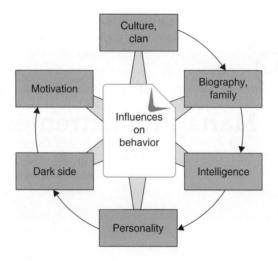

FIG 9.1 / The six dimensions

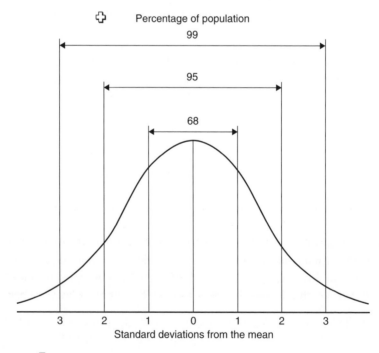

FIG 9.2 / Bell curve

Clearly, most of us will sit somewhere in the middle sections, relatively close to the mean. 'Extreme people', defined as very high or very low on any scale, who are generally perceived as positive (intelligence, physical attractiveness) or negative (neuroticism, narcissism) are by definition unusual and may display unusual behaviors as a function of their 'statistical abnormalities' which they are unable to control.

Many management books focus on the more common, predictable behaviors – it makes sense in terms of numbers. But most would recognize that it is those who are toward an extreme of any of our six elements that are likely to cause most problems. Even when publications provide advice on handling difficult individuals, all too often some risks are downplayed or overlooked. A neurotic manager's behaviors will be more readily handled due to the obvious destabilizing affect they have on others around them. But, while overtly less damaging, at the other end of the scale the extremely 'stable' may also adopt difficult behaviors – be insensitive to others, cold and a poor listener.

Know yourself

But before we embark on the complex, often frustrating but also rewarding business of assessing others and concluding how we might handle them, we have first to know ourselves. There are three reasons for this.

Firstly, we need to assess the degree to which our personal preferences might distort our judgment of the subject. If a potential partner is like us, we overestimate their abilities, and if they are unlike us we may easily dismiss them or view them unfavorably, sometimes overlooking useful attributes. The same is true of motivation. The ambitious power player may not have much time for the vain and hedonistic and vice versa. But each is worthy of understanding and respect on the basis of what they contribute.

Secondly, we need to be aware of the extremes or vulnerabilities that affect our own behavior (or that of a negotiator or manager dealing with the subject).

Examples of the perils of a lack of self-awareness abound. A woman who hogs the limelight and seeks to be the center of attention can be a difficult companion at the dinner table. She thinks she is the life and soul of the party when in reality others are soon tired of her exuberance and lack of listening skills. If she knows she has these tendencies and is 'colorful and dramatic' to use Dark Side trait terminology, she can choose to adopt more restrained behaviors to avoid the danger of alienating others, or of failing to make the impression she seeks – perhaps as being someone capable on engaging with others on an equal and serious basis.

There are various ways to become more self-aware, but few can rely on friends or even work colleagues. Even if they have the insights they are rarely honest. Self-administered psychometric tests are available that produce detailed reports with insights into personality, motivation and other characteristics. Many also require unusual candidness and detachment to be of real value.

Peter, a senior executive in a major bank completed the Hogan series of psychometric tests. Overall, he found the feedback useful and he discussed with the facilitator how he could change some of the behaviours identified in the reports.

However, there were elements in the report which he did not recognize and which he felt were wrong. One in particular suggested that he could be intimidating to junior staff. The facilitator did not press the point but left it with Peter to think about. On leaving the session Peter mentioned this to his secretary, who immediately confirmed that he was intimidating. Over dinner he mentioned it to his wife who also confirmed the assessment.

Peter was shocked. He always thought he got on with people – of all levels. This was something he definitely did want to change. The second feedback session focussed on this aspect in some detail.

One interesting feature of this is that these Hogan tests are not completed by observers or outsiders. This judgment about Peter was made as a result of Peter's own answers to the questions set by the Hogan questionnaire. Peter had the information but did not recognize it.

Other assessments require a facilitator to administer, aid understanding and to guide toward tackling negative findings. Examples include graphology, much favored in France. Many claim accurate results, although we have found no real evidence of validity. Another form of assessment is projective tests, where people tell stories about pictures they see and project their personality motives. These are also popular but unreliable.

Personality tests, such as the NEO-FFI assessing the Big Five, have a considerable body of research backing up their claim to be both valid and helpful in predicting preferences. In relation to Dark Side behaviors the work of Robert Hogan is worthy of note. In our view his set of tests produces uniquely perceptive people insights.

If we, or the 'influencer', has such test results or feedback they can be useful in understanding personal preferences in dealing with people and situations, as can reading *Revealed* in the spirit of openness and learning. If we are honest, we will recognize our behavioral tendencies, good and bad. *Revealed*'s early chapters also highlight the degree to which we are programmed to act in certain ways, and how difficult it can be to over-ride those behavioral norms. In Chapter 1 – Culture we highlighted the importance of this 'programming' and how cultural differences are cited as a major obstacle to successful international business.

The third and crucial element of self-awareness in terms of influence is taking differences between the 'influencer' and subject into account when devising strategies of influence. This means comparing and contrasting our programming, natural preferences and sometimes extremes, with the subject's. We then need to make efforts to understand how we may unwittingly cause discomfort, offence or simply be misunderstood. Finally we then need to be prepared to adapt. In sum we need to identify, confront and incorporate difference.

In essence this book is all about using people's insights to good effect. Understanding others is only half the story. We need to understand ourselves.

What and how can we change?

Extremes or differences in relation to all of the six elements can cause problems or conflict when dealing with a subject. Here we look at the potential to change actions and behaviors, in order to minimize risk.

As we have seen, personality can be affected by a traumatic event at any stage of life: the unexpected death of a very close relative or friend, observing or experiencing some horrific event such as a bombing, kidnapping or critical illness. As noted previously, to a large degree personality is fixed by our late teen, although it can change over time. We tend, for example, to become more conscientious as we grow older.

So, if personality is largely consistent and immutable from an early age, what scope is there to modify our behaviors to ensure that we behave appropriately with our subject?

An introverted CEO may know that his position requires him to be good with people, to be able to make an apparently effortless speech and to have charisma. He knows his preference is to work with a few trusted people in his immediate office, to communicate by email and to allow others to step into the limelight. To be effective in his job, he must draw a distinction between personality preferences and behaviors over which he has some control. He is able to take effective action by recognizing that easy oral communication is not his natural preferred behavior, understanding the benefit and importance of modifying his behaviors (a prerequisite of any adult learning) and seeking help. Given his natural introversion the best training is likely to be around active listening, engaging in 'small talk' with strangers who may, in fact, be his own employees, rather than forcing him speak up and take centre stage. This may continue to be done more effectively by others without undermining his position.

A senior Director in the UK's Foreign and Commonwealth Office admitted to his Head of Training he just did not know how to make small talk. He and his fellow directors had just been criticized in the annual staff survey for 'Lack of visibility' – something common to many companies and organizations. The FCO director viewed with dread the prospect of going 'walk-about' in the registries unannounced and without some stooges to help.

The Head of Training provided some practical solutions, but most of all offered the hitherto unrecognized observation that the Director was actually quite introverted and that his feelings of fear were quite natural and shared by many others.

The Director was never entirely at ease going walk-about, but he knew what he had to do and accepted that in his leadership position this was expected of him. He now knew how to change his behaviours.

In the same way, we can proactively manage specific, one-off situations, for example, a negotiation or pitch for business. We may like the noisy, busy environment of Hard Rock Café, but if trying to win over someone we have identified as an introvert, as a venue for an important meeting we would more appropriately suggest a quiet restaurant where there are private booths with little, if any, background music. When faced with a conscientious interviewer during a job application, we can enhance our chances of success greatly by showing signs of organization and order in our life, even if they don't come naturally to us.

Some people do not find it easy to 'over-ride' consistently their own preferences and adapt to someone else's, and particularly to temper their more excessive personality traits. However, even small changes can make a difference to how people relate to us. If disorganized and shambolic in our administration when staying at the home of a more organized friend, we can a make conscious effort to leave the bedroom and bathroom tidy. If we do we are likely to be a more welcome guest the next time round!

Even if we do find it difficult to adapt, in business, we often cannot afford to carry on regardless. We depend on influencing others – employees, competitors, potential employers or employees. In such circumstances self-awareness and adaptation become necessary tools and not really a matter of choice. Showing respect to Middle Eastern colleagues by reading up on etiquette and sensitivities – such as showing interlocutors the soles of our feet – or, through RPP understanding culturally shaped underlying attitudes to authority and independence, helps us avoid pitfalls and establish rapport. Taking note of a team member's discomfort in certain situations and stepping in when we have relative strengths improves overall performance. While some may object that changing our behaviors is false, that in any case others will see through the changes in behavior and judge the other as insincere, at the very least it shows good intent and a willingness to change. These are fundamental to good negotiation and productive relationships.

Limits to change

But of course there are limits to changing or managing our own and that of a subject we are seeking to influence in some way. This is true particularly when we, or they, are under stress and have Dark Side traits. The more extreme the behaviors, the closer to the 'danger zone' to use Robert Hogan's terminology, the harder they will be to change or influence.

Of the Dark Side traits, the most difficult to manage is the mischievous, manipulative sociopath. Individuals with these tendencies are not motivated to care about others' feelings. They may look like they are acting without self-interest, but that is their manipulative nature coming through – they want something from you. Compassion and sensitivity are not part of their make-up, though they are often charming and fun to be with.

We also need to assess when extreme behaviors can be helpful or are accepted as the most effective way of getting things done. Leaders have to be tough and, in some circumstances, need to be seen to be hard or decisive. Employees and others may expect these behaviors and, in some cultures, lack respect or not know how to react around leaders who do not act in a certain way, even though their behaviors may be deemed unacceptable elsewhere. In societies where the Power Distance ratio is high, for example, subordinates do not expect to be consulted. In a similar way, when faced with trainers or consultants from cultures with a more egalitarian approach to management, trainees may feel unsettled.

Managing the extremes

In previous chapters we have introduced a large number of variables that go to make up a person's personality profile. Each of the six elements we have identified has various components or sub-sets, and it is not possible to specify how we can manage each and every one of them. We have, however, toward the end of each of the six main chapters given some ideas and discussed the most common approaches and highlighted others which are less intuitive. Additionally, in Chapter 1 – Introduction, we outline Cialdini's six internationally valid influencers. These are reciprocity, commitment and consistency, social proof, authority, scarcity and liking to which we have added another – logic.

These influencers rely on *heuristics* – processes that individuals use in order to speed up decision-making processes. Kahneman and Frederick (2002) suggest that cognitive heuristics work through a process of attribute substitution. According to their theory, when a complex judgment of a target attribute is made, this is substituted with a heuristic attribute that is simpler to calculate. So, without conscious awareness, a simpler question is answered than the originally cognitively straining issue. Heuristics are generally advantageous to decision- making, as they require minimal cognitive effort. In certain situations, however, they can lead to cognitive biases. We may misinterpret or fail to factor in relevant information and so come to the wrong decision or conclusions.

In essence heuristics provide us with straightforward, common sense solutions, but we often become over-reliant on them. We fall back on the same heuristics without really considering whether they are likely to be effective, or the most effective. When wishing to persuade a subject who is 'extreme' in some way and especially if they have Dark Side traits, this can prove particularly risky, provoking an unexpected or undesired reaction.

Then, and always, it helps to have a clear objective and time frame in mind when assessing the scope and options for action. These may be constrained by various factors. In terms of reciprocity, for example, we may need to be sensitive to giving favors that may run counter to company policy or legislation. We can't do much about the fact that we are not good-looking though liking is, of course, not solely dependent on that! As a potential influencer, we need to assess these factors thoroughly and develop appropriate strategies, which may or may not depend on heuristics-based influencers such as those outlined above.

In our personal dealings with others we should ask whether we feel adequately prepared and informed to adopt different or adapt our behaviors appropriately. Would someone else be more suited to manage the negotiation or pitch? As an employer, can we, or our organizations, create situations or roles to suit our subject's preferences or which facilitate management of their extremes? If not, should we take the decision that the effort is not worth the potential return? We may defer from approaching a diligent and conscientious individual to take up a senior, high workload position, despite their many attributes, as we assess the organization is unlikely to be able to meet their on-going information needs or feel that they would be over-sensitive to guidance on prioritizing or handling stress.

Given the many potential difficulties it might be tempting to give up and not invest time and energy in influencing more complex individuals. This of course will not always be an option – we don't often choose our negotiating partner. Even if it is an option, the premise of *Revealed* is that understanding an individual will guide us toward solutions. Differences or extremes in terms of background, thinking style, personality or motivation are not an automatic obstacle to successful outcomes. We might delay a meeting with a convergent thinking German until one of our experts, able to respond to questions regarding the technical detail of a contract proposal, is available to attend. We might go through an intermediary of the same cultural background to negotiate a contract. We might adjust our timescales to address the need to build greater trust. We just need to take time to consider and choose wisely the right approach, based on what we know of our subject and our needs and preferences.

Tips and recommendations

Below we give some tips and recommendations on handling subjects. We break them down in relation to key subcomponents of the six elements discussed in the previous chapters. The list is not exhaustive, and the reader will have to weigh one up against another. In our experience, however, certain common themes and desirable approaches are likely to emerge. These can form the central tenet of both short- and long-term influencing strategies.

Culture

We recommend that the remote personality profiler familiarize themselves with, in particular, the relevant cultural practices to which the subject is likely to adhere (e.g. the etiquette of greetings) and any possible sensitivities/significant facts related to the subject's country, religion, etc.

In addition, having established the degree to which the subject is likely to espouse the values of his national culture, consider using the following influencers in Table 9.1.

Biographical information

We can postulate that someone who suffers a misfortune will be influenced by that event and that the lack of support systems around the individual at that time that will have permanently affected them in some way. However, particularly the non-expert cannot isolate the impact of past individual events or relationships and draw reliable conclusions regarding to which influencers they will be most susceptible or responsive.

However, knowing their background does contribute to our overall understanding of a subject and so is valuable. The achievements of Stephen Hawking are all the more astonishing given the early onset of his condition. The tenacity with which Margaret Thatcher adhered to certain beliefs can be explained.

More practically, knowledge of a subject's cultural, family and social background is useful in building rapport. Your family is from the same region; you studied at the same university; you have the same interest in vintage cars. All useful tools and indicators toward influencers such as liking, authority and social proof.

Intelligence

The greatest challenge is managing those who are not really bright enough for the job. Common sense should prevail. Brighter people learn faster; they see opportunities more clearly. However, we know that people are not always insightful as to their actual abilities. Females are prone to

TABLE 9.1 Influencing different cultures

Variable	Short description	Possible influencers
High power distance	Cultures where authority is conferred unquestioningly and age revered	Rank, seniority and the older person
Low power distance	Authority can be questioned and challenged	Logic, scarce expertise
Individualist	Success is achieved through own efforts	Logic, scarce expertise
Collective	Loyalty to and caring for own community	Commitment, social proof and consistency
Masculine	Competitive and achievement orientated	Offering something scarce and reciprocity
Feminine	Value caring and quality of life	Social proof and liking the other
Avoidance of uncertainty	Uncomfortable with uncertainty, they like a plan	Will value commitment, consistency, authority and a logical argument
Comfortable with uncertainty	Not stressed by uncertainty	Liking the other will influence
Pragmatic	Ability to adapt to changing conditions	Social proof – this is what others do and liking
A normative culture	Great respect for tradition and concern to establish the truth	Logic, commitment and authority
Indulgent	Act on impulse and like to enjoy life	Liking will be a powerful influencer as will reciprocity and scarcity
Restrained	Little emphasis on indulgence, control their desires	Commitment, consistency and authority

humility and under-estimation and males to hubristic over-estimation of their abilities.

If people are aware they are 'intellectually challenged' in some way, perhaps in terms of their over-reliance on crystallized rather than fluid intelligence or 'engineer's' intellect rather than more empathetic/emotional approach, it is relatively easy to help. The answer is often to appoint an assistant or set up consultation mechanisms that will support or complement them. Less intellectually able people who are nonetheless self-aware often do surround themselves with smart people anyway to aid with complex decision-making or to provide technical expertise.

The problem is much more difficult when a subject has no such self-awareness, over-estimates their abilities or believes 'I might not have a degree but I am street smart.' This is often accompanied by proclamations of their reliable commercial antennae, their gut feelings and general 'nouse'. Patience, charm and working on the interpersonal skills are the most likely weapons to wear them down.

Convergent and divergent thinkers need different handling. Convergent thinkers will want spread-sheets and data. Divergent thinkers will be happy to have a discussion about concepts and to be more philosophical. Each will be bored by the other approach. At best a divergent thinker will recognize that someone has to look at the figures, but they will always remain more interested in 'blue sky' thinking. Steve Jobs is an interesting example of someone who picked up on his own preferences early on and made sure others with different, more scientific approaches backed him up. Baron-Cohen's distinctions between empathetic and systematic thinkers also indicate preferences in terms of information processing. 'Empathizers' are more likely to pick up on non-verbal communication – body language, eye contact and feeling, as opposed to 'systematizers' who would pay greater attention to detail, rule-based and factual information.

Personality

Any extreme of personality can be wearing. There are two aspects to managing them: how to influence them positively so, for example, you win the negotiation, and how to cope with or compensate for the undoubted weaknesses that a subject will display.

Table 9.2 gives some tips on the most effective approaches to such people.

In Chapter 5 – Personality, we also looked at the issue of trust and integrity. Those who inspire trust – people who are competent, benevolent, principled and constant or predictable in their behaviors – tend to value others exhibiting similar qualities.

Managing Dark Side behaviors

Arrogant and self-confident

Arrogant people exhibit an inability or unwillingness to listen to others. They are convinced they are right, and it is hard to move them away from that belief. They get to the top because they passionately believe in their vision and they compound this by believing that they, and only they, can take the organization

TABLE 9.2　Influencing the Big Five personality traits

Trait	Developing the relationship	Cialdini/logic
Extravert	They need stimulants of many sorts: choose restaurants where there is a lot of 'buzz'; keep the PowerPoints short and with lots of striking imagery; offer an environment which is stimulating and varied; match their energy levels – if they want to walk around, encourage them to; appeal to their sense of responsibility; promise physical rewards such as sports or food	Liking, reciprocation
Introvert	These people need calm space and time for reflection and contemplation; choose a private cubicle in a restaurant with only a couple of people to deal with; they are comfortable with longer PowerPoints; don't rush them; resist the urge to bring in other people; use non-physical rewards (honorary degrees, diplomas); don't get too close physically; appeal to their uniqueness as a person, avoid sexual or aggressive humor; remind them of the names of things	Authority, commitment, logic, scarcity, reciprocation, liking, social proof
Neurotic	They will often need a lot of reassurance; worriers they see problems you have never even thought of. Take these problems seriously, don't push them away or ignore them; minimize distractions, maximize distance between you; appeal to their pride in the organization and family; emphasize what's in it for them, show the appropriate emotion to support your position	Social proof, reciprocation, authority, liking, commitment, scarcity
Stable	It may seem these people are not a problem, but they may be insensitive to the anxiety of others. You should not appear worried or anxious about forthcoming issues. They may be too laid back and you will need to alert them to issues, but in doing so provide the solution as well; be reasonable; make your limits clear; don't interrupt them; ask how they see the alternatives and build on mutual ones	Authority, logic
Open	They will relish new experiences and may need to be forced to look back at existing issues. Refer to individuals who developed the idea or product; emphasize the uniqueness of the idea or product; don't oversimplify; use metaphors; take your time; appreciate their unusual sense of humor let them take credit; refer to the theory behind the application; appeal to the their sense of innovation; give big picture first; be prepared for them to change their minds; appeal to their curiosity, use reason	Scarcity, logic

Closed	Emphasize the tried and true aspects of your proposal; walk them through the proposal step by step; play up to their need to compete and win; don't waste their time; be specific; give examples; refer to established companies that have used your product or idea; use mainstream humor, but be generally serious; avoid complex vocabulary; emphasize conformity with policies and procedures	Authority commitment, social proof
Agreeable	Emphasize how specific groups of people will react; show how your agenda relates to human values; push for closure on the basis of your proposal's impact on people; enquire about their hobbies and family; emphasize the ethical tightness of your proposal; take time to develop the relationship, emphasize how your proposal will help others; because of their tendency to defer, ask questions that draw them out	Reciprocation, liking, social proof, commitment, authority, scarcity, logic
Tough	Push for closure on the basis of bottom line results; emphasize the logical tightness of your position; be sure to do what you say you will do; have alternatives drawn out with plans for each; encourage their criticism and build on their skepticism; build on their need to win and to be right; avoid references on the need for consideration for others; don't take apparent belligerence personally, be flexible	Reciprocation, liking, logic
Conscientious	Set goals and point by point agenda; be sure to arrive on time; give warning of changes to plans; relate to their good health and record of achievement; identify with their favorite way to exercise; to avoid a premature decision against your position, agree on specific steps or follow up or future meeting dates; let them know if you're going to be late; emphasize a good work ethic; be sensitive to their needs and respect for structure; use logic with clear identified priorities and goals; emphasize that they are in control	Authority, reciprocation, commitment, social proof, liking, logic
Disorganized	Help them identify what they need in order to make a decision; emphasize your flexibility; summarize the discussion frequently; be patient if they make you wait or make you late; permit yourself to be spontaneous; don't rush them; don't insist on your agenda when they want to veer from it; help them manage their time and priorities; be willing to wander off in new and different directions; emphasize the pleasurable aspects of your position; appeal to their role as consultant and advisor	Reciprocation, authority commitment

or company forward. If you are negotiating with such a person, flattery is probably the best tool to get them on side.

They price themselves highly. Consider carefully what their motivations are. It may be that they do not seek money itself but position or the ability to tell others they have a superior role. Image is usually more important than cash. If you want them out of the organization and you have the money to pay them off, they will still want to present their departure in a positive light and you should help them do this. Not only will it be cheaper in the end, but it will also help manage their tendency to exact revenge.

We were asked to provide a profile of a well-known impresario based in New York. He displayed an arrogance and vanity that to our minds almost took him into the clinical extreme of narcissism. The client wanted the impresario to sell some real estate in New York for an arts centre to help up and coming artists. The project was to be low key and low budget. The client wanted to know how best to approach the impresario.

Our advice was that while the proposal was to be low key they would not stand a chance of persuading him to sell – appealing to the great philanthropic giver might just, or possibly a grand dinner with the President to help launch it.

Within a company, even at board level, they need constructive feedback. Too often they surround themselves with people who play on their vanity and do not tell the truth. Properly facilitated and delivered 360 degree feedback, together with the reward of executive coaching to ensure this 'talented' person's future development is an effective way of getting the message over.

Find the truth tellers in the organization and make sure they level with the individual. Where there has been a setback make sure the individual is aware and use the opportunity to ensure they learn lessons.

Lowen (2004) looks at treating narcissists from a therapist's point of view. He provides some interesting insights into the mind of the narcissist and the problems of managing them: '... most narcissist patients are terrified of surrendering control. They do not fully trust the therapist – and depending on their early life experiences, this may be understandable. They are afraid of being used, as they perhaps were in their families. Therapy relies on transferring power to the therapist, but the narcissist is likely to resent and resist this transfer of control. Negotiators and managers of narcissists can let them keep some power, but it needs to be defined and limited. The narcissist will see his or her natural position in the organization as the leader and it helps to acknowledge this. People with a vanity streak will be attracted to things that are reassuringly expensive – anything that is exclusive, unique and scarce.

Oldham and Morris (2000) offer some useful additional tips for dealing with narcissists:

- Be absolutely loyal: do not criticize, compete or take credit away from them.
- Clarify objectives with them before you start and do not expect direction.
- Don't expect their individual attention.
- But be ready to give them yours – flattery is always welcomed

Solitary and reserved

These people are tough and independent, but also aloof and detached. They respond best to situations that are task-orientated and job-related. They will ignore requests for more and better communications, and will tend to work by themselves. They are not responsive to emotional approaches, nor to interpersonal persuasion techniques – they just are not interested in the feelings of others. They are indifferent to praise or criticism, unless backed by hard evidence.

For them the logical and practical approach will work best. A respected authority figure will have some impact and they will respond to well-argued written papers.

Again, Oldham and Morris (2000) have some relevant advice.

- Don't force yourself upon them, let them be, they are not necessarily uncomfortable with you around nor unhappy just being alone.
- Be alert to less apparent and straightforward than normal signs that they care.
- Ensure they are able to spend plenty of time alone.
- In argument, appeal to logic rather than emotion.

Imaginative and idiosyncratic

These people thrive in front of a good audience, people who appreciate their humor, creativity and spontaneity. They do not handle reversals very well. They will not mind suggestions and recommendations regarding important decisions, and in fact may even appreciate them. Reports should study their problem-solving style, listen to their insights about other people and model their ability to 'think outside the box'.

They work best when they have a relationship of trust with someone, who will help them realize some of their ideas, explain to other people how the idea or initiative can benefit others and how it might work in practice.

Oldham and Morris (2000) provide useful recommendations for working with these oddballs:

- Accept them for who they are.
- Don't expect them to change or conform but do not let yourself be dragged into their world either.
- Express interest in what they enjoy.
- Allow them time to pursue their interests.
- Accept that they will be reluctant to deal with the realities and responsibilities of life and, as necessary, assume that role.

Mischievous and adventurous

These people can be deceitful, cunning and exploitative. They are also often personally successful and can bring great success to a company. They can also bring ruin to a company. Working with them is a nightmare.

One of the problems facing the manager or negotiator is that these people find it hard to recognize they have a problem: 'They see no reason to change their behavior to conform to societal standards with which they do not agree' (Hare 1993). Though happily seen in a less extreme form in the workplace, anyone who has seen 'The Silence of the Lambs' with Anthony Hopkins' frightening portrayal of Hannibal Lectern will know how difficult it is to treat someone who has the clinical condition of the psychopath. The following guidance is offered by Hare (1999) and Hogan (2001).

Recognize the problem: Mischievous people are charming and have strong interpersonal skills. They are therefore hard to spot because they are likeable. More discerning, critical observers may notice a coldness in the eyes but this is rare.

Protect yourself: recognize that for mischievous people information is a commodity to be traded; for them truth has no meaning. Check what they tell you.

Remove the blinkers: if something or someone seems too good to be true, trust your instincts and check them out.

Avoid power struggles: these people need to be in charge, to have control over others. They will be ruthless in achieving that. If your objectives can be achieved without confrontation, follow that path.

To work with them, employees must be prepared to help them follow through with commitments and pay attention to detail, and to encourage them to think through the consequences of their actions. For this they should not expect a lot of gratitude or even loyalty, but people can take some positive lessons from watching how mischievous people handle others and how they are able to get what they want through charm and persuasion.

Oldham and Morris (2000) offer similar guidance, highlighting not only the fun aspects of their character, but also their risk-loving behaviors that are indicative of a lack of sense of responsibility or concern toward others or life in general. Those dealing with them need to understand their own limits, have a strong sense of self-esteem and adapt to them rather than the other way round.

Excitable and mercurial

These moody people need others around them who are prepared to provide them with a lot of reassurance, keep them well informed so as to minimize surprises and give them time to prepare so they know what is coming. Think of trying to soothe a fretful child.

There are many examples of volatile CEOs – Larry Ellison, Harvey Wienstein and Steve Jobs. One day they shout in anger; the next day they exude encouragement and empathy. They have tremendous energy – this needs channeling. Their volatility will include tremendous loyalty and support for individuals though this will not necessarily be long lived. They are not therefore good managers of large numbers of people. And there are real dangers they can be seen as bullying so you need someone close to them to soften their moods.

Oldham and Morris's (1991) advice on dealing with this personality type is:

- Allow them to put you on a pedestal but also step down from it now and again. They need to idealize you, but you will not be able consistently to meet those standards, and they need to accept and be made to understand this.
- Do not be surprised or over-react to their moods which may be out of all proportion to the issue at hand.
- If they are angry or hurt, they will expect you to know why. Save time and ask directly for an explanation.
- Take responsibility for, or at least monitor business matters which their excessive or impulsive behavior may damage or undermine.

- Keep demonstrating your positive feelings toward them. They need to hear how special they are to you.

Colorful and dramatic

Many expect their leaders to have presence, to be able to hold centre stage and to have charisma. The problems come when they come to love the spotlight and presentation takes over from substance. The good news is that these people are not like the arrogant or the narcissist; they enjoy centre stage but they are much more receptive to feedback.

Dotlich and Cairo (2003) suggest the use of videotape of the person in action works well. They can then see whether they are dominating discussion and whether the audience is with them. Persuade the subject to take their time before saying anything.

People working with them have to be prepared to put up with missed appointments, bad organization, rapid change of direction and indecisiveness. But you can learn from them how to read social clues, how to present your views effectively, forcefully, dramatically and how to flatter and quite simply dazzle other people. They will respond well to people they like and to gifts, favors or compliments.

Oldham and Morris (2000) suggest that in dealing with them we should:

- Allow them to be spontaneous, passionate, sensual and to enjoy themselves.
- Take pleasure in it yourself and be sure to give positive feedback and praise. Be honest but also effusive and don't hold back from expressing your emotions.
- Take responsibility for finances if necessary or perhaps better take on the role of supervisor. They are often unable or reluctant to handle certain responsibilities.
- Forgive and forget. They will. It's best not to over-react, be frightened by or to hold on to the anger or irritation that their dramatic or mercurial behavior may cause.
- Be prepared to stand by and let them enjoy the positive attention of others without feeling jealous.

Cautious and sensitive

To work with cautious-type colleagues you need to keep them well informed about activities that concern them where negative outcomes could reflect on them, and to consult them about intended future actions. When rapid action is needed, or when some form of innovation needs to be implemented, it is best to avoid them or put in writing the fact that you recommended action or innovation. Then be prepared for nothing to happen.

Leaders with this kind of dark side won't necessarily recognize the description – they see themselves as prudent or thorough. According to Dotlick and Cairo (2003) they see themselves as accurate and good analysts. In this world of regulation and surrounded by litigious people, it is surprising there are not more leaders with these characteristics.

But they often have a low threshold for criticism and can imagine themselves to be inferior to others: they may suffer low self-esteem and tend to isolate themselves. Their problem is taking decisions, and they will need all the help and encouragement available to do so. Well-argued and detailed papers will assist them as will time to absorb all the information. Those around them must make the unfamiliar familiar, help them prioritize and remind them of past successes where they have taken a good decision.

Oldham and Morris (2000) recommend that we:

- Accept that they will not always be at ease in company and with strangers.
- Do not insist that they do things they are uncomfortable with to please us or others important to them. Rather encourage them to make small compromises.
- Guide or accompany them in the unfamiliar – at a social event, for example – but don't take over.
- Provide reassurance that they will be liked and appreciated.

Dutiful and devoted

These dutiful and conforming people are relatively easy to manage as they tend to be deferential to their bosses. They respect authority and are unlikely to question decisions. In a sense that is their weakness. Good bosses need to have people around them who challenge and who are not afraid of telling them when they are getting things wrong.

As Dot and Cai (2003) point out leaders with these characteristics have usually achieved their position by being astute at figuring out what other people want. They are not necessarily spineless followers; they 'possess a keen political sense and have an uncanny knack of delivering the right resources, information and ideas to the right people at the right time'. The problem is they avoid conflict and contentious debate. These people need help to confront people. Provide them with the evidence needed to manage a difficult situation; they can't please all the people all of the time. They need to identify the best business solution and be given the arguments to carry that through.

Additionally Oldham and Morris (2000) suggest:

- Enjoy the fact that they like to help and please without guilt but don't take it for granted.
- Be sensitive to whether, in pleasing you, they are neglecting their own needs and desires. They are often less confident and assertive than they appear.
- If you need to criticize, disagree with or discuss difficult issues with them, keep calm and be careful to reassure them so that they do not develop self-doubt or blame themselves excessively.
- Don't take their opinions too seriously, they are likely to say what they think you would like to hear.

Leisurely

These people are also concerned with pleasing authority and that, in turn, is pleasing to authority. They are co-operative and cheerful, but they sometimes provide little leadership for those who work with them. Colleagues and negotiators must be prepared for indecisiveness, inaction and lack of leadership. They must also be prepared to take initiative when processes get stalled. Accept that you won't be supported should your initiative fail or backfire.

Hogan and Hogan (2001) believe that to work with these people, you must be prepared to flatter them, to agree with them, to be exploited, to allow them to take credit for your accomplishments, and allow them to blame you for their failures. Do not misinterpret their silence as agreement.

Oldham and Morris (2000) have further tips on dealing with the leisurely passive aggressive type:

- Accept them and like them for what they are, and expect them to demand more sacrifices from you than the other way round. You won't change.
- Let them know your minimal expectations and what is important to you. They may well not figure it out.
- If they assert their right to do as they please or be as they are offer to assist them or to make a deal.
- Recognize the signs of anger. If they procrastinate, forget or refuse to do something prompt them to express their feelings more directly.
- Notice their habits and routines and try and go along with them.
- Give them plenty of love and attention – they revel in it.

Diligent and conscientious

Hogan and Hogan suggest that these are good role models who uphold the highest standards of professionalism in performance and comportment. They are popular with their bosses because they are so completely reliable. Those that report to them may not feel the same way. They are fussy, nit-picking, micro-managers who deprive their subordinates of any choice or control over their work. This alienates staff who begin to refuse to take any initiative and simply wait to be told what to do and how to do it.

Diligent, conscientious, obsessive-compulsives also cause stress for themselves; their obsessive concern for quality and high performance makes it difficult for them to delegate. It also makes it difficult for them to prioritize their tasks. They also have problems with vision and the big picture. Consequently, they have a kind of ambivalent status as managers and can function in some environments at certain levels.

Encouraging such people to see the bigger picture, to cut corners, to compromise on being perfect is not easy. They have to trust others and rarely can they bring themselves to believe that others can do an adequate job. The encouraging thing is that most people with this tendency, even those with an obsessive compulsive disorder, recognize they have a problem. Those working with them have to recognize the excellence of their work but point out gently that it is time to move on, delegate the smaller tasks and look for the bigger picture.

Dot and Cai encourage the perfectionists to look at the costs of their behaviors: stress, missed opportunities and diminished productivity from subordinates.

Oldham and Morris (2000) offer tips for dealing with these types:

- Put up with their nit-picking habits with as much humor as possible and focus on what they bring to the relationship.
- Be flexible. They are unlikely to change so rather look for ways in which you can contribute your own strengths.
- Do not look for compliments or open signs of affection, it is not in their way of expressing appreciation.
- Avoid arguments – they feel they must win.

Argumentative and vigilant

These people focus on the negative and are distrustful of others. There are many examples of leaders who suffer this characteristic.

To work with these people, colleagues have no alternative but to agree with them, because they will defeat objections in a way that makes sense to them. If the objections are sufficiently strong the vigilant type will develop a conspiracy theory implicating those who oppose them. In their eyes, subordinates are either for or against.

Oldham and Morris (2000) suggest:

- Let them know frequently that you respect them. They are not as confident, tough, independent and assertive as they may seem.
- Persevere in getting to know them. Reserve is not necessarily a sign of indifference and it will take time for them to reciprocate and trust you.
- Don't compete and go head-to-head with them. They need to feel in control of their destiny.
- They are defensive so avoid direct criticism and blame. If you need to confront them express how you feel rather than finding fault.
- Take the lead socially as getting to know people does not always come easily to them.
- Don't tease. Vigilant people often have a good sense of humor, but not about themselves.
- Reassure them that you take seriously any concerns they have about loyalty.
- Be wary of slighting them. They have a long memory and will be slow to forgive.

Manipulative

Niccolo Machiavelli's political philosophy was incorporated in his short treatise *The Prince*. Commentators have mostly viewed it in a pejorative way: a philosophy where immoral means are justified by the ends. Others believe it is simply a realistic approach to managing people and problems, not just in a political environment but in all organizations. In modern psychology it describes one of the dark triad personalities (along with narcissists and psychopaths), characterized by a duplicitous interpersonal style.

Manipulative types depend on being able to operate in some secrecy. They may say one thing to one person and another to someone else. Their immoral approach may encourage them to break or bend the law, so they may, for example, seek the help of private investigators to acquire information on competitors, negotiators or colleagues. They will be willing to offer bribes or favors to individuals to persuade them to support their cause.

The law these days in Europe and North America inflicts harsh penalties on those committing bribery or fraud and in many cases the law does not differentiate between the briber and their boss – both are equally guilty. Openness and a clear policy of zero tolerance of bribery and fraud will discourage the manipulator but not eradicate the problem. They are devious and clever and may just make greater efforts to conceal their actions.

In a negotiation having a manipulator on the other side of the table means you have to keep your base negotiation line secret and be absolutely sure of the loyalty of those working with you. Be prepared for the opposite side to use 'dirty' tactics. Of course having a manipulator on your side in a negotiation is fine as long as you know they are staying on the right side of the law and that they operate within the ethical values of your organization.

Motivation

In Chapter 7 we identified the nine motivators we believe capture most people's reasons for going to work. Ultimately, it is an accurate assessment of the subject's motivation or, more likely, set of motivations that will be of most value to negotiators, managers and recruiters.

Sometimes it is easy to detect a person's motivation: the person openly strives to get awards and 'badges of achievement', and is eager to be an in-group or to be a celebrity. Some are driven by powerful religious or

> The nine motivators
>
> • Achievement
> • Recognition and vanity
> • Power and influence
> • Pleasure and hedonism
> • Beliefs and creeds
> • Acceptance and inclusiveness
> • Risk and excitement
> • Materialism and possessions
> • Safety and security

political ideologies and willing and able to give up everything to achieve a particular end. Others have an abiding love of jewels and trinkets.

Three points need to be born in mind about motivation.

• Sometimes people are very open to persuasion as a function of a hidden motivation that is not easy to fulfill. A powerful underlying need, drive or fear (perhaps of rejection, failure or intimacy) means they seem never to get enough of the experience they believe will satisfy them. Once one discovers their 'drug of choice' they may be very open to persuasion and the best influencers easily identifiable.

- Our motivational profile will reflect motives of differing strength, some of which may be in conflict. Thus, a person may have a very strong need to be accepted by a group but also be a pleasure-seeking hedonist of whom group members disapprove. There is often a trade-off.
- People may or may not be able to articulate what motivates them. If they can they may still be reluctant to 'confess' what really drives them because they know or sense it is socially unacceptable.

A great deal of therapy is aimed at uncovering a person's history and so be able to understand what motivates them. Motivation is perhaps the most intriguing of all the six elements but often also the most difficult to uncover. Once again, a broad knowledge of their background and preferences will help.

Alphafox

In Chapter 8 – Remote Personality Profiling, we presented the case study of Alphafox, a Spanish-origin entrepreneur being considered as an investor in, and board member of, a British company.

In Table 9.3 we use our RPP framework (Annex 2) to summarize our findings and recommendations – some tips and 'influencers'. The action planning grid is left empty, as this is something which the client is best placed to decide, although, Remote Profiler is also able to assist.

Conclusion

We have in this book highlighted the six elements that have the greatest influence on individuals and broken them down into different aspects, presenting reliable evidence that they are critical in establishing behavioral patterns and tendencies. The range of possible combinations of variables is enormous: five cultural variables (at least), up to six biographical variables, six different kinds of intelligence to calculate, five personality factors with virtually unlimited variations between their extremes, 12 dark side behaviors and nine motivations. As we have said before – humans are supremely complex.

TABLE 9.3   Alphafox: RPP framework

Subject: *Alphafox* **Motivation:** *Strongest: Power and influence/ materialism; Recognition. Also: hedonism and beliefs* **Information gaps:** *Investigate further his personal life and Spanish persona*		**Your/Influencer's profile:** *No one 'influencer'. Regular contact with, primarily, British board members* **Purpose of assessment:** *To ensure he is a loyal and committed board member, able to respond to change and handle media and other stakeholder relations* **Operational constraints:** *No significant constraints*	
Element	**Key risks/opportunities**	**Recommended tool(s) of influence/ tactics**	**Action planning**
Culture: Key differences in practices/values Subject's adaptability Situational factors to be taken into account	*Adaptable and at ease in a multinational environment and au fait and accepting of all British practices. Loyalty to certain (unknown) in-groups. Dislike of uncertainty and open challenges to his authority. Relaxed attitude to time so may not respond well to protocol of board meetings*	*Liking and reciprocation Make him feel part of in-group with favors given and received* *Authority – appeal to his sense of self-worth* *Planning but with some flexibility*	
Biography: Shared understanding/ experiences Skills or knowledge (or deficit of) Out of the ordinary?	*Highly experienced entrepreneur with good business networks in UK. Keeps his personal life private Proud of Omega. Keeps up with technology*	*Liking and reciprocation* *Identify mutual contacts whom he likes and trusts Appeal to his 'Spanishness' – it is part of who he is and makes him different/ valuable*	
Intelligence: Level and type Thinking style Personal strengths Willingness to learn	*Crystallized intelligence with sound analytical powers but by preference an intuitive thinker, i.e. somewhat flexible in his thinking styles. Curious and values formal education highly. Responsive to intellectual flattery*	*Scarcity and logic Offer him privileged or scarce access in terms of information/ learning opportunities Mixed presentations inciting his curiosity but with logic and detail to back them up*	

Personality: Preferences Extremes Awareness and management of tendencies Integrity	Moderately extravert and enjoys the good life though does not socialize widely. Somewhat unstable, being inclined to moodiness and disliking changes of plan. Tough and fairly low on EQ so in all likelihood a poor people manager. Dislikes team-working, but generally open to new ideas. Sensitive to questions concerning integrity but secretive, meaning unclear often what his intentions are. He should be very discreetly monitored.	Scarcity, reciprocation Provide him with access to stimulating and varied activities Provide reassurance regarding plans and his performance Appeal to his curiosity Allow him to be right and to win Appeal to his sense of worthwhile confirming priorities with him	
Dark Side: Extremes Ability to control Possible Triggers	Unable to control his behavioral extremes. He is excitable and mercurial and sensitive to slights. He is also argumentative and vigilant, so suspicious. Also shows arrogant behaviors, meaning he appears to have a high opinion of himself and his worth, making him susceptible to flattery. May react badly to media pressure and become irritated by need to engage widely with stakeholders	Liking and trust Flattery and rewards (including financial) Emphasize respect for him and be wary of appearing to undermine him Don't take him on head-to-head Constructive feedback Allow him to feel in control Reassurance Keep them well-informed Keep calm and ask for explanations if angered	

The remote personality profiler has to accept that there will always remain aspects of an individual that remain hidden or undiscovered and that a degree of uncertainty will always persist. No matter how complete the evidence collected a subject will still be capable of surprising us. While some aspects are more constant than others, people do change (though radical change, such as a neurotic becoming entirely stable is very unlikely). Also people can and do modify their behaviors to suit their needs, obscuring often less positive aspects of their personality and motivation. In such cases the profiler must be alert to smaller tell tale micro-actions that give away their true self.

However, it is also true that individuals are more constant and have less control over their actions than perhaps we assume, due to the processes of enculturation and socialization and biological inheritance. The analyst's job is made easier because most people are consistent, and the indicators show a pattern of behaviors that is assessable and enables us to draw sensible conclusions about what is likely.

Based on the remote profiler's possible findings we offer in this chapter guidance on how to identify our own preferences and default behaviors, and to manage differences and extremes in others in order to influence them more effectively. It comes down to understanding, the flexibility of approach and acknowledging that in some cases we can only increase the chances of success, not guarantee it.

Recommended reading

Aubuchon, N. (1997) *The Anatomy of Persuasion.* New York: AMACOM.

Cialdini,R (2001) *Influence: The Psychology of Persuasion*. New York: Quill.

Dotlich, D. and Cairo, P. (2003) *Why CEOs Fail.* New York: Jossey Bass.

Hogan, R. and Hogan, J. (2001) 'Assessing Leadership: A view from the dark side'. *International Journal of Selection and Assessment*, 9, 40–51.

Lowen, A. (1984) *Narcissism: Denial of the True Self*. New York: MacMillan.

Oldham, J. and Morris, L. (1991) *Personality Self-Portrait*. New York: Bantam.

McIntyre, M. (2005) *Secrets to Winning at Office Politics*. New York: St Martins Griffin.

Thompson, L. (2011) *The Truth about Negotiations.* New York: Pearson.

Case Studies

chapter **10**

Revealed asserts that by researching an individual's past, level and form of intelligence, personality and Dark Side traits, we move closer to being able to understand them, their motivations and so predict and, to a degree, influence their behaviors.

In this chapter to illustrate the validity of our approach, based primarily, but not exclusively, on Internet searches, we profile five well-known individuals – John Lennon, Margaret Thatcher, Mohamed Fayed, Steve Jobs and Edward Snowden. Famous people from the West, of course, tend to have a strong presence on the Internet, which facilitates research. With others reliance on personal contacts will be greater, although, as outlined in Chapter 8, a lot can also be gleaned from written and audio-visual sources. It should also be borne in mind that research does not have to be as detailed in order to glean valuable insights into a potential business contact or negotiation partner.

Famous people

John Winston Lennon British musician, singer and songwriter and founder member of the Beatles, who rose to fame in the 1960s and are one of the most successful bands of all time. He was shot and killed at the age of 40 outside his New York apartment.

Culture

Lennon lived in and around Liverpool as a child, raised by his mother's Welsh family. In the 1970s he became aware of his Irish roots on his father's side and began to identify increasingly with Ireland and its politics, causing some controversy at the time. For much of his life he does not seem to have identified strongly with the UK, and is quoted as saying that he regretted not being American, choosing to live in more 'happening' Greenwich Village from 1971, although toward the end of his life he spoke of being homesick and his desire to return to the UK.

As a member of the Beatles he was very much associated with working class Liverpool, although in reality his upbringing was middle class. He played along with this portrayal, saying that although accents were looked down in the UK 'show business' tended to prefer that he exaggerated his Liverpudlian accent. In some other ways he could also be considered very British. The humor of Faulty Towers and Monty Python (which he said he would rather have been in than The Beatles) very much reflected his own wit and humor. He also demonstrated British 'stiff upper lip', giving a front of not being upset by his mother's death when he was 17, although he was deeply affected by it. Paul McCarthy has also commented that you could punch him in the face and he wouldn't let you know it hurt.

Looking at Hofstede's masculinity dimension, much has been made of rivalry between Lennon and McCarthy being a factor in their creative success and subsequent break-up. Britain's high masculinity scores suggest that its citizen's are motivated by wanting to be the best, are success oriented and success-driven. Evidence exists to suggest that Lennon was all these things. However, we do not believe that he pitched himself against others to 'win', rather to give free reign to his spirit. He once described himself as more of a gardener than a career person. As an artist he said his role was 'to try and express what we all feel. Not to tell people how to feel. Not as a preacher, not as a leader, but as a reflection of us all.'

Lennon gave great importance to individualism, a dimension on which Britain also scores particularly highly (this may also account for his attraction to the United States which scores even higher). He was an extremely independent thinker and very much took matters into his own hands. Despite his headmaster and aunt having to intervene to get him into art college, he squandered this opportunity through bad behavior. He challenged politics and the 'system' and was prepared to opt out rather than conform, especially when he did not think it was in his interests. His departure from The Beatles (he was bored) and transfer of responsibility for his financial affairs to Yoko Ono (cynical of others' motives) are further examples. They also demonstrate an ease with uncertainty, another dimension on which Britain scores high.

Britain has a relatively high score for indulgence, a society willing to exhibit their impulses and desires, Britons are positive and optimistic. Optimism and hedonism are, of course, also particularly associated with the 1960s when of course Lennon was most visible. Although Lennon might be described as more of an idealist than optimist, in other respects he fits this profile well, seemingly being at ease with doing as he pleased – his famous nude pictures and bed-in with Yoko Ono, being just two examples.

Biography

Lennon was born in 1940, but his father was serving in the Navy at the time and Lennon saw little of his father who then went AWOL, only returning to the family at the end of the war. This must have caused some tension, both at home and in the wider community, and he and his mother, who by this time was pregnant with another man's child, divorced.

Lennon lived with his mother, but his aunt Mimi reported to Social Services her concerns about conditions at home and Lennon came to live with her from the age of six. She and her husband were childless, but Lennon continued to see quite a lot of his mother and got on well with his two younger stepsisters. His mother's death in a car accident when he was 17 left him heartbroken. He took to drink for a couple of years afterwards. He would go to shows in Blackpool with a cousin whom he continued to visit after he had moved to Scotland. He had little contact with his father until the late 1960s, and they were only reconciled shortly before his father's death.

Lennon was a rebellious child and troublemaker of whom the school and other parents disapproved. Mimi and her husband provided a strict but loving home environment. McCarthy contradicts reports that Mimi was cruel saying she was 'mock strict' with a 'good heart' and that she 'loved John madly'. Lennon later talked of 'five fantastic, strong, beautiful and intelligent women' in his childhood, of which Mimi and his mother were two. Throughout his later life Lennon kept in weekly contact with his aunt and when widowed bought her a bungalow in Dorset. She and her husband encouraged him to read at an early age and his uncle also encouraged his musical involvement. Mimi was dismissive of his musical aspirations, although later claimed to have bought him his first guitar (which in fact his mother had in 1956). Lennon went elsewhere to rehearse with friends (including McCarthy with whom he enjoyed a close friendship, although also turbulent, particularly after the breakup of the Beatles), and was key to the establishment of The Quarry Men when he was 15. Soon after he set up the Beatles with the help of Brian Epstein, with whom he enjoyed a close relationship until his death in the late 1970s.

Lennon was married twice. He married Cynthia in 1962 and had a son, Julian. He saw little of them and the marriage was short-lived and abusive, as were many of Lennon's relationships, something he said he regretted. The marriage's breakdown has also been attributed to his LSD usage and relationship with Yoko Ono, whom he married in 1969. They subsequently separated for 18 months, a drug and alcohol-fuelled period which Lennon referred to as 'the lost weekend' but then came back together and had a son in 1975 for whom Lennon was primary carer until his death.

Intelligence – highly divergent thinker

Lennon gained a place at grammar school at 11 but subsequently failed to live up to his academic potential. He failed all his GCE O-level examinations, his unruly behavior undoubtedly being a factor. This continued at the Liverpool College of Art only where he started wearing Teddy Boy clothes and acquired a reputation for disrupting classes and ridiculing teachers, eventually being thrown out before his final year.

But while he might have had a disregard for formal education, he did value intelligence. He is quoted as saying 'I dislike stupid people. Can't stand to be around slow-witted dumbheads.' In interviews too he seems at times barely able to conceal his frustration with sweeping statements or simplistic questions.

As a child Lennon was drawn toward more whimsical literature and was encouraged in his reading. His favorite book was Lewis Carroll's Alice in Wonderland. At school he wrote a cartoon book – The Daily Howl – which featured stories and poems and in the mid-sixties published two books of his own, the titles of which use wordplay and feature nonsensical stories and rhymes. These illustrate well his keen, and sometimes acerbic, wit and attraction to the absurd. Anecdotes from those who knew him as a child paint a picture of a divergent thinker with an extremely questioning mind. In art college he became a member of a group calling themselves 'The Dissenters' and later in life, in his interviews, creative work and actions, he appears to be perpetually questioning, seeking some higher truth. He was highly experimental along the way, using drugs and espousing various religious beliefs and practices.

Personality – open, disagreeable, somewhat unstable and low on conscientiousness

Lennon's most defining personality trait is his openness, as indicated in the previous section. His creative spirit, pursuit of idealism (though disappointment with the world and its people), questioning of authority and quirky and often mischievous behavior all define him as such.

He could also be disagreeable and always had an edge to him. This could be entertaining but also cruel and unsettling, such as with his relationship with Epstein whom he teased for being a Jew and homosexual. Many of his behaviors (and clothes and appearance) were ostentatious and often gave the impression that, though charming at times, he was hard-headed, shrewd and not all that he might seem. He was not the easiest person to be around.

Earlier we referred to his British stiff upper lip, but there are indicators that he was prone to stress and anxiety. He was very insecure about his appearance – disliking his nose and for many years refusing to wear glasses despite his extreme short-sightedness. His drug-taking and erratic behaviors could be attributed to the stress induced by the rapid and extreme success of the Beatles, but there are earlier signs that he was not always in control. He had a tendency to violence, ranting and moodiness. His first wife and others also undermine the impression in the media that he was calm over the controversy his statements about the popularity of the Beatles versus Jesus had caused, saying that privately he sobbed and was bewildered, frightened and unable to cope with the pressure.

In terms of conscientiousness, he was disorganized. He often rushed out songs to meet deadlines and spoke of his relief at being able to hand over his business affairs to Yoko Ono. When bored of projects, he had no hesitation in moving on and appeared frustrated when held back, such as when he decided to leave The Beatles.

In respect of extraversion we would judge him to be somewhere in the middle. He showed some introvert tendencies – he spoke at times of wanting to withdraw and surround himself with high hedges and isolation. He also bought an uninhabited island with a view to building a home there (though his plans never saw fruition). He also, however, appeared to enjoy company and be sociable and assertive.

Dark Side – excitable and mercurial, imaginative and idiosyncratic

Lennon's up and down relationship with McCarthy, his own accounts of his behavior toward women, his at times vitriolic correspondence with the media and others, and story of an incident when he severely assaulted a man in a drunken fight who he felt had insulted him testify to the difficulty Lennon had controlling his emotions. He acknowledged it, most dramatically perhaps when he said he only stopped kicking the man on the ground when he realized he could kill him. He also brought along his lawyer to a televised interview at the time when he was seeking residency in the United States, clearly concerned that he might be provoked into saying something he should not. In his life it is also apparent that he searched for some sort of peace and calm, the stabilizing element of his relationship with Yoko Ono being something he clearly valued, though others were alarmed at his absorption with and dependency on her.

What Lennon will be most remembered for, however, is his imaginative and idiosyncratic approach to life. He said, 'Surrealism had a great effect on me because then I realised that the imagery in my mind wasn't insanity. Surrealism to me is reality.' As his legacy shows, he could channel his perception of reality into creative and well-received output in the form particularly of his music and lyrics. However, at other times, especially after he left The Beatles, that his dress, actions and beliefs were considered eccentric and alienated him from sectors of society. He referred to himself on more than one occasion as a freak and, certainly there were many times, when he was labeled odd and even dangerous, reinforcing the impression that his more impulsive, reckless and unstable tendencies were never far below the surface

Motivation – beliefs and creeds and pleasure and hedonism

Lennon said that there were two motivating forces in life – fear and love, suggesting a belief in both.

He would often talk about the limitations of fear and in his own life challenged, both as a child and in his later professional and political life, the idea that he should be somehow buckle under. He was, however, a believer in 'Love' and other universal concepts such as 'woman', 'peace' and 'happiness'.

Particularly in the late sixties and seventies, as reflected in his creative output from the time, he pursued various political, religious and philosophical ideologies to these ends. None of them seem to have stuck, although he highlighted the importance of 'rituals' in life. Right up until the end of his life he persisted in seeking personal happiness (a concept which he recalls his mother saying was the 'key to life'), latterly talking with enthusiasm of the peace and contentment he found cooking and in the care of his second son.

In all likelihood it was his open and questioning mind that led him to experiment with so many belief systems, something for which many criticize him. His earlier partying days and drugs experimentation could also be seen as part of his search for happiness. His pursuit of pleasure and hedonism, however, were constants throughout his life. He might have expressed some dis-ease with his wealth, and recognized the conflict between what he said and what he did, but he persisted in pursuing pleasure in material things right until the end, something for which he was fundamentally unapologetic. While with Yoko Ono he also acquired a number of properties and had a luxurious lifestyle. To some extent, like the fans who risked destroying the Rolls Royce in which he travelled, he doubtless felt that he deserved to be able to enjoy it. They had paid for it. He had earned it.

In sum

Lennon's childhood, with some suppressed anger and a sense of being an outsider due to his unconventional family circumstances, could have lead to failure rather than success. As it is, however, his imagination and wildness found an outlet in music, and his mother's sister provided enough stability growing up for him to understand the importance of channeling his efforts into something worthwhile. Fortunately he found music, a creative partner in the form of McCarthy, and belief that there was order and a way forward. The sixties was a time for fun and experimentation, and Lennon was able to capitalize on this as well as channel his artistic talent into something that would bring him success.

Baroness Margaret Hilda Thatcher

Brief

To what aspects of her character and past can we attribute Thatcher's success and failures as a politician?

Culture

A strong sense of patriotism, belief in hard work and personal responsibility coupled with a willingness to challenge the status quo and established ways of operating.

'We shall have to learn again to be one nation, or one day we shall be no nation.'

As a child and young adult Thatcher witnessed the struggles of ordinary people in the inter-war period and WWII and the community's tremendous resilience and resourcefulness in the face of adversity. Her family was heavily involved in the Methodist church, local community and politics, and she would have been exposed from an early age to jingoistic debate and key British values and beliefs identified by Hofstede, leaving lasting impacts on her outlook and behaviors.

Power distance (the British rank as low in this dimension): She had a fundamental belief in equality, contributing to her resolve to break into political circles, at the time predominantly the domain of men and the upper classes. Being accepted at Oxford and subsequently rising up the political ranks, she considered herself living proof that, despite a relatively humble upbringing, given opportunity and hard work, advancement was something everyone could achieve.

She was candid about the benefits of a privileged background, but she was not in awe of it. She judged colleagues and others primarily according to how well they fulfilled their role or how useful they were to her ambitions. This could cause a mixture of upset and dislike amongst those who perhaps felt that their background and position were worthy of more acknowledgment, but also admiration. Even as prime minister she did not baulk from menial tasks, such as darning socks or cooking a simple supper rather than ask junior staff, with whom she was known to be highly courteous and thoughtful, earning her huge respect and loyalty.

Masculinity (the British rank as high in this dimension): Her personal drive and desire to succeed is legendary. At school she worked hard, enjoying debate and putting herself forward for positions of authority, and demonstrated huge persistence in her studies and as a junior MP. She had a highly developed sense of competition from an early age. Some even suggest her marriage to Dennis was largely strategic in that it gave her an easier route into the circles that would enable her to rise up the political ladder.

Her focus was always work rather than family and leisure. She trained and qualified as a barrister while pregnant and a new mother of twins, only later in life admitting to some regret for spending less time with her family. In what many might consider an un-British fashion, rather than adopt a more self-effacing and understated approach she reinforced the belief in equality, particularly prevalent amongst the British educated classes, by making no secret of her self-belief and achievements. She was often criticized for not doing more for women in politics and business but to do so would arguably have weakened her position. As it was, in the male-dominated polite upper-class circles she was intimidating and difficult to oppose. This may have contributed to her latterly developing a greater sense of superiority and infallibility than warranted.

Individualism (Britain ranks amongst the highest on this dimension): Thatcher wholeheartedly applauded individual initiative, the idea that personal fulfillment is happiness and that it is down to each of us to make our way and contribute to society. Her father was particularly influential in this respect in that he was actively involved in politics, the church and community. He taught her by example to stand up for what she believed in and that it is only through action that change can happen. In addition the war years were a time when society exhorted everyone to do their bit and develop independence. Choosing Granville, the town of her birth, for her peerage is indicative of the extreme importance of the role her early years there played in building the character and beliefs that led to her success.

Uncertainty avoidance (low): A low ranking on this dimension indicates that a society has a clear vision of where it wants to go but shows a degree of pragmatism and creativity in how it gets there – the process does not have to be set in stone.

Thatcher urged respect for history and tradition but was unafraid to challenge the current way of doing things. She was impatient with those who were too lazy or reluctant to go back to fundamental principles and chose instead to rely on tried and tested formula. She had a passion for detail, but she did not let herself be hidebound by it. Her approach was rather to analyze situations in the light of the best and widest current information and only then decide what action to take.

Her willingness to take a principled stance on issues of importance, in the face of often great uncertainty and lack of precedent, is one of the aspects of her leadership which has attracted most admiration in her and other British figures such as Winston Churchill, by whom she was deeply influenced.

Indulgence (middle-high): Britain ranks relatively high in terms of indulgence, though this is something not associated with Thatcher, perhaps due to the over-riding influence of her early years. She did not seek gratification in terms of luxury and leisure. She could be extremely frugal and where she was indulgent, for example, in her dress and appearance – something perhaps bolstered by her mother who was a seamstress – it also had a degree of functionality – to create the right impression. Her idea of relaxation was polishing shoes, mending clothes or tidying, and just occasionally listening to opera or a musical and watching a film or thriller on TV. She rarely took time off and was most energized when employed in some task.

In some ways Thatcher came to symbolize a more austere and careworn era from which by the 1990s the younger generation in particular were keen to move on. This was undoubtedly a factor in the fall in her personal popularity and her move toward more lenient and forgiving policies.

Biography

A family that imbued her with a strong sense of moral duty and a heightened sense of ambition and self-worth. Practical experience of hardship in the form of war and poverty and overcoming barriers to senior political circles.

> I owe almost everything to my father. He taught me that you first sort out what you believe in and then apply it. You don't compromise on things that matter.
> Life was not to enjoy ourselves. Life was to work and do things.

When Thatcher came to power Britain's image was tarnished by labor disputes and economic woes. She spoke to a generation with memories of a more unified, respected and dynamic Britain with passion and conviction, successfully instilling the belief that those days could be recreated through personal initiative and responsibility. Abroad she also sought to resurrect perceptions of Britain in earlier times, reveling in her image as 'The Iron Lady' which she felt reflected accurately not only her own resolve but that of the people of Britain when facing adversity.

Margaret Thatcher (née Roberts) was born in 1925 to a strict close-knit Methodist family in the market town of Grantham, Lincolnshire. Her father, a shopkeeper, preacher and alderman influenced her heavily, involving her in his political and community activities from an early age. Thatcher's keen interest in clothes, thriftiness and family duty – she cooked Dennis' breakfast every day – is thought to have come from her mother, a quiet figure. She had an elder sister with whom she corresponded regularly, especially in her late teens and early twenties, who married one of Thatcher's first beaux, at Margaret's instigation.

Thatcher married Dennis, a successful businessman twelve years her senior, in 1951. It was a good match, he being content for her to follow her heart and ambitions. 'What a husband. What a friend'. She was a dutiful if not particularly loving parent, assiduous in attending school meetings and events but only late in life developing a close relationship with her grandchildren.

She was one of the few women at the time to get a scholarship at Somerville College, Oxford, where she said she wished she had been able to say she'd studied at Cheltenham Ladies College. She worked hard to suppress her Lincolnshire accent, some criticizing her for trying to hide her background, while it was likely a practical response to her perceived need to be more readily accepted. She was President of the Oxford University Conservative Association in 1946, the beginning of a long career in politics, an early and perhaps defining influence being Friedrich van Hayek, who condemned economic intervention by government. Additional influences were in all probability her interest in Israel due to the family taking in a Jewish refugee when she was a child and in 1967 a six-week International Visitor Leadership Programme to the United States when she met various politicians and institutions such as the IMF. She first became an MP in 1959 and went on to be Cabinet Minister in 1970 and Prime Minister in 1979.

Intelligence

Clever but not brilliant, analytical brain with strong desire to learn. Overdependence on those with similar thinking styles or able to present arguments in a format which resonated with her, making her at times unreceptive to criticism or other points of view.

> A second-rate brain.
> Do your best and never follow the crowd.

Condemned by one of her Oxford professors as having a 'second-rate brain', in reality Thatcher demonstrated a keen analytical mind powered by a strong need for personal advancement and ambition. Encouraged by her father she did well at school demonstrating enormous academic discipline and interest in learning from a very early age.

Expressed in executive intelligence terms, her greatest strength was in getting a solid, meticulous grasp of situations and using this knowledge to shape policy and strategy – meeting the challenge of a task. As a politician she always prepared meticulously, with a huge capacity for detail that she used to great effect in political argument. This meant that often she came to meetings seemingly with her mind made up, while in reality she enjoyed debate and could be persuaded if a case was argued well or she had developed trust in her interlocutors.

When dealing with people, this same analytical brain, trained her into always seeking the weaknesses in other people's arguments. She was genuinely open to discourse and debate, and willing to adopt new ideas and approaches, but looked for equals in argument. Few had her work ethic or thoroughness, and she was often disappointed. Many found her impatient, dismissive and humorless. She deployed acerbic wit, reportedly the only humor in which she actively engaged, with those she felt were on an equal footing to her. This could cause offence and discomfort, particularly amongst men unused to public humiliation, and lead to many distancing themselves or being intimidated into silence.

This had a deleterious effect on her ability to regulate self. As the years went by, she was forced to rely on fewer and fewer trusted advisors – mostly those who spoke or presented in her language and shared her beliefs – contributing to reduced access to and acceptance of other points of view and so her greater sense of her infallibility.

Personality

Savvy and charming when managing people and situations to meet her aims but with a single-mindedness and extreme conscientiousness that could make her appear unfeeling and unsympathetic to others. In reality her actions were unselfish and underpinned by integrity, compassion and understanding of others:

> Defeat – I do not recognise the meaning of the word.
> You know if you set out to be liked, you would be prepared to compromise on anything, wouldn't you, at any time, and you would achieve nothing.

This quote might suggest that Thatcher was unconcerned by others' opinion of her, which in a sense she was. In her private life she tended to rely on a few close friends and colleagues and by nature she was somewhat of an introvert, often appearing aloof, serious and intense in company. Nonetheless, she was adept at charming and mixing with people and cutting a figure – clearly understanding the importance and political expediency of mixing in the right circles and engaging in debate. 'Personal' did not really come into it, as in her actions and mind she did not separate herself from what she stood for and was prepared to sacrifice popularity to achieve her political aims. Everything else was of secondary importance.

Whether Thatcher did or did not only sleep five hours a night, her reputation as being a tough workaholic, who worked relentlessly and with passion and determination, is perhaps what defines her most clearly in people's minds. She worked on countless redrafts of speeches, was utterly thorough, ordered and disciplined in her approach to everything she did. She set high standards for herself – whether in dress, speeches or being a dutiful wife and mother – and was prepared to be judged on her performance. She sought out others with similar integrity who were selfless and prepared to stand up for what they believed in. She was extremely intolerant of others she considered responsible and yet who failed in their task through lack of dedication or hard work.

Given her tough public persona, her capacity for compassion, loyalty and consideration may come as a surprise to many. She wrote personally to all those who lost relatives in the Falklands War, always showed an interest in the welfare of her Downing Street staff, remembering birthdays and family members and unfailingly supported them if she felt they were in danger of being unfairly treated. Having built and achieved so much based on the image of the Iron Lady, she under-estimated the importance of highlighting her softer, more 'feminine' side.

Dark Side traits

Extremely diligent and conscientious which led her to be demanding of others if she felt that they failed, without reason, to live up to her high standards. In later years developed an unassailable belief in her own views and abilities:

> You turn if you want to. This lady's not for turning.
> Eyes of Stalin/Caligula and voice of Marilyn Monroe.

Thatcher, for many, at home and abroad, was the epitome of a strong, decisive leader. These quotes might suggest that with that power she could be utterly ruthless and focused on a task at the expense of all moral considerations, Machiavellian perhaps. In reality she did not have the win-at-all-costs amoral approach that this term implies. True, she was not adverse to using her womanly charms if beneficial and embraced the image of Battling Maggie – the Iron Lady – when she thought it gave her the profile she needed to get things done, but she was always guided by a strict sense of duty, honesty and service. She had extraordinary self-belief but also belief in the need to act in accordance with what is morally and intellectually defensible.

Far more notable in terms of dark side traits was her extreme conscientiousness and diligence. As highlighted above, ultimately this resulted in her increasing isolation, arrogance and heightened sense of superiority and self-confidence.

Toward the end of her tenure as Prime Minister and beyond she displayed symptoms of the Hubris Syndrome identified by Dr David Owen. The strength of character, conviction and leadership so valued in her early years when Britain was suffering an economic crisis and during the Falklands War led to increasing isolation and contempt for others. Her error came in increasingly thinking that her approach was more informed and sound than alternatives proposed by those around her. Her frequent use of the word 'we' signaled her inability to distinguish between herself and some higher cause. Indeed, toward the end, she branded those who disagreed with her as disloyal both to her and so, in her mind, to the betterment of Britain. Ultimately her tendency to self-refer in the first instance, immunity to criticism and reluctance to acknowledge mistakes and other points of view were her downfall.

Motivation

Highly motivated by achievement orientated toward upholding the beliefs and values instilled in her when growing up, power and influence were a means to an end rather than motivation in themselves:

> These beliefs or values were something that you need to act upon.
> It's not what you've done that counts. It's what you do next.

While highly ambitious from an early age, Thatcher is said to have had an intrinsic disregard for the trappings of power or office. She was frugal in her home life, unconcerned with material possessions or pleasure pursuits, was prepared to take risks and cared very little for what others thought of her, except if it could help her or, conversely, threatened to get in her way.

Her interest was above all action and action orientated not toward personal gratification but toward the fundamental community values and beliefs instilled in her as a child. She was in every sense a conviction politician with power, influence and recognition only important to the extent that they allowed her to get things done, to achieve something worthwhile.

In the end, however, her conviction about how Britain could realize her vision of greatness was not shared by the populace, and nor was her conviction in her unique ability to help the country chart its course toward success. Times had moved on, and her formula of strong leadership and government was rejected in favor of individual effort and achievement, ironically the very values she had sought to promote.

In sum

Thatcher's early influences set her on a course which, coupled with her unassailable self-belief, conscientiousness and sense of duty to the British people, led her to overcome many of the obstacles she faced in politics – primarily male dominance and a perception that the state and organizations should somehow compensate for a lack of individual effort and responsibility.

Her vision of a united and strong Britain, built on the values and beliefs with which she was brought up, was compelling at a time of economic crisis and political disarray. However, in a period of greater prosperity built on the values of personal freedom and initiative that she espoused, the iron resolve for which she was known, and which she exhibited to the exclusion of consensus and debate, ultimately undermined her position.

Mohamed Al-Fayed

Culture and biographical background

Mohamed Al-Fayed was born in Egypt but came to the UK in his mid-thirties and says he considers it home. He speaks fondly of meeting British soldiers stationed in Alexandria as a child, but in more recent years his relationship with the UK has been somewhat fractious and volatile. This could in part be accounted for by two cultural values at the heart of Egyptian society that are at variance with those of his adopted country – attitudes toward authority and the need for belonging. In Egypt there is a far greater tendency to accept ascribed status unquestioningly and to enjoy a reciprocal or at least protective relationship with, primarily family, but also others to whom you show loyalty. In the UK, there is a greater expectation that someone in a senior position has earned their status. Relationships tend to be secondary to getting the job done.

The seemingly disproportionate emphasis Mohamed places on these values could be accounted for by the lack of his family status when he was growing up – his father was a lowly schools inspector and they were by no means affluent. His family was also somewhat difficult. His mother died when he was very young and he had a bad relationship with his father who married someone he disliked. The despair at the breakdown of his own first marriage after just two years was perhaps exacerbated by his own failure to establish a good family life as well as weakening the links with his wife's more successful brothers.

Mohamed has consistently sought to hide aspects of his past that do not conform to these idealized values. He speaks of his own family being happy and loving and a good relationship with his mother even though he was four when she died. He gives Fayed as his place of birth, allowing obvious conclusions to be drawn, when in fact he was originally from Alexandria. The addition of 'Al' to his family soon after leaving Egypt for the first time presumably was also designed to enhance his status. Again consistent with traditional Egyptian values, he highlights 'wisdom' rather than formal learning in his success, claiming his grandfather was a merchant at whose knee he acquired his business acumen.

Now retired, as a boss/manager he was autocratic and expectant of complete loyalty. A wide range of previously favored employees were sacked and punished with 'loss of face', 'face' being an important concept in Arab nations. Their dismissal was often supported by fabricated newspaper stories or accusations in court, most of which proved unfounded. His vendetta against members of the establishment and the royal family could also be seen as frustration caused by his lack of acceptance. His failure, despite two attempts, to be granted a British passport clearly rankles with him and is countered by his acceptance by Scotland where his efforts to support local heritage and the economy have been formally recognized.

Other aspects of his behavior are also more typical of Arab countries: expressing emotions more readily, finding conflicts very threatening and a strong desire to impose a version of truth which is at variance with the facts. While these behaviors and characteristics may not have claimed him the acceptance and status to which he aspired, it is indisputable that his deployment of them, particularly during his early business years, when much of his success derived from his business ventures outside the UK and particularly in the Middle East, served him well.

Intelligence

Fayed's academic achievements are limited. He was a disruptive secondary school student appearing to set little store by formal education, and far more value on experience – his own and that of others, such as his grandfather whom he esteemed. He tends to rely heavily on intuition rather than analysis and to get carried away with particular ideas or details rather than acquire a broad understanding of a situation and get to grips with all the factors that come into play. If they don't fit his version of events or meet his needs, he would tend to dismiss them, grow angry or impatient and move onto other things. When confronted irrevocably with his own mistakes, he tends to try and cover them up, blame others or move on and place his focus elsewhere rather than take effective action to overcome obstacles. This can make him appear unreasonable, impulsive, stubborn and inflexible. His sense of humor is not particularly sophisticated and nor is his vocabulary. It tends to be quite limited and littered with expletives when under stress.

In sum, he does not exhibit many of the executive intelligences to which one normally attributes success, and yet he has over the years achieved considerable fame and fortune. He undoubtedly has a nose for an opportunity, but one senses that his bravado and the mystique surrounding him, a man from a relatively misunderstood but important part of the world, contributed significantly to his prominence in the business world. It is in understanding how to take people in that perhaps his true intelligence lies.

Personality

Fayed is someone who needs to be handled with care as he exhibits several extreme tendencies. His most defining characteristics are his high neuroticism and disagreeableness/toughness, which spill over into dark side behaviors (see below). On the other personality scales, although enjoying a party, or at least being seen in the company of the great and good, many of his pursuits would tend to indicate introversion. He rarely invites people to his home, spends time at his Scottish estate or on his yacht and works hard to present a public persona, rather than actually let someone in. His true character, however, emerges particularly at times of stress, again as discussed below. In terms of conscientiousness or laissez-faire, he is highly driven but does not necessarily stick with a project and certainly not to the rules unless they suit his purpose.

Dark Side traits

Fayed is a dangerous cocktail of dark side traits. He is argumentative and vigilant with extreme sensitivity to perceived affronts. He is always on the alert for disloyalty and reacts viciously if he feels that in some way he has been wronged or an employee or associate has failed him. He frequently lashes out, denigrating others and making false accusations that have on occasions resulted in court cases and ostracism. Classic examples were his long-running feud with Tiny Rowland. His statements regarding the British establishment (who have refused him a passport) and the British royal family who, having withdrawn their patronage of Harrods and failure to acknowledge Dodi and Diana's relationship, suggest he did not feel he was treated with due appreciation or respect. To some extent his extreme reaction to rejection might be attributed to the fact that so much of his early success depended on the maintenance of an image that has little basis in fact.

The second most notable dark side trait he exhibits is being excitable and mercurial. As described above, he can react violently and employees are often nervous around him, and with good reason. Someone can rapidly fall from grace. Sensitive to criticism and with a keen sense of entitlement, a strong need to feel in control and be liked, any challenge to his self-perception and ambition can elicit a violent or emotional response. This was the case very early on when he and his first wife were divorced, and his association with the family that gave him the status and opportunity he lacked through his own background was under threat. He was apparently distraught.

In public and private he often rants and makes wild accusations designed to bolster his position and authority but which over the years have in fact eroded it. In this sense, he also demonstrates a tendency to be colorful and dramatic. He can be entertaining, flirtatious and the life and soul of the party, a showman, but gets bored and loses interest once the party is over or a project is underway. He strives for attention, praise and gratitude, getting the limelight no matter how – by dressing up as a pharaoh, buying friendship through flattery and generosity and courting controversy in the media.

His most defining trait is Machiavellianism. At various junctures over his career, he has managed to manipulate and deceive others. Early on he posed as a Kuwaiti sheikh to develop business in Haiti and throughout has been intensely aware of the importance of appearances, whether cultivated by immaculate dress, his Finnish model wife, exquisitely furnished offices or photographs with celebrities. Early on, he was able to capitalize on the sense of opportunity presented by the oil-rich Gulf States, claiming close associations with its rulers and taking in investors unfamiliar with the region. His abuse of these friendships often led to a total breakdown in relations with those who had helped him early on. Usually by then, however, he had moved on, managing to convince others of his credentials and achievements. It is doubtful that he would be able to do so in this era of open information despite the guile and cunning that has served him so well. Indeed, much of his fall from grace has come about from greater scrutiny of his past.

For many years he was able to maintain the fiction and through his skill in identifying opportunities and clever manipulation of people and facts enjoy considerable success. He has amassed a wealth of over a billion dollars and wielded huge power – whether through his acquisitions – Harrods, Fulham Football Club, his Scottish estate – or through attracting media attention. By any measure his achievements have been remarkable. Hubris is perhaps not an unexpected consequence.

Motivation

As with most of us, several motivators can be attributed to Fayed. Chief amongst them is the need for recognition and vanity. He has set up a charitable foundation which bears his family name and upholds one of the key tenets of Islam – philanthropy – and expresses other contributions in terms of loyalty – a donation to Great Ormond Street Hospital recognition of the role its doctors played in saving Dodi's life – or fulfillment of some great destiny, ordained by God. At one stage he even referred to Harrods as 'Mecca'.

Even now in semi-retirement he courts publicity, stating, for example, that he will donate a 'statue of liberty', the figure of Scota, the daughter of an Egyptian pharaoh, should Scotland vote for independence. His enduring affection for Scotland is doubtless fed by their acknowledgment of his contribution to its development in the form of granting him 'Freedom of the Highlands' in 2002. This and many of his statements smack of a need for acceptance and inclusiveness of this sort. When he has taken on the British establishment he has repeatedly expressed the belief that the British people understand him and are on his side. Rejection is taken hard and tends to provoke a violent reaction and desperate search for acceptance elsewhere.

Power and influence are also important. He lives an ostentatiously luxurious lifestyle and often portrays himself as someone who has earned his success and position by 'rising to the challenge' and 'saving the day'. On his website he suggests that he almost single-handedly built Dubai, saved the British economy in the 1970s and is ready to be Scotland's prime minister at any moment. He bought Fulham FC with the express goal of taking it into the first division (which he did). He highlights his personal vision and role in high-profile projects such as the restoration of the Ritz in Paris and the French villa used by Edward and Mrs Simpson for prosperity. Again, he expresses frustration at the lack of recognition.

He often attaches monetary value to his achievements – perhaps a hangover from his poor childhood. In itself, however, it does not appear to have been a motivator, rather a useful or strategic indicator of power, influence and success. Similarly, although he likes to give the impression of a *bon viveur*, he reportedly clashed repeatedly with Dodi over his playboy lifestyle and his lack of serious achievement, indicating that he himself did not consider this a worthy pursuit in itself.

In sum

Fayed has achieved phenomenal business success, which he would have us believe is due to innate entrepreneurism and greatness. In reality it is doubtful that he could achieve similar success in this day and age. Where he excelled was at portraying himself as something he was not, thereby gaining the trust and business of those who knew no better and were reliant on someone to provide access to unfamiliar markets and networks. In later years, unable to obscure his background and sustain some of the fabrications, coupled with his own loss of reality, bolstered by many years of success, his position and businesses have diminished in importance. Perhaps, had he not taken on the high-profile symbol of Harrods or felt such a strong need to get back at those who rejected him or threatened to upset his image of himself, he would have sustained the myth that his ability was what got him where he was. Perhaps indeed in earlier years, he was more sane and savvy. The fact is that now, he is largely discredited and unable to gain the acceptance that, since childhood, has been a major motivating force.

Steve Jobs – former CEO and creator of one of the most successful IT companies of the twentieth and twenty-first centuries.

Cultural background

Jobs's worldwide influence in terms of technology products and personality is beyond question, as is the contention that few, if any, countries other than the United States, could have incubated such success.

The United States is the most individualistic country in the world, meaning, amongst other things, that people are judged on merit, initiative and expected to be self-reliant. It also ranks low on power distance. Communications are informal, direct and participative. It scores high on masculinity – toughness is admired and competition – internal or external – sought out and taken head-on. It also allows innovation and holds freedom of expression as one of its fundamental principles.

Jobs' personal, visionary and at times brash and abrasive style on stage was not unlike that of many other American CEOs, albeit more extreme. Nor, sadly, are some of his more aggressive management practices.

He had a tough, best-in-field, 'can-do' attitude and had high expectations of individual employees, often chastising publicly and viciously those who gave up or highlighted problems rather than solutions. He set similar standards for himself, responding to his removal from the board of Apple in 1986 by raising capital to form new technological ventures (NeXT and Pixar). He integrated the ideas he developed at NeXT when he took back the reigns of Apple a decade later. He did not look back but moved forward and expected everyone else to do the same.

On a more personal level, a friend said Jobs hated the idea that his real parents did not want him. Jobs remembered his adoptive parents empathetically dismissing the idea, saying slowly and directly that they picked him because he was special, a notion that he obviously cherished.

The United States is also the country of ideas and innovation, and Jobs marketed his company on this basis, emphasizing that he did not have to look outside, do market research to find these. His products evolved from his own needs and aspirations. He intuitively understood the attraction of the fresh and new, particularly to Americans such as him.

Biography

Jobs was born in 1954 in California. His biological parents were of Syrian (father) and American/German (mother) origins. His American-born adoptive parents, Steve and Clara Jobs, brought him up from a very early age. He said he considered them '1000 per cent his parents'. He did track down his mother and establish a close relationship with his younger biological sister, but having researched his father he expressed the desire not to get to know him.

Jobs was brought up in humble but loving surroundings. His father was a mechanic and carpenter and mother did accounts. Neither had gone on to higher education, but both spent time with him to encourage his learning. His mother taught him to read before he went to school and his father how to work with his hands by tinkering with machinery in the garage.

Jobs had a mixed experience at school. He was a prankster and socially awkward. Fights were a daily occurrence, and he was often bullied. He insisted his parents put him in a different school and when they resisted he told them he would quit going. His parents found the best school and scraped together enough money to move house so they could live in a 'nicer' district. He nonetheless continued to resist authority and was often in trouble. Putting an explosive under a teacher's chair and printing fake posters for the school were standard behaviors for the young Jobs. His parents later also paid for him to attend expensive Reed College, from which he dropped out, bored, within a year.

In his late teens he travelled to India with a friend. The trip had a profound influence on him, sparking, for example, his interest in different religions (he maintained a life-long appreciation of Zen Buddhism) and also a more superficial one, leading him to alter his dress and appearance. He considered entering a retreat and around that time also experimented with LSD. In later photographs he showed a degree of conformity in dress, but he was never afraid of taking his own path. He was vegetarian, followed various diets and tried to treat his pancreatic cancer, which was first diagnosed in 2003, through all sorts of therapies, including psychics. He later said he regretted his delay in getting conventional treatment.

He had a daughter with a girlfriend in his early twenties, although initially denied paternity (claiming he was sterile) and for some years gave limited financial support. He later acknowledged her and they were reconciled. He married in the 1990s and had a further two daughters and son.

Intelligence – high, divergent thinker

At an early age Jobs' teachers tested him and, realizing he was bright, suggested he went up two grades. His parents resisted and in the end he went up one (which he said was the right decision). When undisciplined in his learning and disruptive, his parents did not hold him to account; they blamed the teachers instead. He speaks of a fourth grade teacher as somewhat of a saint, bribing him to study and leading him to understand that learning could be interesting. On the whole he continued to be an unapplied student, dropping out of all but calligraphy courses at Reed.

Jobs said he always thought of himself as a humanities person and that he had 'read something that one of my heroes Edwin Land of Polaroid, said about the importance of people who could stand at the intersection of humanities and sciences, and I decided that's what I wanted to do.' He had always shown a disregard for crystallized intelligence, and was far more interested in possibilities. An oft-published picture of Jobs shows him staring at the camera and his business partner at the papers on his desk. He was a classic divergent thinker who surrounded himself with others able to contribute the technical expertise they required to come to fruition.

Personality – chameleon

Jobs was so extreme in so many ways, that in a sense it is difficult to categorize him according to standard personality dimensions. At times he seemed to handle stress well and productively, as when he was ousted from Apple in the 1980s. At other times he was known to be moody, to rant and lash out in anger. He at times thrust himself forward and sought stimulation, but was also attracted to contemplation and Buddhism and withdrawal from the world. He could be both charming and a bully, inspirational and demotivating, seemed to seek new ideas but yet to reject them out of hand. He was known as being hard working and dogged, but then others say that they had never met anyone who changed their mind as frequently as he.

Dark Side traits

There seems evidence that Jobs had a great number of Dark Side traits. First he seemed to be mercurial and unpredictable, blowing hot and cold. He also seemed highly imaginative and creative, which is often very difficult to deal with. He also manifested considerable arrogance and mischievousness.

When looking down the list of behaviors associated with Dark Side traits, Jobs also seems to defy easy categorization (as indeed he did in life). At various times he exhibited behaviors characteristic of most, and these seem to have had both positive and negative consequences. As evinced by his success, at least in a business profit and loss sense, the pluses must have outweighed the minuses. Here we highlight the most significant.

Imaginative and idiosyncratic – well documented. His fascination for Indian philosophy is good evidence for this. His manner and personal life-style also showed some eccentricities. He bought large houses and often left them virtually unfurnished.

Another eccentricity was his perfectionism, caring about the precise shade of color on the early Macintosh PC: The Pantone company, which Apple used to specify colors for its plastic, had more than 2000 shades of beige. 'None of them were good enough for Steve', Mike Scott marveled. 'He wanted to create a different shade, and I had to stop him.' When the time came to tweak the design of the case, Jobs spent days agonizing over just how rounded the corners should be. 'I didn't care how rounded they were', said Scott, 'I just wanted it decided.' His ideas and insistence on small, to others insignificant details were the foundation of much of Apple's success.

Argumentative and vigilant – Quoted as saying 'I'm willing to go thermonuclear war on this' and 'I will spend my last dying breath if I need to, and I will spend every penny of Apple's $40 billion in the bank, to right this wrong', he was reacting to what he saw as a betrayal of trust and friendship on the part of Google employees with whom he had earlier collaborated and whom he had mentored. He was always very secretive and suspicious of others. In this case, and on other occasions, his reactions were extreme, but in all probability his suspicious and caution nature protected Apple from many IP violations, something he felt was one of the greatest threats to the United States.

Solitary and reserved – he showed at times a callous disregard for others' feelings in his private life – toward his long-time girlfriend and mother of his first child, and toward the many employees who would work long and late to bring his ideas to fruition, only to be criticized and their efforts dismissed. This dispassionate approach also enabled him to remain focused and keep going against all odds. 'If it was three in the morning and Steve had a thought or a question or complaint, he picked up the phone and called, right then. The concept of "that can wait until the morning" did not apply.'

Excitable and mercurial – his colleagues never knew what to expect – avoided him in the corridors in case his attention moved on and they were no longer required. In good moods he could inspire, in others he could bring about despair.

Motivation – achievement, power and influence, risk and excitement and beliefs and creeds

For the last nearly 10 years of his life, Jobs labored on, often in poor health and under the shadow of an early death. Despite his vast wealth and achievements he chose to continue at the head of Apple until his cancer finally took hold and he was forced to acknowledge that remaining would only damage the company he had built.

You have to wonder how many people would have remained at the helm when they had so little time and so little to prove. Fundamentally, he seems to have been motivated by the sheer challenge and excitement of his ideas, the desire to see them converted into products that validated his belief that how we use technology has a profound and positive impact on our lives. He achieved all this and, along the way, ensured that the success was always associated with him. According to his sister his final words were 'oh wow, oh wow, oh wow. It seems that sense of excitement never left him.'

In sum

Jobs is one of the most talked-about business 'personalities' of all times and with just cause. His commercial judgment, vision and drive brought huge success to Apple and transformed the way the world uses technology.

As many leaders, however, his success eclipses less attractive aspects of his character – a Dark Side. Many found him irascible, unfeeling and an unreasonable manager, and at times that his desire to control may have led him to be immoral. People were both in awe and in fear of him. But while some may not admire his methods, few do not admire his success.

Edward Snowden – A former US Government IT employee and contractor who became a whistle-blower at the age of 28, causing major and continuing upset at home and amongst its allies.

Culture

Snowden was born to American parents and lived the first 10 years of his life in North Carolina, thereafter moving to Maryland. He did not travel outside the United States until his early twenties, when he lived in Switzerland (which he disliked), Japan and Hawaii. However, his interest in Japan predates that time. A solitary teenager, he studied Japanese, became interested in anime and manga and spent much of his time playing online martial arts games.

Both Snowden's parents (and later his elder sister) worked in government service. In Maryland there is also a high level of government employment amongst the local community, most notably in the National Security Agency (NSA). On leaving school in 2004 he enrolled in the army (though was dismissed after four months – he says he broke both his legs in a training exercise) and later worked for a number of government contractors.

Relating to Hofstede's power distance and individualism dimensions, American citizens tend to set great store by the Constitution and the rights and freedoms it guarantees, holding dear the principle of 'liberty and justice for all'. It is also a country where people are not afraid to hold and speak out about strong beliefs.

Snowden's belief in what America and the American government stand for was in all likelihood strengthened by his family's record of government service, the veil of secrecy and importance surrounding the institutions in which the Maryland community worked. He also lived through an era of post 9/11 rhetoric, promoting an uncharacteristic concern for security in a country which ranks low on uncertainty avoidance. The government repeatedly assured the people of its competence in 'defeating' the threat.

On joining the army he says he was shocked that many army cadets seemed more interested in killing Arabs than defending freedom. A further catalyst for his disillusionment was that the CIA should use slightly underhand methods to get a Swiss banker onside (taking advantage of a traffic incident when he was drunk). Shortly after he said he was hugely disappointed that Obama did not change the nature of the NSA in his second term. All this suggests an idealistic naivety that could be considered typical of someone of his age. (Several international surveys show that his actions have far more support amongst the younger than older generation.)

As previously noted, he spent much of his youth playing online martial arts games in a virtual world. He says 'I grew up in the internet', referring to himself its 'son'. An interesting but unprovable theory is that his online habits might also have been a major influence on his values and behaviors. It appears to have given him a sense of identity and community. Both these were lacking in his normal life. His teachers and peers at school say he was unremarkable, many in fact did not remember him. When speaking of the Internet he expressed some wonder that he had come to 'embody it in this unusual almost avatar manner'.

In terms of behaviors, clearly his IT expertise has given him the access to the information he holds, but it also seems to have shaped his behaviors. Both his delay in going public with the information and choice initially to remain anonymous when talking, making his revelations to *the Guardian* journalist, could be seen as a period of adjustment from the isolated virtual world where he had come to feel more at home. As discussed below, however, we believe that he displays arrogance, enjoying being able to hide behind an image he chooses to project whilst simultaneously enjoying recognition and praise. This would also explain his decision to reveal his identity, even though he said he knew he would be persecuted for the rest of his life.

The language he uses also smacks of aggression. 'I am living proof that an individual can go head to head against the most powerful adversaries and the most powerful intelligence agencies around the world and win.' Masculinity is a dimension on which the United States scores highly, but Japan the highest in the world. It places a high value on toughness and competition, evidenced in the Japanese virtual games to which Snowden showed an obsession as a young adult.

Biography

Snowden was born in 1983 and lived with his parents, who, having married young, stayed together for over 20 years, divorcing in 2001. Lonnie Snowden (his father) was an officer in the US Coast Guard, and his mother is a clerk at the US District Court in Maryland. His father remarried and moved away. By all accounts they are decent people. His father has visited his son in Russia and, although initially stunned by his action, is now broadly supportive; he says that he would like him to stop divulging secrets so he can return to the United States. His mother, who continued to deliver him groceries weekly when he first moved out of home, is described as quiet, of high integrity and has made no comment to the press.

Those who remember Snowden as a teenager describe him as skinny, a 'very nerdy kid/guy with big glasses' and a 'computer whiz-kid'. His closest relationships seemed to be online. He appeared regularly on forums and websites to discuss games, technology, anime, manga and was a prolific contributor to technology blog Ars Technica. Early on he worked for the website of Ryuhana Press which sold anime art. In his forum entries on Ars Technica, Snowden frequently spoke in favor of Hong Kong and its attitude toward free speech and policies. Snowden was a strong supporter of the Electronic Frontier Foundation and the Tor Project, wearing their hooded jumpers and displaying stickers on his laptop.

Snowden was living with his girlfriend (Lindsay Mills) a pole-dancer in Hawaii at the time of the leaks (2013). Reports from friends, family and Lindsay's blog posts suggest that they were in a close and stable relationship, looking to get engaged in the near future. From sections of Mills' blog that have remained since it was closed down, it appears that Mills was surprised by Snowden's disappearance and had no inclination of what he was going to do. Neighbors describe them as a polite but reserved couple socially.

In terms of employment after work at Ryuhana Press and continuing his studies, he spent four months in the army and worked as a security guard at a public university – the Centre for Advanced Study of Languages – before holding a variety of government IT posts. He moved to Geneva to work for the CIA in 2007, and later Dell in Japan and for Booz Allen, a government contractor, in Hawaii, a post from which he was sacked following his revelations. During his time in Geneva a colleague said he appeared to have a crisis of conscience. Snowden claims to have raised his concerns at the time with superiors (although there is no record). He resigned from the CIA in 2009.

He made his revelations in Hong Kong and, having spent a short period there, his American passport was revoked and he was granted temporary residence in Russia from where he continues to seek political asylum in various countries.

Intelligence – moderately high, analytical brain

Snowden describes himself as being 'no stellar student'. He never stood out academically and dropped out of high school. His father points out that this was due to illness and that he went on to attain his General Educational Development (which in the United States and Canada certifies a high-school level of education). His family's attitude toward learning is unknown, but Snowden has developed and pursued various interests independently, including Japanese language and culture, Mandarin (in which he claims to have attained a basic level) and more recently Russian and Russian literature. He has at times given a false account of his academic achievements, saying he studied at Maryland College, the University of Liverpool and John Hopkins University. The latter has no enrolment record and, while the others state that they do, he did not complete his studies.

He is described as smart, articulate and geeky. His ability in the field of IT and computer programming is proven, early examples being his success in programming new keyboard moves into computer games. Later he obtained a series of well-paid IT jobs, always impressing supervisors with his technical expertise.

He is described by a former colleague as introspective (sometimes prone to brood) and highly analytical, someone who would have carefully studied the consequences of his actions, calculating the fall-out long before he acted. Snowden's father's describes him as 'a deep thinker' and a 'sensitive caring young man'.

Personality – ambivert with some indicators of disagreeableness and extraversion

Snowden demonstrates clear concern that someone could be watching his every move, and acts accordingly. He first showed concerns about his online security by posting questions to fellow bloggers in 2003. Glenn Greenwald of *the Guardian* reported that when Snowden entered passwords onto his laptop, he would put a red hood over his head and the laptop and got them to agree to put their mobile phones outside the room or in the fridge. He does not, however seem paranoiac by nature.

Greenwald, who first interviewed him in Hong Kong, says that he appears in control, shows a mature approach, and arranges and conducts meetings in a calm and disciplined manner. As Snowden said, 'I have been a spy most of my adult life.' Arguably these are sensible precautions, given what he knows about how the Internet and security forces work and more recently his desire to provide information and remain at liberty. If he were high on neuroticism he would likely panic and worry excessively. We do not find evidence in his personal life or relationships of nervousness, distrustfulness or unfounded fears, suggesting that these concerns might have been acquired. We judge him to be stable.

Being suspicious and skeptical about others' motives are indicators that someone is disagreeable, and though there might be some justification for this, we feel there is some evidence to suggest he tends toward agreeableness.

People's reactions to Snowden are mixed, although often colored by their own views on his political actions. He appears at once both charming and shrewd, outspoken and complicated.

He portrays himself as a 'social hero' who has martyred himself for the sake of the people of America with no self-interest. At the same time, however, he almost seems to work too hard to prove that he is not self-centered. He says his biggest regret is the impact of his actions on others – family, friends of colleagues and those whose names he could have revealed. There is little real evidence that he has taken them into account. He did not warn his girlfriend of his intentions, although she had only moved to Hawaii to be with him shortly beforehand, and left her and his family completely shocked and bemused by his departure. He has ultimately left the decision of what is published to members of the media. He expresses the hope that they are responsible, thereby exerting pressure while to a degree exonerating himself. It seems he calculated that he could bypass the Espionage Act in this way, as it could not be said that he has ever sold the information to an enemy, but rather freely gave it to his own people.

Every response he gives in interviews is very carefully thought out, every action meticulously executed, and he has chosen the words to perfectly represent what he wants to portray. In that sense he is very conscientious, aware of and deliberate in his actions. In relation to his chosen ends, he can indeed be said to be conscientious. Whether this is a more general character trait, however, is less certain. Snowden's childhood and early career are speckled with unfinished courses, tasks, and commitments. To commit to so many things and never finish them displays a tremendous lack of conscientiousness and willingness to see something through. Furthermore, low consciousness is linked with behaviors such as counterproductive-work behavior and criminal activity.

This analytical and controlled approach might give the impression that Snowden is somewhat introvert. In fact, early online posts suggest that he is not, if anything tending toward extraversion. There are photos of him fooling around with his trousers down, looking calmly and confidently directly at the camera. There are posts boasting of 'liking Japanese, girls, my girlish figure that attracts girls and I like my lamer friends'. He also boasts of sexual marathons from sunrise to sunset. After his recent engaging and confident TED discussion, you see him confidently staring out from a series of 'selfies' with fans.

Dark Side traits – arrogant/self-confident and Machiavellian

'I really am a nice guy … You see, I act arrogant and cruel because I was not hugged enough as a child, and because the public education system turned it's (sic) wretched, spiked back on me.'

The main symptoms of Snowden's Dark Sides are an overwhelming sense of grandiosity, moral high ground, charm, yet paranoia. When young he faced a series of failures – at school and then in failing to get into the Special Forces.

He shows considerable vanity. In early online posts he boasts about his sexual prowess and his ability as an IT expert with few formal qualifications to get well-paid jobs and live 'in paradise' (though the pay was not as high as he implied). These early tendencies seem to have been fed by the ease with which he found employment (despite, as he points out, having few formal qualifications) and was given greater responsibilities on the basis of his IT skills. He was in an environment which few could share – given top priority access to highly secret and confidential material.

This provided him not only with the means but also the 'mission' which he sees himself as having fulfilled by making the government's monitoring activities public.

Some say he has adopted the persona of the unwilling social hero. His interviews are littered with references to higher goals with which he associates himself. He talks of bringing justice and equality to the American people and the world. He has enlightened and freed the world of something that it did not want nor ask for. He presents himself as an example that 'no matter how embedded someone is within their government, how faithful they are … they can still learn.' He first made contact with journalists using the name 'Verax' which translates from Latin as the 'truth teller'. And we have already mentioned his wonder at coming to embody the Internet. He is the one to bring them that learning.

He uses emotionally charged language and gestures to describe his goals. He points and chops with his hands, indicating a sense of authority. He asks 'what I can do for the American people' to protect the 'basic liberties for people around the world' – then talks of the lack of privacy representing an 'existential threat to democracy' resulting in 'no room for intellectual exploration and creativity'. The language highlights his personal achievements. He is fighting the 'Architecture of Oppression' – and yet he seems to say, look at me, I am still holding the enemy to account.

Despite consistently saying he is an 'ordinary American', that he is 'no hero' and that it is the message that matters, that having handed over the documents, others can do his work, he still keeps in the limelight and graciously accepts awards on behalf of the principles he upholds. His suggestion that he is a reluctant leader does not ring true. 'I had been looking around for a leader but I realized that leadership is about being the first to act.' Effectively in saying this he is labelling himself a worthy leader. No-one else rose to the challenge.

All this suggests an exaggerated sense of public service and moral high ground. His sensitivity to any erosion of that view is illustrated by his current attitude.

By any measure he is in a tough situation and yet during a period of great uncertainty it matters to him that he maintains at all costs his own sense of achievement and self-worth. In response to an interview question regarding his feelings toward his political exile, Snowden responded saying: 'I have already won.' On another occasion he enhances his persona as selfless: 'The only thing I fear is the harmful affects on my family, who I won't be able to help any more. That's what keeps me up at night.'

He is far more comfortable being in control and able to maintain this image of himself. In another recent interview he shows reluctance to talk about his time in the Special Forces. Whilst he is loquacious with regard to the nobility of the service (and his associative nobility through his application to join them), he is reserved, reluctant and emotionless when discussing his time there; the interviewer eventually squeezes out an answer from him which is short and blunt in comparison with the rest of his dialogue. Snowden apparently does not react well to being questioned on or considering past events where he has been less successful.

He also has a tendency to manipulate and present the truth as he would like to see it and be seen. This is the Dark Side trait of Machiavellianism and can be seen in his mannerisms, speech and actions.

He appears calm and somewhat suave or debonair with an easy smile. His speech is eloquent, articulate, seemingly well rehearsed and delivered with confidence. In an interview he calmly details how authorities within the United States have disclosed they would like to see him dead, something he seems to brush off with guile and a smile. 'There are significant threats, but I sleep very well … I'm still alive and I don't lose sleep.'

We have made previous reference to how all his actions appear cunning and painstakingly planned. He chose to dictate what he knows to journalists whom he carefully researched to clarify their willingness to speak out (although he over-estimated *the Guardian* journalist's expertise in decryption). Early on he justified his refusal to return to the United States by criticizing the US system saying he would be denied an open trial. His concerns may be justified, but having no alternative but to return he would use the opportunity to enhance his status as a martyr and rally against the forces he says act against freedom and the American people.

He frequently implies that he cannot control the forces against him and yet is also at pains to show that he does. His cultivated hero status means that many are willing to act on his behalf, and he gives a sense of being a puppeteer

242 *Revealed*

behind the scenes. While other journalists are awarded, he is present. While saying that he holds no files on his computer, when it was suggested that he could have given the identities of US informants to Russia, he says with steely eye 'That door is always open.' A thinly veiled threat which it is hard to interpret as being in the public good, though he would hastily dismiss the idea that he would 'cash in'. He manipulates to achieve his ends, and it is not at all apparent that the public good is at the forefront of his mind.

Motivation – recognition and vanity, power and influence (creed and beliefs and risk and excitement)

Snowden cites a series of incidents that led him to become a whistle-blower, his disaffection with the government and security services on 'moral' grounds being the underlying cause.

When speaking of his decision he also frequently mentions the fear of reprisals that prevent others in government service from speaking up. He also says that his greatest fear is that others 'won't be willing to take the risks necessary to stand up and fight to change things to force their representatives to actually take a stand in their interests'.

Such exchanges could be taken at their face value. Few work colleagues are willing to be interviewed about Snowden or his work, which could indicate fear. People also tend to take the easier path and don't choose to translate their beliefs into action.

They could also be used to back up the contention that Snowden must be strongly motivated to break the veil of silence for his beliefs in freedom, privacy and democracy. Or that he is motivated by recognition and vanity, relishing the power and influence his super-hero status gives him over government and the security services. Or that he just enjoys the risk and excitement of it all.

Snowden professes he has no interest in being a hero and emphasizes that it is what he stands for that matters. However, it is hard to explain his rise from 'skinny nerd' at school with minimal qualifications other than through his own self-belief and sense of self-importance. True, he clearly had computer skills that made him stand out, but most of those who do remain behind a screen, seemingly content in their small world. In reality he will have a mix of motivations but, given his vanity and Machiavellian tendencies, we tend to think that his actions are not as risky or self-less as he would like to have us believe.

In sum

We believe that the same analytical intelligence that made him an 'IT genius' also enabled Snowden to plan an escape from a controlled environment which did not suit his personality and aspirations, to a world in which he could take control.

He has manipulated aspects of the truth in his own past and, despite seeking to give the opposite impression and portray his actions as conceived and executed for the public/America's/the world's good, we also believe that his regard and concern for others is secondary to his regard for himself. Now holed up in Russia, hardly known for its civil liberties, he claims he has won the battle and to be happy to sit back and others take control. Simultaneously, however, he keeps in the public eye and rigs things up so he and his interests remain intact.

Annex 1

RPP Research Questionnaire

We recommend that this be completed by the researcher having read Chapter 8 – Remote Personality Profiling. This chapter provides further guidance and explanations.

National culture

Power/distance:

- Does the subject openly challenge authority?
- How do they react when challenged by others in subordinate roles?
- Do they favour clear lines of responsibility?

Individual/collective:

- Does the subject exhibit a concern for loss of face and giving face to others?
- Would they feel comfortable giving preference to a family member seeking employment?
- Do they exhibit loyalty to particular in-groups or rather choose friends more on the basis of common interest and compatibility?

Masculine/feminine:

- Does the subject set clear-cut targets and enjoy competition?
- How do they resolve conflict – through assertive or conciliatory methods?
- Do they express sympathy for the underdog and try to protect them or rather respect the strong leader?

Uncertainty avoidance:

- Describe how the subject plans their day/week? Do they keep a detailed diary and keep slavishly to it, or do they rely on memory and have a relaxed attitude to appointments?

- Would they express their emotions more or less openly?
- Would they give their support to the recognized expert or the generalist who can cope under all circumstances?

Pragmatism:

- Does the subject like to save and invest for the future?
- Do they adapt well to new circumstances?
- Are they comfortable with not being able to explain everything and not always knowing the truth?

Indulgence/restraint:

- Does the subject seek enjoyment without worrying too much about appearances?

Time:

- Does the subject show a preoccupation with time, not liking to be late, 'living fast' and seem driven to complete tasks and get on?
- Do they make a clear distinction between work and play?
- How do they view the past, present and future? Which appears the most important to them?

Biography

Family and early years:
Basic biographical details:

- What was the subject's date and place of birth?
- Did they have any major moves before the age of 15?
- Could they in any way be considered out of the ordinary in terms of physical appearance or on the basis of sex/sexuality?

Parents:

- Were the subject's parents close/separated/divorced?
- What was their parenting style – tough, loving, absent?
- Did someone else assume the role of carer?

Social status:

- Does the subject come from a wealthy or poor background?
- Did they share a bedroom?
- Were or could they be considered as being from a minority? If so, which?

Parental approach to learning:

- Are the subject's parents intellectually strong and did they provide an intellectually stimulating environment during childhood?

Siblings:

- How old and what gender are the subject's siblings?
- What is their relationship with them like?

Misfortunes:

- Did the subject suffer any major misfortunes or traumas in early childhood (up to the age of say 15)? This can include parental loss, messy divorce, witnessing a horrid death in war or closer to home, sexual abuse.
- Did illness affect them in any way?

Emotional and practical support:

- Did the subject have supportive friends and family or others around them?
- Who were the most significant/influential people in their early lives?
- Did they feel in any other way deprived?

Education:

- What kind of school did the subject attend?
- Were their teachers competent and supportive?
- Were they successful in their studies?

Social:

- Was the subject brought up in a rich social environment with many friends from culturally or socially different backgrounds?
- Did they travel a lot?

Later life:
Education:

- What topics and disciplines did the subject study at higher level and where?
- Did they do post-graduate studies?
- Have they undertaken any other personal development activities?

Work:

- What were the subject's first jobs?
- Did they work in a family firm or for other known individuals?
- Have they changed job frequently?
- Have they had supportive bosses and colleagues?
- Have they had any bad experiences at work?

Experiences:

- Has the subject undergone any major trauma, illness or unusual or difficult experience and, if so, how did they cope?

• Have they lived or worked abroad on a short or long-term basis? If so, how well did they settle?

Own family:

- Is the subject single/married/have a partner?
- Are they divorced?
- Do they have children?
- Are they a hands-on parent?

Interests:

- How does the subject spend their leisure time/holidays?
- Are they members of clubs/associations?
- Do they read a lot?

Intelligence

General intelligence:

- Does the subject spend their spare time in intellectually challenging and knowledge-enhancing pursuits such as reading, chess or bridge?
- Are they articulate and do they use a wide vocabulary?
- Are they quick to solve problems and able to see others' points of view?
- Do they approach problems logically or perhaps glide over the detail and rely more on their powers of persuasion?
- Do they tend to put off decision-making and seem reluctant to commit?
- Are they witty?
- Do they often make mistakes?
- Do they like to be challenged in argument?
- Are they comfortable dealing with large volumes of information?
- Does the subject listen to and take account of others when reaching decisions?

Thinking style:

- Would others generally describe the subject as creative?
- Do they enjoy brainstorming?
- Do they base arguments on facts or ideas?
- Are they comfortable speaking off the cuff or do they tend to structure meetings/presentations?
- Do they show an interest in systems, collecting or classifying data?
- Do they have any repetitive or obsessive tendencies?
- Do they express feelings openly?
- Do they have many or few close/intimate friends?
- Are they concerned with others' feelings?

Learning quotient:

- To what extent did the subject's family support their learning?
- Did they enjoy school and do well relative to their peers?
- Have they studied outside their professional field?
- Do they appear confident in their abilities?
- Are they naturally inquisitive?

Personality

Neurotic – Stable:

- How does the subject respond to pressure?
- Are they anxious, irritable, calm, even-tempered?
- How do they respond to the consequences of their own negative actions – e.g. giving a bad annual report, sacking someone?
- Do they display an absence of regret or suffering?
- Are they resilient and optimistic?
- Are they prone to depression or many minor illnesses?

Extravert – Introvert:

- Where does the subject choose to spend their leisure time?
- Do they often invite people to their home?
- How do they react when faced with the prospect of going to a large party where they know few people?
- Do they leave their office door open for any visitors/sit in a corner of an open plan office with their back to others?
- How do they interact with other people?
- How do they respond to other people's moods?
- Are they active users of social media?
- Do they trade accuracy for speed?
- How well do they listen to others?

Agreeable – Tough:

- Is the subject friendly and welcoming?
- Were they popular as a child and do they retain friends easily?
- Describe how they approach conflict. Do they put store on maintaining harmony?
- Are they cooperative or competitive?
- Are they considered courteous and to have good old-fashioned manners and charm?
- Do they tend to spare people's feelings or tell it the way it is?
- Are they able to confront poor performance?

Conscientious – Spontaneous:

- Does the subject have a reputation for being reliable and hard-working?
- Are they usually well-organized and willing to put in time for success?
- What is their attitude to organizational/societal rules?
- What value do they put on doing a good job?
- To what extent do they work alone or with others?
- Are they impulsive?
- Did they get in trouble at school and do they enjoy taking risks?

Open to experience – Practical:

- How does the subject respond to new situations or challenges?
- Would you say they had insatiable curiosity?
- Are they imaginative and creative or more practical?
- How much do they contribute to brainstorming or offer up new ideas?
- Which has greater priority – getting the job done or experimentation?
- Are they easily bored?

Trust and integrity:

- Do former colleagues speak well of the subject and their performance at work?
- Are people generally at ease around them or are their mood and behaviour difficult to predict?
- How prepared would they be to bend the rules or apply them inconsistently?
- Have they ever been implicated in any counter-work behaviors?
- Do they score high on extraversion, neuroticism and psychosis (see Dark Side behaviours below) or exhibit tendencies to excitement or stimulus-seeking behaviors?

Emotional intelligence:

- Does the subject ever apologize for their behavior or acknowledge their failings?
- Do they provide constructive feedback to others and handle situations sensitively?
- Are they prone to outbursts or do they manage their emotions appropriately?
- Are they sensitive to the emotions of others?
- Are they able to manage their own extreme emotions, and that of others?

Dark Side Traits

Argumentative and Vigilant (habitual distrust/paranoid):

- Is the subject trusting or doubting? – please give examples
- How do they respond to other people's views?
- Do they take credit when it is not always warranted and blame others when things go wrong, failing to acknowledge their own errors or mistakes?
- Do they appear self-assured and even charismatic?

- Do they take decisions easily, requiring no outside reassurance or advice?
- Are they cautious about entering into dealings with others, preferring to size them up before entering a relationship?
- Are they good listeners, with an ear for subtlety, tone and multiple levels of communication?
- Are they feisty and ready to stand up for themselves, especially when under attack?
- Are they alert to criticism but without becoming intimidated?
- Do they place a high premium on fidelity and loyalty, work hard to earn it and don't take it for granted?
- Do they enjoy and believe in conspiracy theories?
- Are they alert to being mistreated? Do they retaliate readily and decisively?

Solitary and Reserved (aloof/schizoid/cold):

- How does the subject respond to new people joining the office?
- How do they respond to controversy?
- Do they prefer to work alone?
- Are they indifferent to the feelings of others and prefer to work with data not people?
- Are they self-absorbed and focused? Do they shrug off criticism?
- Do they have many/any close friends?

Imaginative and Idiosyncratic (eccentric/schizotypal):

- Does the subject have dozens of new ideas? If so, how well do they follow up on them?
- Do others consider their ideas offbeat or take them seriously?
- Do they enjoy entertaining others with their unusual perceptions and insights?
- Are they constantly alert to new ways of seeing, thinking and expressing themselves and use unusual forms of self-expression?
- Do they seem bright, colourful, insightful, imaginative, very playful, and innovative, but also as eccentric, odd and flighty?
- Under stress and heavy workloads do they become upset, lose focus, lapse into eccentric behavior and not communicate clearly?
- Are they at times moody and with a tendency to get too excited by success and too despondent over failure?
- Will they do anything to get attention, approval and applause?

Manipulative (sociopaths/psychopath/guiltless/callous):

- How does the subject respond when faced by rules and regulations that are preventing them from getting ahead?
- Do they become bored easily? If so how do they respond?
- Do other people, who know them well, trust them?
- When faced with explaining a mistake how do they respond? Do they use charm?

- Do they appear smooth, polished and charming?
- Do they turn most conversations around to a discussion of themselves?
- Do they discredit and put down others in order to build up their own image and reputation?
- Do they lie to co-workers, customers or business associates with a straight face?
- Do they consider people they outsmart or manipulate dumb or stupid?
- Are they opportunistic?
- Do they hate to lose and play ruthlessly to win?
- Do they come across as cold and calculating?
- Do they act in an unethical or dishonest manner?
- Have they created a power network in the organization and do they use it for personal gain?
- Have they shown regret for making decisions that have negatively affected the company, shareholders or employees?

Excitable and Mercurial (volatile/borderline):

- Is the subject unpredictably moody?
- Do they have emotional outbursts or tend to withdraw?
- How do they react to minor mistakes?
- Are people ever worried about approaching them?
- Are they hard people to talk to?
- Do they have a history of failed relationships?
- Have they changed jobs frequently?
- Do they evaluate information as it relates to them personally?

Colourful and Dramatic (melodramatic/histrionic):

- How does the subject behave when in a group where they are relaxed?
- Do others describe them as fun, attention-seeking or quickly bored?
- Do they deal with stress and heavy workloads by becoming very busy?
- Do they enjoy high-pressure situations when they can be the star?
- Do they tend to evaluate themselves by how many meetings they attend rather than what they get done?
- Do they need and feed off approval without acknowledging their need for it?
- Do they persist in trying to be a star even after their lustre has faded?

Arrogant and Self-confident (bold/narcissistic):

- To what extent does the subject listen to feedback?
- Do they accept responsibility or blame others?
- Do they dominate others and are they competitive?
- Do they take decisions easily and require no reassurance or advice from others?
- Do they have surprisingly high self-confidence?
- Do they expect others to recognize them as special?

- Do they react very badly when criticized?
- Are they quick to blame others, rather than themselves, when things go wrong?

Cautious and Sensitive (excessive caution/avoidant):

- How does the subject respond to plans for change?
- How do they engage in office debates/meetings?
- Do they offer new ideas and strong opinions?
- When they are stressed do they begin to adhere to established procedures rather than rely on new technology or a fresh approach?
- Are they controlling of staff?
- Do they follow instructions precisely and try to ensure that staff members do the same?
- Do they react badly to criticism?
- Do they appear rigid and resistant to innovation and change?

Dutiful and Devoted (eagerness to please/dependent):

- How does the subject respond to their boss? Do they accept requests and ideas without question?
- How flexible are they in their dealings with other people, particularly more senior people?
- How do they respond to tough people issues?
- Do they seek approval and acceptance and suck up to people, especially authority figures?
- Are they hyper-alert to signs of disapproval and to opportunities to ingratiate themselves and to be of service, to demonstrate their fealty and loyalty to the organization?
- When they think they have given offence, do they redouble their efforts to be model citizens?
- Are they thought of as polite, good-natured, cordial and indecisive?

Leisurely (passive resistant/two-faced/passive-aggressive):

- To what extent does the subject demonstrate consistency between what they say and what they do?
- How do they respond to other people's requests? Do they ignore them, become resentful, say they will do something but don't?
- Do they tend to get angry and slow down, even more when asked to speed up?
- Do they tend to feel mistreated, unappreciated and put upon?
- When they sense that they have been cheated do they retaliate, but always under conditions of high deniability?
- Do they manage to hide their annoyance quite well, by pretending to be co-operative, making their peevishness and foot-dragging very hard to detect?
- Do they often arrive late for meetings?

- Are they stubborn and hard to coach?
- Do they avoid direct confrontations?
- Are they prickly, unpredictable and unrewarding to deal with?
- Do they manage to build teams?

Diligent and conscientious (perfectionist/obsessive/compulsive):

- What is the subject's working environment like?
- How do they respond to other people's work output? With constant redrafting and attention to tiny details?
- Are they great sticklers for order or cleanliness?
- Can they discard worn-out or worthless objects even when they have no sentimental value?
- Do they hoard rubbish at home and in the workplace?
- Do they reluctantly delegate tasks and work with others unless they submit exactly to their way of doing things?
- Are they tenacious despite the price to pay?
- Are they miserly, hoarding money for future catastrophes?
- Do they keep within budget?
- Are they rigid and unpleasant to work for?

Machiavellian (calculating):

- Does the subject remain aloof and uninvolved in other people's problems?
- Do they tend to tell people what they want to hear?
- Are they prepared to cut corners to get what they want?
- Do they flatter important people?
- Do they give away their real motives?

Motivation

Achievement:

- To what extent is the subject motivated by doing a good job, whether or not their role in its successful completion is recognized?
- How energetic are they in driving projects to completion?
- Do they speak about group achievements?
- Have they always been eager to get awards, certificates and other signs of success? Will they do anything to be a winner?

Recognition and Vanity:

- To what extent does subject seek publicity for their achievements?
- Do they care about their appearance?
- Do they become angry if not praised?
- Do they like prizes and seek the adulation of others?

Power and Influence:

- To what extent does the subject seek and value senior positions in the organization?
- How would they see their role in three years' time – leading or staying where they are?
- Do they seem confident or nervous when faced with a new social situation or a new challenge at work?
- Do they enjoy competition?
- Are they assertive and directive when leading a group?

Pleasure and Hedonism:

- To what extent does the subject value and pursue fun and frivolity in the office?
- Do they have a relaxed attitude to lunch hours?
- Do they prioritize leisure time over work?
- Are they described as fun-loving?

Beliefs and Creeds (altruistic/ideological):

- What is the subject's attitude to voluntary work? Do they expect personal advantage from such activities?
- Does associating the organization's goals with the public good matter to them?
- To they make their views and beliefs explicit?
- Are they prepared to make sacrifices in order to stand up for a cause or belief?
- Do they talk in terms of morals, things being right or wrong?
- Are they attracted to ideologies of any kind?

Acceptance and Inclusiveness (affiliation/need to be included):

- How significant is the social environment at work for the subject?
- How frequently do they join colleagues in the pub or bar after work?
- Do they seek people out to have lunch together in the canteen or do they bring in sandwiches and sit alone eating them?
- Is it important to them to be in the 'in-group'?

Risk and Excitement:

- How does the subject view risk – personal or commercial?
- To what extent do they seek excitement?
- Would they rather spend their holidays on a beach or abseiling down some mountain?
- Do they enjoy meeting celebrities and other important people?
- Do they avoid boredom at all costs?

Materialism and Possession (avarice/commerce):

- To what extent is the subject interested in making money?
- How interested are they in non-financial objectives?

- Are they hoarders?
- Do they flaunt their wealth and possessions?
- What is their attitude to money?

Safety and Security (tradition):

- To what extent does the subject value the organization's history or values?
- How do they respond to initiatives concerning experimentation or innovation?
- Do they enjoy daily routines?
- Do they make regular savings?
- Do they prefer to live by rules and regulations?
- Are they conservative in their attitudes and values?

Annex 2

RPP Framework

Subject: (name, position/role)
Motivation: (Achievement/Recognition and Vanity/Power & Influence/Pleasure & Hedonism/Beliefs & Creeds/Acceptance & Inclusiveness/Risk & Excitement/Materialism & Possessions/Safety & Security)
Information gaps: (Areas for future research)

Your/Influencer's profile: (Background /Personality traits/Dark Side tendencies)
Purpose of assessment: (Recruitment/negotiation etc.)
Operational constraints: (Resource/Time/Skills/Information)

Element	Key risks/ opportunities	Recommended tool(s) of influence/ tactics	Action planning
	(Based on research findings)	(Scarcity, reciprocation, social proof, liking, logic, authority, commitment and consistency)	(Priorities/ responsibilities)
Culture: • Key differences in practices/values • Subject's adaptability • Situational factors to be taken into account			
Biography: • Shared understanding/experiences • Valuable skills or knowledge (or deficit of) • Out of the ordinary?			
Intelligence: • Level and type • Thinking style • Personal strengths • Willingness to learn			
Personality: • Preferences • Extremes • Awareness and management of tendencies • Integrity			
Dark Side: • Extremes • Ability to control • Possible triggers			

Notes

2 Culture

1. This dimension has evolved from the Long-term Orientation dimension researched by Michael Bond in 1991.

4 Intelligence

1. The answer is 197 – all the others are squares.
2. The answer is Madrid – all others lie on latitudes of approximately multiples of 10°.

Bibliography

Adair, J. (2002). *John Adair's 100 Greatest Ideas for Effective Leadership and Management*. Oxford: Capstone Publishing Ltd.

Adler, N.J. (2001). *International Dimensions of Organisational Behaviour* (4th edition) South-Western, Div of Thomson Learning.

Al-Khatib, J., Malshe, A. and AbdulKader, M. (2008). Perception of Unethical Negotiation Tactics. *International Business Review*, 17, 78–102.

Arnold, M. (1867–1868). *Culture and Anarchy*. Cornhill Magazine.

Asch, S.E. (1951). Effects of group pressure upon the modification and distortion of judgment. In H. Guetzkow (ed.) *Groups, Leadership and Men*. Pittsburgh, PA: Carnegie Press.

Austin, E., Farrelly, D., Black, C. and Moore, H. (2007). Emotional Intelligence, Machiavellianism and Emotional Manipulation. *Personality and Individual Differences*, 43, 179–189.

Babiak, P. and Hare, R. (2006). *Snakes in Suits*. New York: Regan Books.

Baron-Cohen, S. (2011). *The Essential Difference*. Harmondsworth: Penguin.

Bolchover D. (2012). Competing Across Borders. How cultural and communication barriers affect business. *Economist Intelligence Unit*.

Bourdieu, P. (1984). *Distinction: A Social Critique of the Judgement of Taste* (R. Nice, Trans.). Cambridge, MA: Harvard University Press.

Bower T. (1998). *Fayed*. An Unauthorised Biography. London: MacMillan.

Bracken, D.W. and Timmreck, C.W. (2001). Guidelines for multisource feedback when used for decision making. In Bracken, D.W., Timmreck, C.W. and Church, A.H. *The Handbook of Multisource Feedback*. San Francisco, CA: Jossey-Bass.

Brislin R.W., Cushner K., Cherrie C. and Yong M. (1986). *Intercultural Interactions: A Practical Guide*. Beverley Hills, CA: Sage Publications Inc.

Brody N. (1992). *Intelligence*. San Diego, CA: Academic Press.

Brooks-Gunn, J. and Duncan, G. (1997). The Effect of Poverty on Children. *The Future of Children*, 7, 56–71.

Carnegie, D. (1936). *How to Win Friends and Influence People*. New York: Pocket Books.

Cash, T.F. (1988). The effects of male pattern baldness on social impression formation. Unpublished manuscript.

Cattell, R. (1987). *Intelligence.* New York: Springer.

Cheung, E.M., Leung, K., Zhang, J-X. et al. (2001). Indigenous Chinese Personality Constructs: Is the Five Factor Model Complete? *Journal of Cross-Cultural Psychology*, 32, 407–433.

Church A.T. and Katigbak M. S. (2002). The Cultural Context of Academic motives: A comparison of Filipino and American College Students. *Journal of Cross-Cultural Psychology*, 23, 40–58.

Christie, R. and Geis, F. (1970). *Studies in Machiavellianism.* New York: Academic Press.

Cialdini, R.B. (2001). *Influence: Science and Practice* (4th edition). Boston, MA: Allyn & Bacon.

Cialdini R.B. (2009). *Influence: The Psychology of Persuasion*. HarperCollins e-books.

Clutterbuck, D. (2012). *The Talent Wave.* London: Kogan Page.

Collett, P. (1994). *Foreign Bodies.* London: Simon and Schuster.

Convy M., Hess, R.D., Azuma, H. and Kashiwagi, K. (1980). Maternal Strategies for Regulating Children's Behavior: Japanese and American Families. *Journal of Cross-Cultural Psychology*, 11, 153–172.

Costa, P. and McCrae, R. (1992). *Revised NEO Personality Inventory (NEO-PI-R) and NEO Five-Factor Inventory (NEO-FFI)*. Odessa, FL. Psychological Assessment.

Costa, P.T., McCrae, R.R. and Kay, G. (1995). Persons, Places and Personality: Career Assessment Using the Revised NEO Personality Inventory. *Journal of Career Assessment*, 3, 123–139.

Cotterell, N., Eisenberger, R. and Speicher, H. (1992). Inhibiting Effects of Reciprocation Wariness on Interpersonal Relationships. *Journal of Personality Social Psychology*, 62, 658–668.

Dinda, S., Gangopadhyay, P.K., Chattopadhyay, B.P., Saiyed, H.N., Pal, M. and Bharati, P. (2006). Height, Weight, and Earnings among Coalminers in India. *Economics and Human Biology*, 4, 342–350.

Dotlich, D. and Cairo, P. (2003). *Why CEOs Fail.* New York: Jossey Bass.

DSM-IV: American Psychiatric Association (2000). Diagnostic and Statistical Manual of Mental Disorders. (4th edition Rev.). Washington, D.C.: APA.

Earley P.C. (1993). East Meets West Meets Mideast: Further Explorations of Collectivistic versus Individualist Work Groups. *Academy of Management Journal*, 36, 319–348.

Ekman, P. (2004). *Emotions Revealed.* New York: Phoenix.

Ekman P. and Friesen W.V. (1975). *Unmasking the Face.* Engelwood Cliffs, NJ: Prentice-Hall.

Eysenck, H. (1967). *The Biological Basis of Personality.* Springfield, IL: Thomas.

Ferri, E. (1976). *Growing up in a One-Parent Family*. London. NFER.

Fox K. (2004). *Watching the English.* London: Hodder & Stoughton.

Furnham, A. (1989). Quartet for a damp land. *Times Higher Educational Supplement.* May.

Furnham A. (2005). *The Psychology of Behaviour at Work*. Hove: Psychology Press.

Furnham, A. (2008). *Personality and Intelligence at Work*. London: Routledge.

Furnham, A. (2010). *The Elephant in the Boardroom*. Basingstoke: Palgrave.

Furnham, A. (2014). *The New Psychology of Money*. London: Routledge.

Furnham, A. (2015). *The Work Values Questionnaire: A Motivational Measure*. London: ABRA.

Furnham, A. and Bochner, S. (1986). *Culture Shock*. London: Methuen.

Furnham A. and Bochner, S. (2001). *The Psychology of Culture Shock*. London: Methuen.

Furnham, A and Taylor, J. (2011). *Bad Apples*. Basingstoke: Palgrave.

Furnham, A., Richards, S. and Paulhus, D. (2013). The Dark Triad of Personality. *Social and Personality Compass*, 7, 199–216.

Galen, C. (170) Theory of humours (see also Kraseon (1938)).

Galtung J. (1981). Structure, culture, and intellectual style: An essay comparing saxonic, teutonic, gallic and nipponic approaches. Social Science Information, 20, 817.

Gardner, H.(1983). *Frames of Mind*. New York: Basic Books.

Gelfand M.J., Nishii L.H. and Raver J.L. (2005). On the Nature and Importance of Cultural Tightness-Looseness. *Journal of Applied Psychology*, 91 (6), 1225–1244.

Gesteland R.R.(2005).*Cross-Cultural Business Behaviour* (4th edition). Copenhagen Business School Press.

Ghorpade, J. (2000). Managing Five Paradoxes of 360-Degree Feedback. *Academy of Management Executive*, 14, 140–150.

Gibson S., Maznevski M.L. and Kirkman B.L (2009). When Does Culture Matter? *Cambridge Handbook of Culture, Organisations and Work*. Cambridge: Cambridge University Press.

Gladwell M. (2008). *Outliers*. London: Penguin Group.

Goffman, E. (1981). *Forms of Talk*, Philadelphia, PA: University of Pennsylvania Press.

Goldsmith, D. (1922). The Use of the Personal History Blank as a Salesman Test. *Journal of Applied Psychology*, 6, 149–155.

Goleman, D. (1995). *Emotional Intelligence*. New York: Bantam Books.

Goodman M.E. (1967). *The Individual and Culture*. Homewood, IL: The Dorsey Press.

Gosling, S. (2009). *Snoop*. New York: Basic Books.

Great British Class Survey (2013).

Gunter, B. and Furnham, A. (2001). *Assessing Potential*. London: Whurr.

Guéguen, N. and Jacob, C. (2001). Fund-raising on the web: The effect of an electronic foot-in-the-door on donation, *Cyber Psychology & Behavior*, 4 (6), 705–709.

Hall, C. and Lindzey, G. (1957). *Theories of Personality*. Chicester: Wiley.

Hall, E.T. (1989). *Beyond Culture*. New York: Anchor Books.

Hare, R.D. (1999) *Without Conscience: The Disturbing World of the Psychopaths Among Us*, The Guilford Press.

Harrison L.E. and Huntington S.P. (2000).*Culture Matters: How Values Shape Human Progress*. New York: Basic Books, A Member of the Perseus Books Group.

Hawking, S. (2010). *The Grand Design*. New York: Bantam Books.

Heine S.J. (2005). Where Is the Evidence for Pancultural Self-Enhancement? A Reply to Sedikides, Gaertner and Toguchi (2003). *Journal of Personality and Social Psychology*, 89.

Henry Nicholas, *Business Week*, October 6th, 2011.

Herrnstein, R. and Murray, C. (1994). *The Bell Curve*. New York: Free Press.

Hill Richard (2002). *We Europeans*. Brussels, Europublic SA/NV.

Hoecklin L. (1995). *Managing Cultural Differences*. Addison-Wesley Publishers Ltd and The Economist Intelligence Unit.

Hoffman, E. (1989). *The Right to be Human: The Biography of Abraham Maslow*. Wellingborough: Aquarian Press.

Hofstede G. (2010). *Cultures and Organisations: Software of the Mind*. New York: McGraw-Hill.

Hogan, R. and Hogan, J. (2001). Assessing Leadership: A View from the Dark Side. New York, *International Journal of Selection and Assessment*, 9, 40–51.

Hogan, R., Barrett, P. and Hogan, J. (2009). *Hogan Business Reasoning Inventory Manual*. Tulsa, OK: Hogan Assessment Systems.

Honey, P. and Mumford, A. (2000). *The Learning Styles Helper's Guide*. Maidenhead: Peter Honey Publications Ltd.

Hope-Hailey, V. (2012). *Where Has Trust Gone?* London: CIPD.

Howard, P. and Howard, J. (2010). *The Owner's Manual for Personality at Work*. Austin, TX: Bard Press.

House R.J., Hanges, P.J., Javidan M., Dorfman P.W., Gupta V. and GLOBE associates (2004*). Leadership, Culture and Organisations: The Globe Study of 62 Nations*. Thousand Oaks, CA: Sage.

Hudson, L. (1966). *Contrary Imaginations*. London: Penguin.

Hsu F.L.K. (1953). *Americans and Chinese: two Ways of Life*. New York: Henry Schuman, Inc.

Inglehart, R. (1997). *Modernization and Postmodernization*. Princeton, NJ: Princeton University Press.

Jefferson, T., Herbst, J.H. and McCrae, R.R. (1998). Associations between Birth Order and Personality Traits: Evidence from Self-reports and Observer Ratings. *Journal of Research in Personality*, 32, 498–509.

Judge, T.A. and Cable, D.M. (2004). The Effect of Physical Height on Workplace Success and Income: Preliminary Test of a Theoretical Model. *Journal of Applied Psychology*, 89 (3), 428–441.

Judge, T.A. and Cable, D.M. (2011). When It Comes to Pay, Do the Thin Win? The Effect of Weight on Pay for Men and Women. *Journal of Applied Psychology*, 96, 95–112.

Kağıtçıbaşı, Ç. (2005). Autonomy and Relatedness in Cultural Context: Implications for Self and Family. *Journal of Cross-Cultural Psychology*, 36,403–422.

Kahneman. *Heuristics and Biases: The Psychology of Intuitive Judgment*. Cambridge: Cambridge University Press. 49–81.

Kahneman, D. and Frederick, S. (2002a). Representativeness revisited: Attribute substitution in intuitive judgement. In Gilovich, T., Griffin, D. and Kahneman,

D. *Heuristics and Biases: The Psychology of Intuitive Judgement.* Cambridge: Cambridge University Press, 49–81.

Kahneman, D. and Frederick, S. (2002b). Representativeness Revisited: Attribute Substitution in Intuitive Judgment. In Thomas Gilovich, Dale Griffin, Daniel Berry J. W., Poortinga Y. H., Breuglmans S. M., Chasiotis A. and Sam D. L. (2011). *Cross-Cultural Psychology Research and Applications.* Cambridge University Press.

Karau S.J. and Williams K.D. (1993). Social Loafing: A Meta-Analytic View of Social Integration. *Journal of Personality and Social Psychology*, 65, 681–706.

Kets de Vries, M. (2006). *The Leader on the Couch.* Basingstoke: Palgrave.

Kluckhohn C. (1954). Culture and behaviour. In G Lindzey (Ed.) *Handbook of Social Psychology*, 2. Cambridge, MA: Addison-Wesley.

Knowles, M. (1998). *The Adult Learner.* Woburn: Butterworth.

Kolb, D. (1984). *Experiential Learning.* New Jersey: Prentice Hall.

Kohn, A. (1999). *Punished by Rewards.* Boston, MA: Houghton Mifflin.

Kottak C. (2011). *Window on Humanity: A Concise Introduction to Anthropology.* New York: McGraw-Hill.

Kurtz, D.L. (1969). Physical Appearance and Stature: Important Variables in Sales Recruiting. *Personnel Journal*, 48 (12), 981–983.

Langlois, J., Kalakais, L., Rubenstein, A., Larson, A., Hallam, M. and Smoot, M. (2000). Maxims or Myths of Beauty? A Meta-analytic and Theoretical Review. *Psychological Bulletin*, 126, 390–423.

Lautenschlager, G. and Shaffer, G. (1987). Re-examining the Components and Stability of Owen's Biographical Questionnaire. *Journal of Applied Psychology*, 72, 149–152.

Leman, K. (1998). *Birth Order.* New York: Revell.

Lamera, K. (1938) Trans Ancient to Modern Greek) Papyros Library: Collected Works of Ancient Greek Writing (Vol 24). Athens.

Livermore D. (2010). *Leading with Cultural Intelligence: The New Secret to Success.* New York: AMACON.

Lowen, A. (2004). *Narcissism: Denial of the True Self.* New York: MacMillan.

Magnusson, P.K.E., Rasmussen, F. and Gyllensten, U.B. (2006). Height at aged 18 years is a strong predictor of attained education in later life: Cohort study of over 950,000 Swedish men. *International Journal of Epidemiology*, 35 (3), 658–663.

Markus H.R. and Kitayama S. (1991). *Culture and the Self: Implications for Cognition, Emotion, and Motivation.* New York: American Psychological Association.

McClelland, D, (1983). *Human Motivation.* Cambridge: CUP.

MCrae R.R., Terracciano A. Personality Profiles of Cultures: Aggregate Personality Traits. *Journal of Personality and Social Psychology*, 89, 407–425.

Menkes (2005). Hire for Success. *Harvard Business Review*, 83, 100–109.

Milgram, S. (1974). *Obedience to Authority: An Experimental View.* New York: Harpercollins.

Murray, H. (1938). *Explorations in Personality.* New York: Open University Press.

Nettle, D. (2005). An Evolutionary Approach to the Extraversion Continuum. *Evolution and Human Behaviour*, 26, 363–373.

Nettle, D. (2006). The Evolution of Personality Variation in Humans and Other Animals. *American Psychologist*, 61, 622–631.

Neyer. A-K. and Harzing A-W. (2008). *The Impact of Culture on Interactions: Five Lessons Learned from the European Commission*.

Nydell M.K. (Omar) (2002). *Understanding Arabs. A Guide for Westerners*. Yarmouth, Maine: Intercultural Press.

Oberg, K. (1960). Culture Shock. *Practical Anthropology*, 7, 177–182.

Oldham, J. and Morris, L. (1991). *Personality Self-Portrait*. New York: Bantam.

Oldham, J. and Morris, L. (2000). *Personality Self-Portrait*. New York: Bartam Books.

Owen, D. (2011). *In Sickness and In Power: Illness in Heads of Government during the Last 100 Years*. London: Methuen publishing Ltd.

Owen, D. (2012). *The Hubris Syndrome*. London: Methuen.

Paulhus, D. and Buckels, E. (2011). *The Dark Tetrad of Personality*. Toronto: DRDC.

Paulhus, D. and Williams, K. (2002). The Dark Triad of Personality. *Journal of Research in Personality*, 36, 557–563.

Pruitt, D.G. (1968). Reciprocity and credit building in a laboratory dyad. *Journal of Personality and Social Psychology*, 8, 143–147.

Rajiv Vaidyanathan and Praveen Aggarwal (2005). Using Commitments to Drive Consistency: Enhancing the Effectiveness of Cause-related Marketing Communications, *Journal of Marketing Communications*, 11 (4), 231–224.

Regan, D.T. (1971). Effects of a Favor and Liking on Compliance. *Journal of Experimental Social Psychology*, 1, 627–639.

Rokeach, M. (1973). *The Nature of Human Values*. New York: Free Press.

Sagan C (1977). *The Dragons of Eden*. New York: Random House.

Saudino, K. (2005). Behaviour Genetics and Child Development. *Journal of Developmental Behaviour and Padiatrics*, 26, 214–223.

Schwartz, H.A., Eichstaedt, J.C., Kern, M.L., Dziurzynski, L. and Ramones, S.M.(2013). Personality, Gender, and Age in the Language of Social Media: The Open-Vocabulary Approach. *PLoS ONE*, 8 (9): e73791.

Seligman, L., Dawson, E., Nitz, M. and Whicker, M.L. (1990). Hair Loss and Electability: The Bald Truth. *Journal of Nonverbal Behavior*, 14 (4), 269–283,

Smith P. B., Bond M. and Kagitcibasi, C. (2006). *Understanding Social Psychology Across Cultures*. London. Sage Publications Inc.

Smernou, L., and Lautenschlagger, G. (1991). Autobiographical Antecedents and Correlates of NeuroticiBsm and Extraversion. *Personality and Individual Differences*, 12, 49–53.

Sorokowski, P. (2010). Politicians' Estimated Height as an Indicator of Popularity. *European Journal of Social Psychology*, 40, 1302–1309.

Sternberg, R. (2003). A Broad View of Intelligence. *Consulting Psychology Journal*, 55, 139–154.

Steve Jurvetson on Steve Jobs, *Business Week*, 6 October 2011.

Steve's Jobs: Restart Apple (Cathy Booth), *Time Magazine*, 18 August 1997.

Stulp, Buunk, Verhulst, and Pollet (2012). Tall claims? Sense and nonsense about the importance of height of US presidents. *The Leadership Quarterly*, In Press.

Sullaway, F. (1996). *Born to Rebel*. New York: Pantheon.

Taylor, J. and Furnham, A. (2005). *Learning at Work*. Basingstoke: Palgrave.

Therivel, W. (2001). *The GAM/DP Theory of Personality and Creativity*. New York: Kirk House.

Triandis H. C. (1994). *Culture and Social Behaviour*. New York: McGraw-Hill, Inc.

Trompenaars F. and Hampden-Turner C. (1997). *Riding the Waves of Culture*. New York: Nicholas Brealey Publishing.

Vaillant, G.E. (1994). Ego Mechanisms of Defense and Personality Psychopathology. *Journal of Abnormal Psychology*, 103, 44–50.

Ward, C., Bochner, S. and Furnham, A. (2001). *The Psychology of Culture Shock*. Hove, England & Philadelphia: Routledge.

Wilke, H. and Lanzetta, J.T. (1970). The Obligation to Help: The Effects of Amount of Prior Help on Subsequent Helping Behavior. *Journal of Experimental Social Psychology*, *6*, 488–493.

World Values Survey http://www.worldvaluessurvey.org/wvs/articles/folder_published/article_base_54.

Zhang Y.C., Kohnstamm G., Slotboom A.M. Elphick E. and Cheung P.C (2002). Chinese and Dutch Parents' Perception of Their Children's Personality. *Journal of Genetic Psychology*, 163, 165–178.

Zimbardo, P. and Boyd, J. (1999). Putting Time in Perspective: A Valid, Reliable Individual-Differences Metric. *Journal of Personality and Social Psychology*, 77, 1271–1288.

Index

Printed and bound by CPI Group (UK) Ltd, Croydon, CR0 4YY